THE ANTHROPOLOGICAL STUDY OF CLASS AND CONSCIOUSNESS

THE ANTHROPOLOGICAL STUDY

EDITED BY E. Paul Durrenberger

OF CLASS AND CONSCIOUSNESS

UNIVERSITY PRESS OF COLORADO

© 2012 by the University Press of Colorado

Published by the University Press of Colorado
5589 Arapahoe Avenue, Suite 206C
Boulder, Colorado 80303

The University Press of Colorado is a proud member of
the Association of American University Presses.

AAUP 1937 / 2012

The University Press of Colorado is a cooperative publishing enterprise supported, in part, by Adams State College, Colorado State University, Fort Lewis College, Metropolitan State College of Denver, Regis University, University of Colorado, University of Northern Colorado, and Western State College of Colorado.

∞ The paper used in this publication meets the minimum requirements of the American National Standard for Information Sciences—Permanence of Paper for Printed Library Materials. ANSI Z39.48-1992

Library of Congress Cataloging-in-Publication Data

The anthropological study of class and consciousness / edited by E. Paul Durrenberger.
     p. cm.
  Includes bibliographical references and index.
  ISBN 978-1-60732-156-9 (hardcover : alk. paper) — ISBN 978-1-60732-157-6 (ebook)
1. Social classes. 2. Classism. 3. Class consciousness. 4. Social stratification. 5. Labor unions. 6. Working class. I. Durrenberger, E. Paul, 1943–
  HT609.A44 2012
  305.5—dc23
                              2011050456

Design by Daniel Pratt

21   20   19   18   17   16   15   14   13   12   10   9   8   7   6   5   4   3   2   1

To the Industrial Workers of the World,
which clearly defined class relations

Contents

CONTENTS

Preface

This is a book about the role of the concept of class as an analytical construct in anthropology and how it relates to culture. We hope this book will give anthropologists permission to use the word *class*.

We should not let the ideologies of neoliberalism deter us from incorporating class as central to our understandings. If "everyone" agrees there is no class, then those who experience it most intensely—for instance, Walmart shoppers who daily live the injuries of class but don't know what to call it—along with anthropologists with insufficient analytical clarity use other concepts and words that disguise those realities. In polite academic circles it may be "race" or "gender." Among the hoi polloi it may be "those Mexicans" or other immigrants. Whether the discourse be elevated or not, these terms are poor substitutes for a viable and vibrant concept of class.

The contributors to this volume explicate the relationships between experience and how people understand their worlds—consciousness—culture, and how both experience and consciousness relate to the realities of positions in economic systems—class.

In the tradition of American anthropology, we include archaeological interpretations to extend our time horizons into the past so that we can better understand long-term processes rather than be confined to contemporary ones. The book begins to answer these questions with archaeological work (Honeychurch, Bolender) that sets the time-span of the study of class and indicates the advantages of confining ourselves to the evidence of material objects and remains so that the ideologies of the living do not interfere quite so much with our attempts to understand the relationship of class and culture.

The contributors all focus on Morton Fried's (1967) notion of class as groups of people defined by differential access to resources. Sometimes differential access is enforced by means of the apparatus of state organizations, but examination of the archaeological and historical record suggests that this is not an inevitable relationship. The central questions that unify this collection of ethnographic, ethnohistoric, and archaeological works from various locales and periods are:

- What are the objective bases for class in different social orders, from chiefdoms to industrial states?
- How do people's understandings of class relate to their conceptions of race and gender?
- How do *ideologies* of class relate to *realities* of class?
- How does the US managerial middle-class denial of class and emphasis on meritocracy relate to the increasing economic insecurity that many now experience?
- How do people who experience economic insecurity respond to it, and what are the political implications of their responses?

THE ANTHROPOLOGICAL STUDY
OF CLASS AND CONSCIOUSNESS

Introduction

E .   P A U L   D U R R E N B E R G E R

> There is a crime here that goes beyond denunciation. There is a sorrow here that weeping cannot symbolize. There is a failure here that topples all our success. The fertile earth, the straight tree rows, the sturdy trunks and the ripe fruit. And children dying of pellagra must die because a profit cannot be taken from an orange.
>
> STEINBECK, 1939:477

Steinbeck was writing of California. We write about the world as the processes he described in *The Grapes of Wrath* have overtaken the planet. He outlined the processes (1939: 324–325):

> And the great owners, who must lose their land in an upheaval, the great owners with access to history, with eyes to read history and to know the great fact: when property accumulates in to few hands it is taken away. And that companion fact: when a majority of the people are hungry and cold they will take by force what they need. And the little screaming fact that sounds through all history: repression works only to strengthen and knit the repressed. The great owners ignored the three cries of history.

> The land fell into fewer hands, the number of dispossessed increased,
> and every effort of the great owners was directed at repression.

In the twenty-first century the processes have become globalized, as Paul Trawick discusses in his paper in this volume. And now the dispossessed in California come not from Oklahoma and Arkansas as they did in Steinbeck's day, but from Latin America where great corporations have replaced the great owners of Steinbeck's time and have exacerbated all of the processes he described. Today we cannot even find the face of the owner, for it is a corporation. And, as Griffith discusses in his work in this book, it is no longer just California that receives the refugees from corporate rapacity but many other areas of the United States as well as other lands.

Wherever ethnographers do fieldwork, we see these processes at work. We see them in the great cities as the burgeoning informal economy (Smith 1990; Hart 1973, in press) or young peasant women working in factories in China and Southeast Asia (Pun Ngai 2005; Mills 1999; Wolf 1994) or Mexican people reorienting their lives from production on their own land to industrial agriculture (Zlolniski 2010) or factories (Heyman 1991) and in whole regions as they adjust to the new economic structures (Narotzky and Smith 2006).

The global flows of capital escape ethnographic attention because they are not localized to any one place for us to see (Durrenberger 2004; Durrenberger and Erem 2010). But we see the results wherever we look (Lewellen 2002; Truillot 2003; Nash 2007; Nordstrom 2004, 2007). When we can look ethnographically at Steinbeck's "batteries of bookkeepers to keep track of interest and gain and loss," (1939:317) as Gillian Tett did, we can see their thought processes at work if not the results of their actions as they try to create wealth out of nothing (Tett 2009). These financiers succeed in benefiting themselves richly at great cost to the rest of us, leading to increased global repression, hunger, and war as the works of Carolyn Nordstrom (2004, 2007) graphically illustrate.

In increasing the disparities of wealth and income both within countries and among them, the processes of globalization have highlighted the distinctions between the local and global owning and working classes. Corporations have become more powerful as they control not only local and national economies but global processes (Bakan 2005; Anderson, Cavanagagh, and Lee 2005). In the United States they have forged a cultural revolution to make these processes appear to be natural and inevitable (Doukas 2003; Fones-Wolf 1995) and to encode these tenets in a mindless media state (deZengotita 2006). The owners have learned the third of Steinbeck's historical lessons. While one of the chief instruments of mind control of ancient states was to insist on belief in counterexperiential religious doctrines (Durrenberger and Erem 2010), modern corporations rely on media manipulations of reality that they can own. Classes vanish in this fog, and all too often contemporary scholars willingly follow the corporate lead.

WHY STUDY CLASS?

Today's globalized political economy accentuates the inseparability of class and culture. As anthropologists who want to understand the nature and dynamics of culture, we must also understand the nature and dynamics of class. The way people understand life is determined by their daily experiences, which are in turn determined by their class positions in their political-economic systems. As Marx famously put it, the windmill gives us feudalism while the steam mill gives us capitalism. The microchip gives us a global economy and a global class system.

The place where I lived in central Pennsylvania in the mid-Atlantic region of the United States is a graveyard of dead economic systems, its landscape cluttered with stone ruins of iron-smelting furnaces, canals and systems of locks, lime kilns, and place names incorporating the words "furnace," "port," and "mill." More recent artifacts such as the mammoth Bethlehem Steel plant go the way of the water-powered weaving factories of Lowell, MA, becoming museum artifacts on a greater scale than the pyramids of Egypt and leaving behind the appellation of "rust belt" for a whole region. The displacement of such a massive industry as steel making—which seemed such a permanent fixture of the landscape and the economy—left a region in shock with a generation of unemployed workers. When US white-collar workers began losing their jobs in the 1980s, awareness of a new economic system slowly began to spread.

In the past some such changes have been so slow that they did not become obvious within a generation. The much accelerated pace of change that has accompanied the microchip revolution reveals these processes and connections more clearly and swiftly, and a generation has entered the twenty-first century with no expectation that they could follow their fathers into the mine or mill for a lifetime of work, a job.

Now not only in the rust belt but all over the United States and much of the rest of the world, both parents work "outside the home" in unstable employment situations to try to make enough money to sustain their households. Neoliberal rhetoric has become the language of expectation as a generation has been taught that it is natural and legitimate to think of people and jobs as disposable and that people need to be flexible to meet the demands of markets, while loyalties of class, family, kinship, region, and other groups are at best passé and at worst an unrealistic and illicit betrayal of self-interest in a neoliberal market system. When everything is a market commodity, there are no collective interests, only individual ones. It is difficult for people who have grown up in the neoliberal "ownership society" to imagine that it was through collective action that preceding generations achieved the work conditions, wages, and benefits that they look back on with envy and perhaps resentment. They may then turn that resentment on unions as somehow causes of their misery rather than potential liberators.

In the United States we hear much about a middle class that, after the economic crisis of 2008, was increasingly guarded about its prosperity. Around the world, we hear much of starvation and the major part of the global population that lives on meager incomes. But the middle class of the global North and the sweatshop workers of the global South are linked in a single global system. The privileges of the one are contingent on the misery of the other, though paradoxically, they have more in common than is immediately apparent to either because they share the same structural position with respect to capital.

To understand these similarities, though, we have to be able to see beyond what is obvious to the people inside the systems, what Marvin Harris (1974) called the cultural dreamwork that obscures the realities of their lives. While some cultures may leave this dreamwork to individuals or make it collective, in the United States it is an industry (deZengotita 2006). Americans live in—and in terms of—a culture that has been manufactured during a long and hard-fought cultural revolution to propel market sensibilities, the gospel of wealth—that capital creates wealth—into consciousness and to erase from that same consciousness such realities as class and the gospel of work—that labor creates wealth (Fones-Wolf 1995; Doukas 2003; Durrenberger and Doukas 2008).

Anthropologist Sherry Ortner (1998, 3–7; 2005) participates in the dreamwork when she recognizes the reality of class but then dismisses it as objectivist discourse and discusses it as "a culturally constituted identity." To insist on focusing on the manufactured "native categories" is to contribute to the problem, not its solution. Such a rhetorical move is akin to the magician's trick of directing our attention to what the left hand is doing while the obscured right hand does its magical work to deceive the eye. This sleight of hand leads Ortner into long discussions of other identity issues such as race and gender, which, while they may also be economically constituted (Brodkin 2000), are not equivalent to class any more than any other issue of identity is.

To say as Ortner does that, culturally, race eclipses class is to ignore, as Schwartz (1998, 15) put it, that "class is no less real than the moon when it is being eclipsed." For Magellan to infer the shape of the earth from its shadow on the moon required that he focus on the earth that cast the shadow and not get lost in the shadow itself. If we want to understand the dietary practices of Hindus, we must understand the ecological and economic role of cattle, not their role in the dreamwork of sacred cows (Harris 1974). If we want to understand class in the United States, we must understand its role in the structure of the political ecology and not its role in the American dream. Thus, what Americans think, if anything at all, about class is not relevant.

To break out of these ideological "native" constructs requires the kind of conscious empirical and theoretical work that the contributors to this volume have done. We mean this book to make class visible to anthropologists and to move toward an adequate anthropological treatment of class both theoretically and empirically.

The contributors have worked together using the classic means of anthropology—ethnographic and archaeological description, holism, and cross-cultural and cross-temporal comparison—to address a series of issues in terms of their separate ethnographic and archaeological experiences to explicate the relationships among people's daily experience and how people understand their worlds—consciousness—and how each of these relates to class—their position in the economic system. Thus, class and consciousness.

The work we make available here in one place brings together historical and ethnographic reference points for meaningful comparisons. While the contributors span the globe from Mongolia to China to Iceland, Mexico, and Brazil, most of the works are anchored in the United States. This moves anthropology away from the comfortable sites of exotic peoples and remote times into the everyday worlds of many of our readers.

Because class is ideologically so prominent, especially by its energetic denial in the United States, China (Pun Ngai 2005), and other contemporary state societies, we all focused on the distinction between the outside realities of class—the etic—and the internal views of class—the emic. In this volume we explore the processes by which class is related to culture and how people think—what we call *consciousness*.

THE INVISIBILITY OF CLASS IN THE UNITED STATES

Discussing matters of class in the United States, editor Lewis Lapham (1988, 3) said:

> Within the free-fire zones of the American language the uses of the words 'money' and 'class' shift with the social terrain, the tone of voice and the angle of the sales pitch. Few words come armed with as many contradictions or as much ambivalence.

In 1901 at its organizing convention, the Industrial Workers of the World proclaimed there were but two classes, the employing class and the working class, which had nothing in common. By the 1950s, the claim that there were any classes in the United States had been labeled as communist-inspired ideology to be avoided at the risk of being un-American. The official American ideology proclaimed a classless society, and people who thought otherwise could be persecuted from their teaching posts and rejected by publishers (Ehrenreich 1989, 25). Some anthropologists today act as though it might still be dangerous to discuss class or to understand it.

Ironically, this was one ideological component that the United States shared with communist nations, which saw any discussion of class to be anticommunist. Sociologists could not deny inequality and could discuss stratification and socioeconomic status along with "roles" that were charac-teristics of individuals, like gender and occupation. Whether one was a bank president or a janitor was a matter of one's choice of role. At the same time, while American sociologists, with few exceptions, denied the existence of class as a meaningful category, they described various socioeconomic sta-tuses and gave us the endearing term "socioeconomic status" or SES as a proxy. Their reference point was their own shared experience of the managerial middle class in terms of which all other class or role behaviors were somehow deviant (Ehrenreich 1989, 25–29).

By 2005, as the rich became much richer and the workers became poorer (but with wider access than ever to consumer goods produced by even poorer workers around the world), the United States appeared less class bound than ever because religion, race, and possessions were not sure guides to a person's place in the social hierarchy. But statistics showed stark class contrasts. Class had become a clear predictor of lifespan, health, residential location, choice of marriage partners, and of who got into universities, much less "good" ones (Keller 2005, xi). As class divisions were becoming greater and more apparent to those who were looking, class became more invisible to most Americans. The stronger the phenomenon, the more we have denied it.

By our inattention to these processes and by our complicity with the process, some anthropologists have contributed to the denial of class, to making it invisible as it becomes more undeniable. With this book, we hope to help reverse that process.

Capital is wealth that that does not have to be consumed, that can be used to produce commodities that can be sold on markets. Some people own capital; most do not. By expanding the meaning of the term *capital* metaphorically to incorporate knowledge (cultural capital) and social relations (social capital), we have performed an ideological magic trick akin to the financiers' magic of creating wealth out of nothing—we have made capital seem universally available.

Everyone has some knowledge and some social relations. If knowledge and social relations are forms of wealth, or forms of capital that can produce wealth, everyone has some and everyone is an owner of capital, a member of the capitalist class, and class divisions disappear. But we are left with the nagging facts of disparate health, longevity, residences, and security not to mention opportunity (Durrenberger 2002, 2006). In the traditional sense of the word, there are still those with disproportionate access to and control of capital, but they have become camouflaged among all the other owners of capital, just like everyone else, not a separate class with distinct interests.

August Carbonella and Sharryn Kasmir (2006) argue that for a historical moment in the second half of the twentieth century, the industrial workers of the United States merged into a culture of consumption that successfully bought them off and disguised their subordinate status with the appearances of prosperity.

Ehrenreich suggests (1989) that the "middle class" is that part of the working class to which the capitalist class has granted perquisites and privileges in return for managing the work of the others. The ideology of meritocratic individualism assures these people that they deserve their privileges because of their talent, hard work, good individual choices, or other measures of merit. At the same time, the less privileged deserve their fates because of some lack of merit or bad individual choices. The work of Katherine Newman in the 1980s (1988) shows how this self-justifying ideology supported those who fancied themselves denizens of this middle class to justify their own access to privilege and then betrayed them when they lost their jobs. Thus, people who thought of themselves as members of this middle class participated in a cultural illusion, part of the dreamwork created to distract them from the realities of their own and others' lives.

Also in the second half of the twentieth century, scholars discovered poverty, defined it as a topic of inquiry, and described the cultural characteristics of the poor as pathologies relative to the life-models of the managerial middle class to which such scholars belong. These works contrasted affluent workers with pathological, racialized ghetto dwellers. Poverty—rather than their structural position in the political economy as unemployed—was a characteristic of the poor: a status, an identity. These studies distanced the affluent working class who were pleased to refer to themselves as middle class, from the inherently poor (Eherenreich 1989).

In his discussion of the ways that newspapers perpetuate the myth of classlessness, Benjamin DeMott (1990) shows what can happen to ethnography when we don't make these connections. In a special report, a *New York Times* reporter cites ethnographic work on drug dealers by anthropologists from the University of Colorado Medical School, the John Jay College of Criminal Justice, and San Francisco State to suggest that the drug dealers chose to reject secure jobs with training, Social Security, pensions, health insurance, and other benefits familiar to the managerial middle class in favor of short careers dealing drugs that result in death, jail, or both. From the point of view of the managerial middle class, this choice is simply stupid.

DeMott concludes that the purpose of this *Times* story is not to elucidate the interior views of the lives of people involved in the drug trade or how their experience of school initiated them into the awareness that they are fated to be losers facing no meaningful job or training opportunities. The distinction the article establishes is the distance "between the middle [class] and mental darkness" (1990:115). Once the *Times* writer establishes that distance, it is appropriate to chide and rebuke those involved in the drug trade. Such stories reassure the meritocratic middle minded that there are no differences of class, only differences of brains, merit, status, and identity—good choices (of the middle class) and bad ones (of the poor). The stupid deserve what they get, as do the meritorious.

Thus the ideology of the managerial middle class is as closed and self-referential as Evans-Pritchard's (1937) description of Zande magic. It makes reasonable all kinds of deficit theories—the idea that some individual deficit is at the root of any problem an individual suffers and the person can remedy it with appropriate effort or help (See Rubin 1994; Durrenberger and Erem 2010). All plane crashes are the result of pilot error.

In this book we make those connections, though they take us into times past and distant places. We show the connections among the denizens of haute couture beauty shops and the primitives living romantically environmentalist lives outside the range of nature-ravaging capitalism—and how these images are part of a corporate campaign to seduce women to purchase simulated experiences of "greenness." We show how the people of the periphery see through the forms of control to formulate populist responses to the realities of corporate global degradation to realize the nightmare scenario of Steinbeck's large landowners. We move class to the center of anthropology and join June Nash (2007) in moving anthropology into the realm of the global nexus.

HOW CAN WE MAKE CLASS VISIBLE?

From an abstract theoretical anthropological perspective, it may not be difficult to define classes in industrial societies, whether capitalist or communist. These orders are first and foremost state societies. The cultural ecologists of decades past taught that states are the institutional forms that guarantee one class privileged access to resources in a system of unequal access that defines classes. Whatever the form of the state, there is a privileged class that is set apart from the rest, and the asymmetry is enforced by more or less disguised use of force on behalf of the ruling class.

Eric Wolf (1999) discussed several ways a ruling class may extract economic value from other classes, including kinship and tribute. In kinship and tribute orders, classes may be more readily visible as there is no particular interest in disguising class distinctions, and typically there are reasons to *accentuate* them. Thus they become visible to archaeologists in succeeding ages.

From the residues of actions that archaeologists recover and interpret in terms of historical and ethnographic analogies, we can make inferences about such reasons. Reasons motivate action and are based on cultural logics that define what is culturally possible and impossible, what is imaginable and unimaginable, what is desirable and undesirable. But these systems of reasons aren't free-floating configurations infinitely variable through time and space as Ruth Benedict might have suggested (Salzman 2001). Rather, they are determined by people's experiences, and people's experiences are determined by their positions in their economic systems. Thus an emperor might marry his sister to guarantee the purity of the blood of his successor, whereas such a match would be incestuous for a peasant. An aristocrat might ride a "high horse" while a peasant might be denied such a lofty mode of transportation. The differences of experience determine the different systems of reason available to each and thus the different reasons each can develop and the different actions available to each.

Reasoning and reasons are forms of consciousness, forms of thought that are determined by people's experiences, which in turn are determined by their positions in economic and political systems and which proceed to inform their actions (Durrenberger and Erem 2010).

Consciousness emerges from action in the social and material world—employing available resources to do things with other people to achieve substantive goals. As class systems constrain people's actions in the world to provide a sense of structure, they also form people's consciousness, their cultures, and their sense of both means and ends—of what is important and ways to achieve those things. Hence the class difference in the assessment of dealing drugs versus holding down a "respectable" job, of incest versus an acceptable marriage, or of acceptable modes of transportation, fishing, irrigation, remuneration, or broadly living their lives. As people act in the world, they also change it (Salzman 2001).

Thus do people exercise agency, interacting with others to achieve their objectives, and thus does agency contribute to change. Agency is a function of goals that our modes of thinking or consciousness define as reasonable.

Finally, experience shapes consciousness. Thus we have a more or less transitive cascade of relationships from experience to consciousness to goals to action in the world and on the world and back to experience.

DeMott provides a compelling analysis of these relationships in his discussion of a US working-class surrogate mother who contracted to be artificially inseminated and carry to term an infant for a couple of the managerial middle class in return for remuneration. When she reneged and wanted to keep the infant herself, a judge awarded custody to the middle-class couple. The court case and related events received considerable press attention in the United States. A frequently posed question was: "What kind of woman would consent to bear and sell her child?" (DeMott 1990, 96).

Lawyers called on psychologists who described her as suffering from various individual deficits from schizophrenia to multiple personality disorder. There was no issue of class, but there was one of occupation (a biochemist and pediatrician versus a garbage truck driver and former barroom dancer), all of which counted in favor of the better-off couple and highlighted the deficits of the less well-off surrogate couple. The language of the experts, the psychologists, described the "surrogate" mom as somehow deranged.

DeMott suggests that the freedom to credibly speak the language of class might have made a difference. Breaking her contract and kidnapping her baby landed the surrogate in court. The prosecution presented her as unstable. The defense argued that she was a victim of social injustice, that "it will always be the wife of the sanitation worker who must bear the children for the pediatrician" (DeMott 1990, 97).

The surrogate broke her contract, DeMott explains, because when she discovered that the couple that had hired her thought of her as an employee, she responded from the experience of people in her class position—people who are accustomed to being the employees of others renting out their bodies as surrogates to do things for their betters, whether it be making steel or babies.

The surrogate did not think of herself as a person engaged in making money, as an employee—in the trade of her body for lucre—but as a person engaged in helping another person who was in need. Experience taught her that people without health or other insurance or reserves of money sacrifice to help one another. Her own mother had had only sporadic employment and called on poor but generous neighbors for help (for ethnographic examples see Stack 1997). The surrogate and her husband had likewise helped friends who suffered accidents or emergencies. We anthropologists call this *reciprocity*, and it seems familiar to us from our study of noncapitalist social orders but somehow out of place in capitalist orders based on rapacity. The surrogate envisaged a desperately troubled couple, threatened by the wife's self-diagnosed multiple sclerosis, who could not cope without her help.

> She had seen people in distress turn to others helplessly, had herself been turned to previously; in her world failure to respond was unnatural. Her class experience, together with her own individual nature, made it natural to perceive the helping side of the surrogacy as primary and the commercial side as important yet secondary. (DeMott 1990, 99–100)

This and similar examples show that media and law separate actions and motives that are unfamiliar to the managerial middle class from their social grounding, because the only language available to understand the connections between actions and backgrounds is the language of class, and that is not allowed, or likely even considered. Science and law conspired to see this woman through the lens of individual diagnosis rather than class and thus remove some people from the perceptual sameness of all people to become, like the drug dealers, incomprehensible, nearly a different species (DeMott 1990, 101).

Katherine Newman (1988) provides another example of these relationships in her comparison of American white-collar and blue-collar workers. Because blue-collar workers have been subjected to layoffs and recalls their whole lives, they know that a layoff has nothing to do with them personally. If the plant is closing or laying off workers, they know it is because of something about management, not about them. Perhaps the plant is moving to another country; perhaps it is shutting down production temporarily; whatever the cause, it has nothing to do with the workers.

In contrast, white collar workers of the late twentieth-century United States expected more or less continual employment with the same employer. Their ideology of meritocratic individualism was based on their schooling and made it obvious that achievement was a function of individual effort and talent; that the more meritorious one's behavior, the higher one would rise in the ranks of the corporation. When these people were laid off due to downsizing, they reasoned that it must have been because of something about themselves. They must somehow be at fault, though often they could find no fault in their work efforts. This conviction repeatedly led to their personal dis-integration because the realities of their lives were no longer predictable by the logic of meritocratic individualism, the ideology that had offered them justifications and refuge while they were employed. Blue-collar workers experienced no such disorientation when they were laid off.

DeMott (1990) like anthropologist Jules Henry before him (1963) points to the ideologies and practices of schools as creating a false sense of equality and inculcating a sense of individual merit. Jean Lave (1988) points to the relationship between schooling and meritocratic individualism and suggests that cognition incorporates understandings of the individual's past, expectations of the future, formation of goals, and assessments of available social and material means, all of which are functions of class position. The trick is to be able to see the importance of that class position in a society that denies its existence in the courtroom, diagnosis, media, and schools. For that, the characteristic means of anthropology are appropriate: ethnography, holism, and comparison.

THE ROLE OF ETHNOGRAPHY

Ethnography gives us first-hand observations. Holism shows how those observations are connected to others. Comparison allows us to see similarities and differences of systems. When the people have perished, we use archaeological evidence. Archaeology contributes a wider comparative view, and the comparative view allows for more detailed archaeological and ethnographic interpretations. It also distances us so we can speak of classes, ruling classes, and states without censure or embarrassment—something American anthropologists have found difficult or impossible to do when describing our own social order.

As capitalist production expands to all corners of the globe it incorporates people of all lands and joins them in the same structure of production. The well-paid unionized dockworkers of Charleston, South Carolina (Erem and Durrenberger 2008), are part of the same system as the Chinese factory girls (Pun Ngai 2005) who produce the container loads of goods the black longshoremen in South Carolina unload en route to Walmarts to supply the culture of consumption of American workers.

As Marshall Sahlins points out (2000), people of different places and times relate and respond to the global system in terms of their own understandings and their own local practices and realities. So there is not a uniform response to globalization, but many different ones.

While we may have produced detailed ethnographic descriptions of various pieces of this global system, anthropologists have ignored the connections among the parts and said little about the relationships of power and force that create specific hierarchies (Carbonella and Kasmir 2006). At one moment capitalism brings people into it as, for instance, it incorporates village women in China. And at the next, capitalism turns upon them as, for instance, when it moves production from the United States or Mexico to China, leaving American or Mexican working people without jobs and with lower incomes—and clamoring for the cheaper goods from Chinese workers inexorably fueling the relocation of the next factory to China (Heyman 1991).

Carbonella and Kasmir (2006) suggest that by drawing these connections we can move anthropology from our historic identity as the ones who study "primitive" people beyond the reach of capitalism and challenge the traditional academic division of labor that has relegated the study of class formation, the working class, and labor unions to sociology. At the same time, this delocalizes anthropology, shifts its vision from the worm's-eye view of ethnography to a global view in order to understand the causal forces that determine the lives of the people we see in the ethnographies. It shifts our focus from the exotic to our homelands in the global North.

Since the explosion of identity politics and cultural studies, ethnography has been appropriated by a wide range of disciplines from English to marketing to sociology (e.g., Fantasia 1988; Burawoy 1991, 2000). Usually, however, what passes for ethnography, even in sociology, is quite distinct from what anthropologists do as ethnography.

Anthropologist Harry F. Wolcott (2008,71) suggests that ethnography is directed at learning about culture. The underlying idea is that *culture is revealed through discerning patterns of socially shared behavior*" (italics original). He admits that there may not be satisfactory resolutions to questions such as how much sharing or agreement is necessary, but others have given formal and methodological answers to such questions (see especially the works of Romney and his colleagues: Romney 1999; Romney et al. 1996; Romney and Moore 1998; Romney et al. 2000; Romney, Moore, and Rush 1996).

It seems that most appropriations have dislodged ethnography as a set of techniques from the larger conceptual framework that gives it meaning in anthropology (Wolcott 2008). Wolcott suggests that articles in the journal *Contemporary Ethnography* and its mission statement indicate the idea of ethnography as "anything that can be studied through a fieldwork approach" (71). For some, it is any qualitative approach and does not entail quantitative methods. Anthropologists such as Romney, on the other hand, seek ways to integrate quantitative methods into ethnography to increase its validity and reliability.

Anthropologists Patricia Sunderland and Rita Denny (2007) argue that in consumer research, ethnography has been appropriated as simply another psychological method in an implicit paradigm "that assumes individual motivation and make-up are the key to consumption practices" (2007, 14). Notice, importantly, how this approach is a projection of the middle-class ideology of meritocratic individualism. Anthropologists may never live up to our ideal of cultural relativity and etic awareness, but we attempt not to project our ideologies. While there are manuals for "doing ethnography," Sunderland and Denny offer a series of case studies meant to indicate by example "how to apply and appreciate cultural analysis in the practice of consumer research" (15). In sum, they "want to show that the real magic and difference of ethnography lies in the cultural approach and analysis, not in a different kind of data gathering" (15).

We agree, and we offer these studies in a similar vein as examples of the ethnographic understanding and study of class and its relationship to consciousness. As anthropologists, however, we extend the time horizon via archaeological interpretations and the geographic horizon to all people.

THE ANTHROPOLOGY OF CLASS

Morton Fried (1967) provided a way of thinking about the evolution of social orders. Egalitarian forms have as many positions of prestige as there are people capable of filling them, and all have equal access to strategic subsistence resources such as land and water. Egalitarian societies would include foragers and some horticulturalists such as Lisu and Gumlao Kachin in Southeast Asia and Tsembaga in New Guinea.

Rank-ordered societies have fewer positions of prestige than people capable of filling them but maintain equal access to resources. These would include "big man" social orders such as those of New Guinea, Gumsa Kachin, and Trobriand Islanders. While some people may organize production for short-term goals such as prestige-granting feasts, there is no compulsion.

Stratification rests on some group of people having privileged access to resources. Sooner or later, the privileged group will develop the mechanisms of the state to maintain order by inculcating in all a respect for law, an ideology that inequality is natural and inevitable, and a bureaucracy to keep track of people, places, and things. Stratified social orders include all of the familiar modern states as well as ancient kingdoms and chiefdoms.

Fried suggests the definition of class as those groups defined by differential access to resources in stratified orders. Some have privileged access to resources and others do not. All of the contributors to this collection used this starting point to address the question of how class shapes culture.

Across time and around the world anthropologists have documented the development and working of many kinds of hierarchical social arrangements. Many share certain features that Morton Fried isolated in 1967 as differential access to resources. That is, some people have privileged access to resources. Classes are groups of people in the same society that do not have the same rights to use resources. Fried suggested that such social orders could not long endure unless they developed the apparatus of states to maintain order by physically and culturally controlling those without privileged access and convincing them to accept their disadvantaged positions.

What counts as a long time varies with perspective, but such stratified societies, even in the absence of states, are remarkably tenacious over at least hundreds of years, as the papers by William Honeychurch on Mongolia, Doug Bolender on Medieval Iceland and Ann Hill on Nuosu of the Southwestern frontier of China all indicate.

A related notion of class favored by Wolf (1999) is that it is defined by place in the process of production. Class position defines who does what to whom and who gets what. This is similar to some definitions of politics, and class is just as much a political as an economic fact. This is the reason that anthropologists who wish to develop comparative understandings of economic and political systems often refer to a political economy—to suggest the necessary linkage between the two spheres.

Inculcating the belief that some people naturally or supernaturally have more power and prestige and rights to use certain things than others results in compliance to hierarchy. Thus class and consciousness—peoples' ways of thinking and acting—are linked. Because the shaping of culture is never complete, people may more or less successfully resist—and change—these institutions and conventions, while others may fight to uphold and reinforce them.

Josiah Heyman, David Griffith, Kate Golterman, Sharryn Kasmir, Dimitra Doukas, and Barbara Dilly suggest, in their chapters about dimensions of class in the United States, that global processes link local class arrangements to more inclusive organizations that are more or less coercive. As cultural anthropologists have confronted the consequences of globalization in our ethnographic work (see Nash 2007), we have tried to understand the workings of complex systems beyond villages and tribes and how they change through time. As archaeological data have accumulated, we have been able to expand the scope of our understandings beyond locales and regions as Honeychurch does in this volume. One of the emerging conclusions of both of these lines of inquiry is that the dynamics of class systems and structures is central.

In the middle of the twentieth century, anthropology moved beyond its early focus on islands and tribal groups to consider peasant villages and nations and more recently to the global systems that link the planet today. For instance, as Kate Golterman shows, a corporation links affluent Americans with Native Americans via the commodities upon which all focus. Paradoxically, as factories began to replace peasants' fields and tourism and industrial agriculture began to intrude into foraging peoples' domains, it is anthropology's insistence on fine-grained ethnographic understanding of people in locales that forced us to consider global contexts.

CLASS AND CONSCIOUSNESS

From the beginning, culture has been a central topic of anthropology, but class has not often been considered a central element in shaping culture, people's awareness of their social and natural worlds, or consciousness. This book develops that topic in relationship to class in several contexts from the prehistoric in Mongolia (Honeychurch) to the historic in Medieval Iceland (Bolender) to the ethnohistoric in the frontiers of China (Hill). Trawick situates the understanding of class squarely in the global political economy. Other papers focus on the fine-grained ethnography of a beauty salon in the

United States (Goltermann), the relations between General Motors and the United Auto Workers as the corporation self-consciously set out to change workers' consciousness (Kasmir), the broad sweep of American history as it affected farm women (Dilly), the complexities of the border with Mexico (Heyman), the details of immigrant workers' lives (Griffith), and developing ideological patterns of the mostly white rust-belt (Doukas).

Why do armed mobile collectives of mounted herders capable of politi-cal independence participate in a large-scale asymmetric system? William Honeychurch makes critical use of archaeological, ethnological, and docu-mentary materials as well as anthropological theory to suggest that while the various states that would become China were warring among them-selves in the Warring States period (475–221 BC), a process of crisis, social disruption, militarization, and centralization was leading to the develop-ment of the Xiongnu polity across the complex environments of what we now know as Mongolia, Inner Mongolia, southern Siberia, eastern Kazakhstan, and Xinjiang with a widespread ideology and a centralized ritual to mediate between heaven and earth. Along with greater mobility that optimized livestock and surplus production came greater social stabil-ity and more predictable productive conditions that favored local groups, so that system of stratification did not have to rely on coercion though it could amass it if conditions warranted. Honeychurch shows how individual and group productive decisions and ideologies coalesced into a thriving system that challenged China for the next four hundred years and whose successors reverberate through history from that time forward.

While archaeology can never reveal the ideas or consciousness of peo-ple to us, it can show us the consequences of their actions, especially those actions that were repetitive and widespread enough to show up as patterns of artifacts or other material remains. In the third chapter, Bolender uses such evidence to reconstruct the process of class formation in Iceland.

He discusses how differential access to rights in land defined land-owning aristocrats who commanded the labor and products of others via rental and wage agreements: renters whose access to land depended on the goodwill of landowners but who commanded the labor of others, and wage workers whose labor was at the command of aristocrats and renters.

Recognizing the limitations of documentary evidence for under-standing the process of class formation, he indicates that archaeological evidence shows a three-stage process. First, large, complex, independent farmsteads composed of chieftains, dependents, and slaves settled in the second half of the ninth century. Within a hundred years all land was controlled by larger and smaller more and less powerful households, each dependent on its own power to defend its land as there were no overarching state institutions.

Second, in about the year 1000, large landowners substituted direct control of labor inside their households for indirect control of labor through rental arrangements on small subdivided farms to increase production and the number of people the land supported. Third, after the Icelanders ceded authority to the King of Norway, the Church became a major landowner, concentrating land ownership in fewer hands without the formation of new households. By the end of the seventeenth century, all land including Church properties belonged to only 5 percent of the people, and a small aristocracy commanded the labor and product of a mass of tenant and dependent farmers.

The ethnohistorical approach to Nuosu of the fourth chapter is intermediate in its time scale and relies on the testimony of the living, which sometimes poses problems of interpretation. Morton Fried (1967) argued that without some institutionalized means for keeping order, those without privileged access would repudiate the system of stratification and institute more egalitarian forms in which there is no differential access. Ann Hill tests these conjectures against ethnographic and ethnohistoric data. As in Mongolia, on the southwestern frontier of China, Nuosu aristocrats have privileged access to resources, but the system has remained in place, though neither uniform nor unchanged, for at least several hundreds of years. Furthermore, she argues, states and empires themselves are not inherently stable as they experience social and political upheavals such as the Communist Revolution in China and subsequent regimes. Thus while class systems are inherent in states, there may be other means to maintain class systems and stratification.

Hill shows that different Nuosu historical trajectories in different locales resulted in slaves owning property and renting it to aristocrats, aristocrats joining immigrant communities of commoners, and other anomalies. Add to this the complexities of the Republican period, the Communist Revolution, and postrevolutionary incorporation of Nuosu into the Chinese polity, and Hill argues that Nuosu represent a complex and long-lived system of stratification without a state.

Paul Trawick's chapter, the fifth, is pivotal because it provides the global perspective that is necessary for the chapters that follow. He points out that globalization has produced a new global class structure. The fossil-fuel-based mass consumption of the North has two consequences: the impoverishment of the South and global warming. The global capitalist class promotes the idea that unlimited economic growth is an unmitigated and general good that informs the ideology of finance capital, the idea that money, itself *symbolic* of value rather than real value, can increase infinitely. Thus they layer symbol upon symbol without creating any real value while impoverishing the planet. The solution, he suggests, is an ancient one that people have invented time and again when they find themselves dependent on a scarce and finite resource such as water: equal and fair sharing of a common pool resource.

Since the working class of the Global North benefits from current arrangements—with cheap food and manufactured goods—it accepts the global capitalists' fantasy of infinite growth. This ideology is equivalent to what Doukas (2003) calls the "gospel of wealth," whereas the views of the Global South are more aligned with what she identifies as the opposing "gospel of work," which seems to have survived among sectors of the US working class, if only as an informal ideology (Durrenberger and Doukas 2008).

In the sixth chapter Doukas focuses on a specific dimension of the ideology of wealth creation or finance capital and its elaboration into various class-based scenarios of an American crash, collapse, or catastrophe. Doukas pays careful attention to the distinction between the external realities of class and the conceptions of class that people share as cultural constructs.

She suggests that narratives of impending catastrophe illustrate class differences that would otherwise remain hidden in a society whose ideology is heavily committed to the denial of class—each class conceives its catastrophe in terms that reflect class position. In exposing an inaccessible and contemptuous global elite, working-class stories of the conspiratorial New World Order reveal an awareness of the differences between owners of capital and those who work for them. The dominant class reveals this awareness in its own way, predicting a crash in terms of the logic of the finance capital it hopes to preserve (the symbolic value Trawick discusses) against the claims of the working-class "mob." On the border between these two classes, the middle class—those of the working class that the capitalist class hires to manage the rest—maintains the self-congratulatory ideology of a classless prosperity for all that disguises its class position. It discusses peak oil and other resource crises as natural catastrophes that can cause the collapse of the global economic system, again in terms similar to the ones Trawick develops.

In the seventh chapter Dilly outlines the dynamic relationships among the evolving realities of class in the United States, young farm women's conceptions of them, and how they informed their decisions about their lives. She explores the class consciousness of young American farm women. Here regional variation is perhaps even more complex than that Hill describes for Nuosu in China. As other writers in this book indicate, race, religion, and immigration status interact with capitalist social and economic structures. Here, these interactions defined gendered divisions of farm labor that limited young farm women's patterns of behavior and thought so that farmers could exploit the labor of their daughters for a wide range of productive and reproductive tasks in the expansion of American agriculture on the frontier as they either resisted or aided in the transformation from household to commercial production. A romantic ideology of kinship, labor, community, and yeoman farming disguised these oppressive practices, which in some ways appear to be analogous to the initial stage of intrahousehold stratification that Bolender discusses for medieval Iceland.

In the eighth chapter Griffith continues the theme of rural labor in the contemporary US Midwest and South. If Trawick develops a global analysis, Griffith sees similar processes from the ground up. Based on his ethnographic study of diverse locales in Iowa, North Carolina, Mexico, and Honduras, Griffith argues that consciousness of class is based on the shared experience of class. The fragmentation process creates opportunities for workers to become entrepreneurs while their household consumption demands require multiple sources of income.

The experience of immigration can also fragment people's social lives along the lines that Heyman discusses such as language, nationality, dress, food preferences, race, and immigration status. Immigrants form entourages based on loyalty and obligation to translate social relations into economic and political gain. People experience similarity and difference not in their economic positions, but in consumption. The semblance of upward mobility that results from earlier immigrants providing services to new immigrants or managing their labor together with the fragmentation of work drive people into identity practices, employer paternalism, and multiple economic roles that militate against the shared experiences that would result in consciousness of class.

In the ninth chapter, Heyman explores the complexities of the United States–Mexico border to unravel the role of class among the many dimensions of social concepts about people. He discusses the long history of economic and political relations for organizing people as labor and how regional social and political arrangements are rooted in larger capitalist processes. The relationships of class and consciousness are convoluted as class intersects with generation, race and citizenship status, nationality, and gender to provide the strategic categories people use as they order their lives for work as factory and agricultural labor, technicians, professionals, government and domestic workers, and in the informal economy across the border.

The tenth chapter is an ethnographic account of the role of class and class consciousness in General Motors's (GM) Saturn plant. Sharryn Kasmir describes the details of the factory, how Saturn workers negotiated contracts that split them from the national-level agreements of the United Auto Workers (UAW), and how GM tried to develop a new worker consciousness based on cooperation with management and a concept of their own elite status within the ranks of GM workers. As insecurity of workers in the Saturn plant increased, they rejected management moves to reaffirm their association with the national UAW and rejected the sense of privilege that GM proffered. Like Hill, Kasmir recommends that we understand the formation of classes and class consciousness in terms of such local details of evolving relations between capital and labor.

Situating the lives of urban beauty shop patrons in their global and class contexts, in the final chapter Kate Goltermann examines class relations in a hair styling salon and their connections with class ideology as well as global commerce. She situates the salon in a network of contradictory perspectives and interests—associations with other salons, media, Native Americans, governments; with the parent corporation and its ideologies, practices, and products; as well as with NGOs and other elements of the global political economy. Paradoxically, while being remade to a certain image, women understand the distance between what they are and male-dominated ideals of beauty, especially with respect to the process of aging. Thus, the experience of the salon, while offering relaxation and prestige, also confirms insecurities. As clients are processed through the salon in a standard set of procedures, the operatives also ratify the ideology of meritocratic individu-alism and convince their clients that they are unique and deserving. In the meantime, reinforcing their own insecurities, the operatives measure the distance between themselves and their clients socially, economically, and physically. In products branded as Native American, often with only flimsy ties to indigenous cultures, the clients perceive authenticity. This suffices to persuade them that they are participating in "green" practices without having to trouble themselves to recycle trash or care about people of color. Consumption of commodities becomes consumption of a system of values and a fantasy of the eternally youthful environmentally aware and authentic person.

CONCLUSION

The papers in this volume show in specific ethnographic and archaeological contexts how class and consciousness are related and how and under what circumstances people may develop consciousness of class. People become aware, develop consciousness, learn their cultures by the experience of growing up when and where they do. Far from being free-floating configu-rations of ideas, cultures are anchored to the material conditions of exis-tence that determine experience. When the kinds of historic processes that Honeychurch, Bolender, and Hill discuss result in people having differential access to resources, class becomes a crucial determinant of experience, and experience determines consciousness.

States guarantee asymmetric access to resources: classes. One of the means they use to do so is the manipulation of consciousness, the creation of dreamwork to obfuscate the realities of these inequalities either by pro-claiming them to be natural, obvious, and necessary as between aristocrats and commoners, or by denying that they exist as communist and consumer capitalist orders do. This book breaks away from the comfortable confor-mity of some American anthropologists with our cultural dreamwork to show just how the inequalities of class structure experience and awareness across cultures and within them.

It is all too comfortable to project the consciousness of the manage-rial middle class and depict a world of individuals making self-interested choices and living the lives that their merit confers on them whether they be of wealth or of poverty. Many American anthropologists have done so. We break from that tradition and return to the tradition of breaking through the dreamwork to depict the underlying realities of etic relationships, positions in economic systems, and how those structure experience and hence consciousness.

In doing so we take anthropology the next step, incorporating global perspectives without sacrificing our strength—empirical description, whether it be ethnographic or archaeological. Our comparative analyses allow us to move beyond the confines of any single system to more general understandings of class and consciousness so that we can see the workings of our own cultural constructs and how they blind us to realities. We don't simply construct realist narratives or objectivist discourses; we describe realities to replace those accounts which have repeated rather than repudiated the dreamwork of meritocratic individualism and the classless middle class. We show that those same self-satisfied denizens of the middle class are etically in the same class position as the sweatshop workers of the global South who produce the consumer goods that the more privileged demand to live out their identities as consumers in a world of goods.

We believe that replacing obscurantism with clarity will not only contribute to more adequate analyses but will also provide a basis for changing those aspects of such systems that are not only no longer adaptive but are endangering our species. To continue to participate in the myth-making not only detracts from the credibility of anthropology; it is ethically reprehensible and politically irresponsible.

REFERENCES CITED

Anderson, Sarah, John Cavanagh, and Thea Lee. 2005. *Field Guide to the Global Economy, Revised Edition.* New York: New Press.

Bakan, Joel. 2005. *The Corporation: The Pathological Pursuit of Profit and Power.* New York: Free Press.

Brodkin, Karen. 2000. "Global Capitalism: What's Race Got to Do with It." *American Ethnologist* 27(2): 237–256.

Burawoy, Michael. 1991. *Ethnography Unbound: Power and Resistance in the Modern Metropolis.* Berkeley: University of California Press.

———. 2000. *Global Ethnography: Forces, Connections, and Imaginations in a Postmodern World.* Berkeley: University of California Press.

Carbonella, August, and Sharryn Kasmir. 2006. "Rethinking the Anthropology of Social Class." *Anthropology News* 47(8): 8–9.

DeMott, Benjamin. 1990. *The Imperial Middle: Why Americans Can't Think Straight about Class*. New York: William Morrow.

deZengotita, Thomas. 2006. *Mediated: How the Media Shapes Our World and the Way We Live in It*. New York: Bloomsbury Publishing.

Doukas, Dimitra. 2003. *Worked Over: The Corporate Sabotage of an American Community*. Ithaca, NY: Cornell University Press.

Durrenberger, E. Paul. 2002. "Why the Idea of Social Capital Is a Bad Idea." *Anthropology News* 43(9): 5.

———. 2004. "Global Processes, Local Systems." *Urban Anthropology* 32(3–4): 253–279.

———. 2006. "On the Invisibility of Class in America." *Anthropology News* 47(8): 9–10.

Durrenberger, E. Paul, and Dimitra Doukas. 2008. "Gospel of Wealth, Gospel of Work: Hegemony in the U.S. Working Class." *American Anthropologist* 110(2): 1548–1433.

Durrenberger, E. Paul, and Suzan Erem. 2010. *Anthropology Unbound: A Field Guide to the 21st Century*. Second ed. Boulder, CO: Paradigm Publishers.

Ehrenreich, Barbara. 1989. *Fear of Falling: The Inner Life of the Middle Class*. New York: Pantheon.

Erem, Suzan, and E. Paul Durrenberger. 2008. *On the Global Waterfront: The Fight to Free the Charleston 5*. New York: Monthly Review Press.

Evans-Pritchard, E. E. 1937. *Witchcraft, Oracles and Magic among the Azande*. Oxford: Clarendon Press.

Fantasia, Rick. 1988. *Cultures of Solidarity: Consciousness, Action, and Contemporary American Workers*. Berkeley: University of California Press.

Fones-Wolf, Elizabeth A. 1995. *Selling Free Enterprise: The Business Assault on Labor and Liberalism, 1945–60*. Champaign-Urbana: University of Illinois Press.

Fried, Morton. 1967. *The Evolution of Political Society: An Essay in Political Anthropology*. New York: Random House.

Harris, Marvin. 1974. *Cows, Pigs, Wars and Witches: The Riddles of Culture*. New York: Random House.

Hart, Keith. 1973. "Informal Income Opportunities and Urban Employment in Ghana." *Journal of Modern African Studies* 11: 61–89.

———. In Press. "The Informal Economy." In *The Human Economy: A Citizen's Guide*, edited by Keith Hart, J. L. Laville, and A. D. Cattani. Cambridge: Cambridge University Press.

Henry, Jules. 1963. *Culture against Man*. New York: Vintage.

Heyman, Josiah McC. 1991. *Life and Labor on the Border: Working People of Northeastern Sonora, Mexico, 1886–1986*. Tucson: University of Arizona Press.

Keller, Bill. 2005. "Introduction." In *Class Matters*. Correspondents of the *New York Times*, ix–xviii. New York: Henry Holt and Company.

Lapham, Lewis H. 1988. *Money and Class in America: Notes and Observations on our Civil Religion*. New York: Weidenfeld & Nicolson.

Lave, Jean. 1988. *Cognition in Practice: Mind, Mathematics and Culture in Everyday Life*. Cambridge: Cambridge University Press.

Lewellen, Ted C. 2002. *The Anthropology of Globalization: Cultural Anthropology Enters the 21st Century*. Westport, CT: Bergin and Garvey.

Mills, Mary Beth. 1999. *Thai Women in the Global Labor Force: Consuming Desires, Contested Selves*. New Brunswick, NJ: Rutgers University Press.

Narotzky, Susana, and Gavin Smith. 2006. *Immediate Struggles: People, Power, and Place in Rural Spain*. Berkeley: University of California Press.

Nash, June. 2007. *Practicing Ethnography in a Globalizing World*. Boulder, CO: AltaMira.

Newman, Katherine. 1988. *Falling from Grace: The Experience of Downward Mobility in the American Middle Class*. New York: Vintage.

Nordstrom, Carolyn. 2004. *Shadows of War: Violence, Power, and International Profiteering in the Twenty-First Century*. Berkeley: University of California Press.

———. 2007. *Global Outlaws: Crime, Money, and Power in the Contemporary World*. Berkeley: University of California Press.

Ortner, Sherry. 1998. "Identities: The Hidden Life of Class." *Journal of Anthropological Research* 54(1): 1–17.

———. 2005. *New Jersey Dreaming: Capital, Culture, and the Class of 58*. Durham, NC: Duke University Press.

Pun Ngai. 2005. *Made in China: Women Factory Workers in a Global Workplace*. Raleigh, NC: Duke University Press.

Romney, A. Kimball. 1999. "Culture Consensus as a Statistical Model." *Current Anthropology* 40 (Supplement, February 1999): 103–115.

Romney, A. Kimball, John P. Boyd, Carmella C. Moore, William H. Batchelder, and Timothy J. Brazill. 1996. "Culture as Shared Cognitive Representations." *Proceedings of the National Academy of Science* 93: 4699–4705.

Romney, A. Kimball, and Carmella Moore. 1998. "Toward a Theory of Culture as Shared Cognitive Structures." *Ethos* 6(3): 314–337.

Romney, A. Kimball, Carmella C. Moore, William H. Batchelder, and Ti-Lien Hsia. 2000. "Statistical Methods for Characterizing Similarities and Differences between Semantic Structures." *Proceedings of the National Academy of Science* 97(1): 518–523.

Romney, A. Kimball, Carmella Moore, and Craig D. Rush. 1996. "Cultural Universals: Measuring the Semantic Structure of Emotion Terms in English and Japanese." *Proceedings of the National Academy of Science* 94: 5489–5494.

Rubin, Lillian B. 1994. *Families on the Fault Line: America's Working Class Speaks about the Family, the Economy, Race, and Ethnicity*. New York: Harper.

Sahlins, Marshall. 2000. *Culture in Practice: Selected Essays*. New York: Zone Books.

Salzman, Philip Carl. 2001. *Understanding Culture: An Introduction to Anthropological Theory.* Long Grove, IL: Waveland Press.

Schwartz, Jonathan. 1998. "High School Classmates Revisited: Sherry Ortner and Philip Roth." *Anthropology Today* 14(6): 14–16.

Smith, M. Estellie. 1990. "A Million Here, a Million There, and Pretty Soon You're Talking Real Money." In *Perspectives on the Informal Economy*, edited by M. Estelle Smith, 1–22. Monographs in Economic Anthropology No. 8. New York: University Press of America.

Stack, Carol. 1997. *All Our Kin: Strategies for Survival in a Black Community.* New York: Basic.

Steinbeck, John. 1939. *The Grapes of Wrath.* New York: Viking.

Sunderland, Patricia L., and Rita M. Denny. 2007. *Doing Anthropology in Consumer Research.* Walnut Creek, CA: Left Coast Press.

Tett, Gillian. 2009. *Fool's Gold: How the Bold Dream of a Small Tribe at J. P. Morgan Was Corrupted by Wall Street Greed and Unleashed a Catastrophe.* New York: Free Press.

Trouillot, Michel-Rolph. 2003. *Global Transformations: Anthropology and the Modern World.* New York: Palgrave Macmillan.

Wolcott, Harry F. 2008. *Ethnography: A Way of Seeing.* Second ed. Lanham, MD: AltaMira.

Wolf, Diane. 1994. *Factory Daughters: Gender, Household Dynamics, and Rural Industrialization in Java.* Berkeley: University of California Press.

Wolf, Eric R. 1999. *Envisioning Power: Ideologies of Dominance and Crisis.* Berkeley: University of California Press.

Zlolniski, Christian. 2010. "Economic Globalization and Changing Capital-Labor Relations in Baja California's Fresh-Produce Industry." In *The Anthropology of Labor Unions*, edited by E. Paul Durrenberger and Karaleah S. Reichart, 157–188. Boulder: University Press of Colorado.

Thinking Political Communities

The State and Social Stratification among Ancient Nomads of Mongolia

WILLIAM HONEYCHURCH

INTRODUCTION

The distant ancestors of today's Mongolians constructed some of the great polities of the Old World. More than 2,000 years ago, the first nomadic state, called by the name Xiongnu, challenged the Han dynasty of China, dividing East Asia into two distinct political spheres for more than three centuries (Lattimore 1940; Di Cosmo 2002:196–199). Eight hundred years ago, most of Eurasia knew only one political order, that which arose from beneath the hooves of Mongol cavalry to become the largest land empire in human history. Despite these notable political accomplishments by the nomadic peoples of eastern Eurasia, surprisingly little is known of the indigenous political traditions from which these organizations emerged.

The vast majority of anthropological and historical literature on early steppe polities repeats a common theme on the organizational potential of mobile herders—that in fact, due to movement, lack of surplus, and fierce independence, they tend not to organize politically, or do so only on a small-scale or temporary basis. To be precise, among pastoral nomads, "hierarchical political institutions are generated only by external political relations with state societies, and never develop purely as a result of the internal dynamics of such societies" (Irons 1979:362). This basic idea has persisted with great tenacity over three decades (e.g., Salzman 2004:98–101) and underlies much recent theory on premodern eastern steppe politics (Khazanov 2001; Barfield 2001; Kradin 2008a).

To be fair, the above statement by William Irons, one of the great cultural anthropologists of nomadic peoples, was offered as an hypothesis to be evaluated. Along with this hypothesis, Irons cautions that he arrived at this conclusion based primarily on twentieth-century ethnographic studies. Since nation-states became the main form of political organization during the twentieth century, nomadic groups not involved with state societies have long been in short supply. Further, there is indeed plenty of good ethnographic and historical case material that demonstrates sound cultural, ecological, demographic, and environmental reasons for pastoral groups to maintain communal access to resources and egalitarian organization (Salzman 1999).

However, one cannot help but be suspicious of centuries-old preconceptions of nomads that are part of the mythology of so many different civilizations. The foundations of political and cultural theory about nomads have roots as deep as history itself and are steeped in long intellectual traditions in which nomads from the periphery are viewed as barbarous and inimical to the heartlands of civilization. Historians such as Herodotus, Sima Qian, Ibn Khald n, and Toynbee all took part in constructing and communicating aspects of what has become an implicit and received tradition. Excessively broad sweeps of the ethnographic brush and pervasive historical tropes offer little benefit in exploring the diversity and variability of human societies. A more comprehensive comparative understanding of human sociopolitics will be one of the benefits of a systematic and open-minded study of nomadic societies, both in the past and present.

The archaeological record has proven effective for evaluating many ideas and concepts offered about mobile herders and is particularly well suited for examining social, economic, and political change over time scales of centuries to millennia. However, like the ethnographic and historical records, archaeology has biases and limitations that must be recognized, and this is particularly true of the eastern steppe region where archaeological research is still very much in a developmental phase. Keeping this in mind, I turn to the problem of sociopolitical organization of large-scale, eastern steppe nomadic polities, specifically with the intent of developing ideas about the intertwining of stratification, productive resources, and ideology. The comparative framework of Morton Fried (1967), himself an expert on East Asia, is a starting point for this discussion. By drawing on past and current ideas on stratification and archaic states, I hope to show that not only did pastoral nomads create complex political organizations, but they did so in ways that may teach anthropologists valuable lessons about sociopolitical process in general.

STRATIFICATION AS TEMPORAL, SPATIAL, AND COGNITIVE PROCESS

Fried (1967:186–187) defines stratification as differences between individuals of the same sex and age categories based upon unequal access to the basic resources needed to sustain life. He maintains a broad and flexible understanding of "basic resources," which might include knowledge, information, technologies, labor, and infrastructure, all allowing an individual to subsist within a society. This socioeconomic aspect of stratification, however, is only one strand twined together with many others that form the complexities of a stratified society. In addition to group segregation based on socioeconomic "haves and have nots," archaeological models for stratification have focused on sociopolitical aspects, "leaders and followers," as well as hereditary distinctions based on endogamous status groups, "elites and commoners" (Barnes 2007:173–174). These different strands of social division all had early precedents among steppe societies, but at some point they coalesced into a novel set of political relationships situated within a novel kind of community.

The question of how and when these traditions were woven into a stratified polity necessitates a conception of stratification not as a descriptive condition or a threshold to be crossed, but as a process of on-going negotiations within society. This process was characterized by variation over time and space in the making of social segregation. A diachronic perspective shows that creating stratification may have involved abrupt or incremental beginnings, false starts, declines and collapses, as well as periods of greater and lesser stability in the segregation of select groups. Spatially, this chronology unfolds across different resource and environmental zones, varied sociohistorical contexts, and involving peoples with distinct beliefs and practices. For the purposes of this study, archaic stratification is not a type of society as much as a variable mode of relations that had to be actively sustained and participated in, day in and day out.

Recognizing process and variation in process over time and space is essential for situating specifically socioeconomic factors in a developing order of conditions and responses that resulted in the stratified polity of the Xiongnu.

Socioeconomic divisions and control of basic resources were not primary structuring factors in steppe stratification until sociopolitical conditions emerged that changed the nature of pastoral production as part of a broader political economy. Therefore, in order to explain the emergence of Xiongnu stratification, I take full advantage of Fried's reluctance to tie the concept of basic resources too closely to the basic elements of production (1967:187), in this case, animals, pasture, and water. These three components of steppe pastoralism were embedded in time, place, social relationships, and knowledges, and the acts of production that directly supported individuals and families involved decision making in reference to these multiple contexts.

Where different social configurations or events alter these contexts, the range of elements that might pertain to the category of "basic resources" can shift or expand. It was these shifts and expansions, derived from political actions, that promoted a version of the pastoral economy allowing for differential control over the productive activity of interregional movement in the early Xiongnu state. The possibility of such movement, however, was itself the product of changes in social scale brought about by the formation of an expansive political community under military leadership.

In this sense, pastoral economics is primarily a social construct contingent on local and regional circumstances and experiencing shifts between modes or configurations (Salzman 2004). These shifts are variable over time and space but are founded on how producers make decisions relative to their immediate settings and the range of possibilities and limitations they perceive. Opportunities for political actors to initiate asymmetric relationships were probably not embedded in the stable modes of pastoral lifeways as much as between modes and new kinds of decision making generated as these fluctuate. This dynamic conception of pastoralism as having varied configurations, scales, and productivity contrasts with a more typological and static view (Khazanov 1994), usually invoked by those dismissing steppe politics as fundamentally limited in scope due to the marginality of pastoral economics.

In order to theorize how and why herders organized a state, we must focus not so much on whether a particular kind of resource base can be exploited for political ends, but instead look at how political communities are negotiated, under what circumstances, and how these initial conditions might radically change the variables upon which common people and leaders alike make choices. It is these contingencies that are important, and how they intersected with information assessment and individual and group decision making can explain why common people participated in a community of organized social asymmetry.

Such an approach shifts the focus of analysis away from economic typology to a more engaging mixture of thought, action, and social relationship as the crucible for social stratification. This decidedly messy tableau is crucial for understanding the way steppe politics emerged and became institutionalized. Following an introduction to the geography, peoples, and setting of the eastern steppe zone, I develop this model for combining small-scale decision making with emergent conditions to explain how the stratified Xiongnu state came into being.

THE EASTERN STEPPE AND XIONGNU EMERGENCE

To begin, it is important to clarify what happened, when, and where, and then to look at explanations for these events of more than 2,000 years in the past. The eastern steppe region can be defined in various ways and is often synonymous with the Inner Asia of Owen Lattimore's (1940) famous historical geographic analysis. I will focus on the core of the eastern steppe, the territory of Mongolia, but will draw as well on data and ideas generated from archaeological work in Inner Mongolia, southern Siberia, eastern Kazakhstan, and Xinjiang.

Archaeologists and historians consider this tremendous geographical area to have been the maximal extent of Xiongnu political influence over the historical duration of the polity from 209 BC to ca. AD 120 (Batsaikhan 2003). Two Chinese dynasties were contemporary with the Xiongnu, namely, the Qin (221–206 BC) and Han (202 BC–AD 220) dynasties, though during this historical period of 400 years, both the Xiongnu and sedentary polities underwent transformations, collapses, and reemergences. I place emphasis on the word *historical* here since the contemporary material culture of the northern steppe, which is convincingly linked to the "Xiongnu" polity of textual sources, dates from as early as 400/300 BC to as late as 250 AD. This discrepancy is related to the large error ranges of radiocarbon chronology and the fact that relatively few contexts have been dated, as well as imprecision in Chinese historical knowledge. The archaeological and textual records are very different bodies of information, and there are substantial factual, geographical, and chronological inconsistencies between them. These problems will have to be addressed as the material record becomes better understood and more developed.

Eastern Eurasian environments are extremely diverse and range from dense coniferous forests of Siberia in the north through gradations of forest steppe, steppe, arid steppe, to the Gobi Desert in the south. Across the Gobi and moving further southwards, grasslands again resume and are transitional to the mountains, river valleys, and Central Plain of China. From east to west, environmental changes are again vegetational but linked more to topography. From the forested mountains of Manchuria, broad rolling grasslands make up most of eastern Mongolia. These are intersected by the north central Khentii and Khangai mountain ranges. These central areas with low mountains and intermountain steppe also have the major river basins of Mongolia, all flowing north to the Arctic watershed. Further to the west, there are arid flatlands, salt lakes, and the foothills of the high Altai mountains, which overlap and link the westernmost portions of Mongolia to Siberia, Kazakhstan, and Xinjiang.

To the southwest, the Altai mountains intersect with the western Gobi, which transitions into the rich mountain valleys of the Tian Shan range of northern Xinjiang, famous for a well-known leg of the Silk Road. South of this range is the formidable Taklamakan desert, which is a western extension of the arid Gobi belt but as a "sand desert" differs ecologically from the Gobi "pebble desert." The diversity of these environments suggests great differences and potentials in subsistence practices, resources, spatial distributions, movement regimes, and productive risk. Clearly, a "one-size-fits-all" approach to pastoralism and its socioeconomics will not have much explanatory value given this degree of variation.

Seasonal herding of sheep, goats, cattle, camels, horses, yaks, and, in some places, reindeer are all part of the pastoral tradition of the eastern steppe. Species composition of herds, timing and number of seasonal movements, distance of movement to new camps, and the number of families in co-residence are all complex variables. They are configured by household-based decision making subject to locality, animal holdings, and season, not to mention the local social and political setting.

Though evidence is still limited, subsistence based on domestic herd animals probably began during the early second millennium BC in Mongolia (Honeychurch and Wright 2008). Pastoralism was (and still is) part of a broader set of productive strategies including small-scale agriculture, hunting, gathering, and fishing where these pursuits were viable (Honeychurch and Amartuvshin 2007). Again, while the evidence is far from robust, the first suggestions of social differentiation may be found in the form of impressive stone monuments and burials of the Late Bronze Age (late second and initial first millennium BC) (Frohlich et al. 2009). Changes in the social relations of local groups have been explained by environmental change, ethnic group migrations, and warfare (Tsybiktarov 2003); the advent of horse riding and shifts in alliance networks (Honeychurch et al. 2011); and elite aggrandizement through feasting and ceremonialism (Allard and Erdenebaatar 2005).

Archaeologists do not have the time resolution necessary to understand events leading up to the Xiongnu polity during the critical period of 600 to 300/200 BC, though a tentative overview is possible. Evidence from Mongolia and surrounding regions suggests that burial practices became more elaborate and included greater assemblages of exotic and wealth items (Derevianko and Molodin 2000; Chugunov et al. 2004; Tseveendorj et al. 2007; Honeychurch et al. 2009). Violent conflict was endemic in some regions, but in others, especially north central Mongolia, there are no clear signs of warfare (Torbat et al. 2007; Honeychurch et al. 2011; Shelach 2009a). Exchange networks and the flow of prestige items increased across the entire macroregion and became increasingly important in negotiating local relationships (Shelach 2009b).

Surveys of Early Iron Age monumental centers in Mongolia show a pattern of multiple and distributed monument construction areas that later became spatially consolidated and more centralized (Houle 2009; Honeychurch et al. 2011). Finally, while elite activity areas were spatially consolidated, the spacing between these centers increased, which suggests expanded political territories in association with greater central control (Honeychurch and Amartuvshin 2007). These assertions are based on data from few study areas across this macroregion and require further substantiation by archaeologists using diverse methodologies. However, from this apparent setting of small-scale but expanding polities, the Xiongnu state emerged most likely in the north central river basins of Mongolia and Buriatiia, Siberia (Honeychurch and Amartuvshin 2009).

XIONGNU STYLES OF STRATIFICATION

While Xiongnu organization certainly changed dramatically over time, there is good evidence that social stratification was a crucial part of the political formula as well as part of the subsequent steppe political tradition (Sneath 2006:4–6). Evidence for stratification comes from both descriptions of nomadic political structure in Chinese historical texts and the material evidence of archaeology. Both records suggest social segregation in favor of a small minority who were indeed rulers, elite, and military commanders and who had access to rare and precious commodities as well as labor. How this minority stabilized their social standing over time and attempted to promote novel ways of thinking and production that favored elite control will be discussed below following a review of evidence for Xiongnu stratification.

The earliest Chinese history that examines the Xiongnu polity is the *Shiji* text authored by Sima Qian (ca. 145–86 BC). This text was recorded at a time when the Xiongnu polity was mature and when the Han Dynasty and the steppe state were engaged in an intensive period of warfare and competition sustained over several decades. Therefore, descriptions of steppe political organization are likely to be based on interaction and reliable information though still subject to cultural misunderstandings, political agendas, and pertaining to the time period in which the record was written. While the textual histories are invaluable reports on steppe peoples and their societies, intrinsic problems with the informational bases of these accounts and their interpretation are not often emphasized, though recently Di Cosmo (2002) has provided a much needed exception in the case of the *Shiji*.

With regard to the study of early steppe politics, great problems arise from misinterpretation of seemingly straightforward statements recorded in the past. For example, throughout this paper, and indeed in all of the scholarly work on steppe history, terms such as "tribe," "clan," and "chiefdom" are commonly used to refer to corporate-political groups. Such terms should not be confused with carefully defined anthropological concepts of the same name. These words are in fact crude translations of ancient group terminology that is still poorly understood by contemporary researchers and was not fully understood by the ancient historians who used their own native terminology to approximate foreign words (Ecsedy 1972:248). Such terminological confusion has also led to a mistaken emphasis on idealized segmentary kinship structure as the basis for steppe territorial and political organization (Sneath 2006; Lindner 1982). In fact, forms of steppe political organization were often more varied and more complex than the standard historical discourse would suggest.

Having considered some of the limitations of the histories, we turn to what the texts say about Xiongnu political organization. In Chapter 110 of the *Shiji* text, Sima Qian provides a description of the Xiongnu state as a socially stratified organization (see Watson 1993:136–137). It was led by a hereditary elite that consisted of a single ruling house and three consort clans that provided senior marriage partners to the highest elite members of the ruling house. Only members of these corporate groups were eligible for the highest political offices, which combined political authority, divine right, military leadership, and elite endogamy (Di Cosmo 2002:176–178). The historical sources provide a great many details on positions and offices that supported rulership; however, debate has long surrounded the question of who made up this intermediate elite and what role the pre-Xiongnu "territorial" aristocracy played in state politics. In fact, one of the major controversies in Xiongnu historical research has been to what extent these hierarchical positions represent a nascent administrative body supporting central authority and either integrating or dispossessing a prior territorial elite (Mori 1950; Yamada 1982).

Archaeological evidence for patterns of elite segregation is most clearly seen in burial contexts. Unfortunately, eastern steppe archaeology struggles with the problem of unrefined chronology, and our data represent blocks of time up to 200 years. Better chronologies will become available but only through more systematic fieldwork followed by extensive and costly laboratory analyses. Despite these limitations, archaeologists have provided evidence for what Gina Barnes (2007; 1986:83, 88) calls "material stratification." In her studies of Japanese state formation, Barnes defines this as distinctive material patterns involving rare items, labor-intensive architecture, and significant locales. These patterns occur over a large geographical region but represent an interacting subset of the regional society that was capable of accessing and mobilizing such resources.

There are two forms of elite burial during the Xiongnu period that might be taken to indicate similar patterns of material stratification: one with an embanked ring surface feature made of stone and soil, and the other with a large platform-like mound and several levels of deeply interred construction (Miniaev 1985). Both forms are labor intensive and contain imported items, precious materials, and prominent cemetery locations. Of these two, the smaller and more widespread form is the Xiongnu period "ring tombs," which have surface features measuring up to 14 meters in diameter and pit interments ranging in depth from 1.5 to 3 meters. In these burials, individuals were placed in a supine position and oriented to the north, northeast, northwest, or in rare cases, to the east. Burial chambers consist of an internal construction that might comprise a simple earthen pit, a pit with stone slab siding, a wooden coffin, or an elaborate coffin in a timber frame enclosure. Finds include the remains of domestic herd animals and wild fauna; ceramic vessels and bone tools; iron, bronze, silver, and gold artifacts; and long-distance goods such as Chinese and Central Asian products. Burial sites can vary from a single burial to groups of over 350 ring burials, sometimes associated with the second type of "platform tombs."

These larger platform-like constructions have the same orientation and consist of a low rectangular or slightly trapezoidal earth and stone mound ranging in dimension from 16 to 29 meters on a side with a height of up to 2 meters above the modern surface. On the south side there appears a sloping entryway as much as 22 meters in length that accesses a deep central burial chamber. The burial pits of these tombs reach 10 meters or more in depth, and the construction work overlying the chamber consists of soil, stone, and wood layers. The burial chamber itself includes an inner and outer wooden construction of hewn logs and wooden planks usually made of larch or pine. Within the innermost chamber, a wooden coffin holding the interred individual is sometimes found, though disruption from pillaging has often destroyed the internal contexts of these sites. These tombs were often richly furnished with precious metals and stones, large ceramic vessels, felt and woven carpets, silks, jade items, bronze mirrors, and lacquer ware. A wide range of horse-related equipment is also commonly found, as is faunal evidence for horse, cattle, Bactrian camels, wild animals, and quantities of domestic grain.

At this time, archaeologists are not able to delimit the chronological range of these two types of mortuary treatment, nor explain the geographical spread of these different practices. Most work has been done on the smaller ring burials, though several multiyear excavation projects are currently underway on the large platform tombs. Some researchers suggest that the largest burial format was related to the ruling houses of the Xiongnu polity. The ring burials, with multiple variations in internal structure, may have been burial treatments provided to different ranks of intermediate elite. At least in one well-documented context at the Siberian site of Tsaram, an elite platform mound was surrounded by several ring burials of male individuals with potential signs of human sacrifice (Miniaev and Sakharovskaia 2002).

Where demographic and genetic studies have been conducted, there is strong evidence that only a relatively few members of society were buried with either of these mortuary practices. In the Egiin Gol valley of north central Mongolia, all Xiongnu period cemeteries located by intensive survey represent a total of a little more than 100 individuals out of an estimated population that reached into the thousands for the time period that these cemeteries were in use (Honeychurch et al. 2007). Based on ancient DNA analysis of a single cemetery at Egiin Gol, which was used over several centuries, it is clear that many individuals shared genetic relationships and that only three to four genetic lineages are represented there (Keyser-Tracqui et al. 2003). Common people were provided with simpler methods of burial, and archaeologists have had little success in documenting the mortuary treatment of the hundreds of people who did not receive labor-intensive platform or ring tombs. Simpler Xiongnu mortuary practices might have included cremations, unmarked burials, or surface exposure of bodies. Otherwise, commoners may have been provided with very shallow pit burials marked with just a few stones scattered on the surface, as has been documented at the Gobi desert site of Baga Gazaryn Chuluu (Nelson et al. 2009).

Settlement sites of the Xiongnu period also show substantial differences in size, construction, and composition, though very few of these settlements have been studied systematically. Archaeologists have located seasonal campsites of herding families as well as large seasonal settlements that may have been associated with local elite activities (Honeychurch and Amartuvshin 2007). In addition to habitation sites, small-scale and larger walled sites have also been discovered and dated to the Xiongnu period. In the Egiin Gol valley, a walled and ditched site perched above the river on a high rise is associated with goods imported from China, but very little evidence for consistent or repeated use has been found. It is therefore difficult to understand the function of this walled site, though it is situated in a prominent and defensible location and could have been used for either protection or ceremonial events (Honeychurch 2004:133–135). Much larger wall sites have been investigated in Siberia and Mongolia and have been found to have planned layouts, often with internal structures and external ditches, and very different kinds of use histories. Some are clearly village-like settlements where multiple resource production and craft specializations were practiced (Davydova 1995; Pousaz et al. 2007), while others may have been related to elite or even possibly administrative functions. The variety of settlements suggests that functional difference was an important aspect of Xiongnu organization, and though more fieldwork is needed, I expect that many such sites will show evidence for association with the political elite.

EXPLAINING XIONGNU POLITICS

Why do herding groups with great potential for political independence participate in a large-scale organization that was founded upon clear social asymmetries as demonstrated in the historical and material records? Theories for the rise of the Xiongnu regional polity commonly relate state formation processes to cultural and economic dependence on Chinese neighbors. Some explanations emphasize sinocization processes in which peripheral peoples directly adopted cultural and political models from Chinese states and applied them on the steppe (Honey 1992). Others argue that an unstable pastoral nomadic economy required agricultural supplements from China, and so steppe nomads organized at comparable levels to coercively extract these resources (Fletcher 1986; Barfield 2001). Finally, many anthropologists and historians simply doubt the complexity of nomadic organization altogether and argue that centralization was sporadic and consensual, and that local leadership was primary (Yamada 1982; Khazanov 1994:166–198).

Archaeology, along with historical research critical of sinocentric texts and a reassessment of anthropological theory on nomadic pastoralism, have effectively challenged these explanations (Di Cosmo 1994, 1999; Humphrey and Sneath 1999; Sneath 2006; Honeychurch and Amartuvshin 2006; Rogers 2007). While the Xiongnu polity is certainly secondary in that it emerged within a setting of adjacent states, the relationship between early China and surrounding polities, including those in Korea and Japan, was complex, variable over time, and is today highly controversial. Throughout the centuries leading up to the formation of the Xiongnu polity, Chinese states were busy annihilating and incorporating each other during the aptly named Warring States period (475–221 BC). State competition, regional instability, and the brief consolidation under the Qin empire in 221 BC certainly affected distant groups, but indirectly (Di Cosmo 1994; Honeychurch 2004; Shelach 2009b).

The emergence of the Xiongnu state involved indigenous processes unfolding within a setting influenced by adjacent regions but also with regard to 800 or more years of steppe experimentation with social differentiation, central leadership, and political technique during the Late Bronze and Early Iron Age. A model that better reflects this indigenous perspective has been offered by Nicola Di Cosmo (2002:178–186). He explains how the Xiongnu regional polity may have formed through a sequential process of crisis and social disruption, militarization under a charismatic leader, and centralization around that leadership position. Di Cosmo's stepwise sequence is a good framework for introducing concepts of shifting circumstance, decision making, and negotiation to the problem of enduring social asymmetry among steppe nomads. The following discussion uses Di Cosmo's broad outline of events and the above concepts to explore connections between thinking, stratification, and nomadic statehood. Given an emphasis on assessment and choice, what conditions made participation among commoners in the early Xiongnu state probable? To answer this question, I focus on the initial creation of political community, increased scales of pastoral production, and new opportunities for political control made available by increases in social and economic scale.

NEGOTIATING POLITICAL COMMUNITY

Political community has been defined variously but generally refers to a body politic composed of those people who identify with a polity and its territory (Weber 1978:901–903). I use the term to discuss, not a type of group, but a change in group affiliation, associated with statehood, in which a social collective is created by way of a single political relationship to an individual or a subgroup. This political relationship is uniform for every member of the community and is the basis for collective identity and action (Fried

1967:236). The community incorporates narratives justifying the centrality and ascendency of this individual or core subgroup and connects the maintenance of the political community to the actions and decisions of these core members. Affiliation has the capacity to dissolve prior forms of political identity as well as social and cultural boundaries internal to the community, though this process may be negotiated, resisted, or manipulated for political ends.

Territorial expansion through warfare was the beginning of the Xiongnu state and constituted the initial political community. During times of destabilization on the eastern steppe, numerous historical examples show how a successful military leader and supporters translated armed conflict against neighbors into a social movement with political potential (Di Cosmo 1999). Sima Qian reports such an account of the building of the initial Xiongnu political community under the leader Maodun (Watson 1993:134–136). According to Di Comso (2002:174–176), this occurred during a period of crisis on the steppe caused by Qin Dynasty expansion into northern pasturelands at ca. 215 BC. While the sources and reliability of this account are not known and the historical and archaeological chronologies show discrepancies, it is remarkable how consistent the story of Maodun is with ethnohistorical cases of state formation. If step-by-step instructions for state consolidation could be imagined based on cross-cultural accounts from the past 400 years, as proposed by Flannery (1999:14–15), then Maodun literally built his state "by the book."

This correspondence suggests that there may be more than legend and myth involved in the account of Maodun. As recounted by Sima Qian, Maodun was a member of an existing elite lineage though he was disenfranchised from attaining the highest political positions. He usurped power by innovating new military techniques and organization, assassinated his father to acquire a position of leadership, and rapidly expanded against neighboring groups. Archaeologists believe that rapid construction of large-scale political communities through warfare was not uncommon in prehistory, and many such collectives formed and just as rapidly fell apart, leaving few archaeological traces (Wright 2006). The transformation of a mobilized collective into a regional organization that maintains asymmetric political relationships requires the creation and application of contextualized political technique or "statecraft." This can be defined as actions, events, techniques, and traditions that frame factional negotiation within a political community based on the divergent agendas of community participants, both elite and nonelite (Rogers 2007:264–265).

For example, the success of his build-up allowed Maodun to control people, territory, and resources but more importantly, it endowed him with a broadly recognized prerogative for generating relationships based on authority and loyalty. Regional scale conquests made possible such relationships between the leadership and an unprecedented number of followers. Through a series of both intentional acts and unintentional occurrences, this relationship between "leaders and followers" was translated into an homologous relationship between "rulers and ruled," which was then tenuously maintained over time. Evidence for this conversion of roles within the early Xiongnu political community includes techniques that distinguished the ruling segment while simultaneously joining the regional and diverse collective together. One such set of techniques was the investment of initial military success and prerogative in public modes of belief about the exceptional nature of central leadership, beliefs which later became state ideology.

XIONGNU RULERS AND STEPPE BELIEF SYSTEMS

Political community is defined by participation. Choices in favor of participation over resistance on the part of newly integrated groups is a crucial first step in state building. Novel ideologies and revisions of cosmology were common sources of influence over decision making within many political communities, and both were powerful motivating factors in the creation of the Xiongnu state (Kürsat-Ahlers 1996a; Fletcher 1986). According to the historical texts, the state ruler of the Xiongnu, known as the *Shanyu*, was considered to be the single ruler "chosen by heaven." The new title suggests the emergence and promulgation of the concept of a king-making deity, which was likely an enhancement of existing religious beliefs and distinct from the Chinese "son of heaven" concept (Di Cosmo 2002:172). This position also made the *Shanyu* an explicit intermediary between the political community and heaven, and placed communal ritual privilege in the *Shanyu*'s hands (Kürsat-Ahlers 1996b: 35).

Revised cosmology was accompanied by a shift in political worldview that strongly emphasized essential cultural differences between the steppe peoples and those of sedentary China. In a famous letter to the Han Emperor

Wen (ca. 176 BC), *Shanyu* Maodun declared himself uniter of all those who draw the bow into one family. In reply, Emperor Wen affirmed his domain over all southern peoples who wear hats and sashes (Di Comso 2002:196). Communications from the Shanyu to the Chinese usually emphasized the pastoral way of life by referencing movement and the herding of animals, especially cattle and horses (Yü 1990:123). Though Chinese cultural rhetoric has some role in the reporting of these texts, to the extent that the letters represent the leadership of two competing states, they suggest that cultural dichotomies were important in reifying both the Xiongnu and Chinese polit-ical communities. Similar cultural ideologies have been reported in many pastoral-based polities and provide a model for their political function.

The Tuareg camel pastoralists of North Africa and the Nkore Bahima cattle herders of East Africa are examples in which the ideal of the nomadic lifeway not only identified the community but was exemplified by the elite who assumed the preeminent role of nomadic warriors and protec-tors (Sáenz 1991; Karugire 1971). To some extent, the steppe versus sown dichotomy found in the cultural ideologies of many nomadic and sedentary civilizations is probably more a product of politics and ideology than of subsistence economics (Chang 1993:689).

Eastern steppe rulers manipulated this perceived dichotomy not only in their appropriation of the nomadic warrior ideal but also in the promo-tion of the concept of China as the main cultural enemy against whom steppe rulers explicitly protected nomadic commoners. The best evidence for this practice comes to us through the earliest writing by steppe peoples discovered on the inscribed stelae of the post-Xiongnu polity known as the Second Türk empire, ca. AD 682–742. The monumental standing stones of elite tomb sites in the Orkhon valley of central Mongolia still retain texts in the Türkic script in which the Chinese kingdom is depicted as intrinsically hostile and the paternal protection of Türk rulers the only protection from that threat (Sinor 1990:310–11). Ironically, Türk leaders often made close political alliances with the Chinese state, demonstrating an important differ-ence between state ideology and elite practice. During the Xiongnu period, evidence for a parallel belief might be found in patterns observed by histo-rians for each new *Shanyu* to solidify his position by mounting large-scale attacks against the Han Dynasty frontiers to demonstrate heaven's favor and legitimize the *Shanyu*'s role as culture hero and protector, in addition to procuring wealth (Yü 1990:124; Chang 2007:142). These examples show the

importance of continually restabilizing large-scale asymmetric social organization via the promulgation of ideas, concepts, and beliefs.

MATERIAL SYMBOLS OF COMMONALITY AND DIVISION

While cosmology and ideology are best known through textual sources, a
third technique for stabilizing political community, based on broad inclusion of commoners but incorporating elite distinction, was through material symbols and community practices. The production of material cultures
has been studied extensively by archaeologists, specifically in the context of
forming new political identities (Pauketat 2001; Schortman et al. 2001:312–
313). Xiongnu period material culture, in general, comprises a wide range
of practices and end products including iron and ceramic technologies,
ceramic vessel forms and styles, artistic motifs and symbols, weapon types,
clothing, jewelry, and architecture. Some of these materials, like clothing,
archaeologists are only able to recover from ideally preserved contexts,
which are extremely rare. The styles and artifacts that comprise this material culture certainly shared in prior steppe traditions, but as an assemblage
they constitute a dramatic change from prior material patterns of the Early
Iron Age.

Material cultures have multiple levels of meaning, and all material
culture communicates and influences social interaction to some extent.
For that reason, objects and technologies have potential for playing political roles, and in the case of the Xiongnu, the construction of novel burial
architecture and the use of foreign prestige items both had political consequence. Some argue that the presence of certain burial forms and imported
goods among nomads of the Xiongnu period can be explained as an emula-
tion of Chinese culture (Kürsat-Ahlers 1996b:27–28). While some products
and practices did originate in the south, China was only one source of nonlocal and exotic materials exploited by steppe peoples. Furthermore, place
of origin, whether China or elsewhere, was probably less significant than
the new meanings these materials obtained through their use in politically
significant practices. For example, the burial forms and nonlocal objects
that became part of Xiongnu material culture from the earliest periods had
characteristics suggestive of broad inclusiveness while at the same time
emphasizing the segregation of an elite subgroup (cf. Schortman et al.
2001:313).

The burial practices of the Xiongnu period have long been a point of contention among steppe archaeologists. Mortuary behavior has long been conceived as a generally conservative set of practices and an avenue for discovering the origin and identity of the nomadic group that constituted the pre-polity "Xiongnu." The search for these origins depends upon the assumption that the name *Xiongnu*, as described in the Chinese histories, belonged originally to a discrete "ethnic" group whose name became the designator of the later polity. Since the 1960s, archaeologists have attempted to trace the geographic origin of the initial core Xiongnu group by analyzing Early Iron Age burial constructions to see which culture-region had practices that most resembled those of the Xiongnu period (Miniaev 1985). This search for exact origins has largely proven fruitless and, in fact, no region seems to have had prior mortuary practices that show a clear match.

What is interesting, however, is the extent to which different components of the Xiongnu burial tradition are found across the eastern steppe and northern China region prior to and including the third century BC. Surface stone and earth features, pit constructions, the use of stone slabs, inclusion of domestic animals, northerly orientation, wooden chambers and wooden coffins—all are distinct grave components found in various combinations from the Altai to Northern China. This suggests that Xiongnu mortuary culture was the product of a composite tradition that combined diverse practices of peoples located across the geographical extent of the polity. This phenomenon is best explained not by an original "ethnic" group, but by far-reaching political consolidation that incorporated the diverse peoples of the east Eurasian region (Wu 1990).

The burial forms used by local and regional Xiongnu elite groups had elements that were recognizable in every corner of their political territory and likely served as physical emblems of inclusion and integration. Furthermore, Xiongnu tombs were large-scale and labor-intensive constructions and contain faunal and ceramic evidence for ceremonial feasting activities in association with mortuary events. Large groups of commoners and elite likely gathered from dispersed regions within the polity and perhaps beyond the polity proper to participate in mortuary ritual. We can interpret Xiongnu cemeteries as the remains of public events at which commoners likely took part in building and ritual activities in recognition of the elite dead and living (Honeychurch et al. 2007). In this way, different regional groups were brought together and integrated through common labor and common understandings of the material construction they made. Through participation, commoners enacted and at least tacitly accepted the social distinctions marked by such elaborate burials. Xiongnu burial architecture is a good example of material culture created from a synthesis of older and diverse practices that actively integrated a widespread population and affirmed by way of integration, the preeminence of elite sponsors.

The display and use of rare objects that were widely understood and valued, but possessed by only a small segment of society, likewise accomplished the joining of a new community founded upon elite division. In Xiongnu archaeological contexts, such items came from many geographical regions such as China, Central and South Asia, and the forest zone of Siberia. These objects and constituent materials from external regions, found mostly in burials, include lacquer ware, coins, silk, bronze mirrors, beads, precious stones and nephrite, glass and amber, carpets, decorative plaques, artistic styles, and in some cases, even complete Han Dynasty chariots (Miniaev and Sakharovskaia 2007; Honeychurch et al. 2007). All of these object types or materials fit into older traditions of "value" recognized on the steppe from as early as the second millennium BC, especially mirrors, small and rare decorative items, carts/chariots, and plaques. This material culture was therefore selected according to indigenous priorities and cultural meanings (Rogers 1990:17–21).

From a political perspective, the significance of these external goods and materials was both their broad recognition as item categories having indigenous traditions of value, but also as external productions having cultural novelty and potential for redefinition in the steppe context. As used by elite owners, these objects became materials around which new relationships could be structured based on gift giving, display, disposal and conspicuous consumption, or as badges of rank. If burial assemblages are any indication of the importance of these materials for structuring relationships, then a comparison of Egii Gol valley cemetery finds from the Early Iron Age and Xiongnu periods is instructive. A threefold increase in categories of external goods in Xiongnu mortuary assemblages suggests a much greater investment in material support of complex relationships (Honeychurch et al. 2007). Similar to the case of burial construction, members of the elite with access to the networks circulating exotic material culture used such items to appeal broadly to a diverse steppe population while creating visible social distinctions between themselves and their people.

BENEFITS OF AN UNSTABLE ECONOMY

Despite a surrounding context of warfare, disruption, and reconsolidation, steppe peoples neither blindly accepted belief and symbolism, nor did they participate in these practices without question. Nor was mere belief in polity sufficient to sustain it (Fried 1967:230). While some may have been true believers in divine appointment of rulers, steppe leaders as culture heroes, and elite-sponsored collective symbols, many groups must have found other circumstances persuasive for participating in the Xiongnu political order. These combined some degree of straightforward coercion or coercive threat as well as techniques for power sharing; however, an economic basis for either political participation or political control is rarely explored in models for steppe states.

In his study of ethnohistorical state formation, Flannery (1999:10–13) points out that in most of his cross-cultural examples, state leaders reorganized subsistence production in some manner that effectively bound commoner lifeways directly to central leadership. In contrast, some historians and anthropologists argue that steppe states organized with little or no integration between regional politics and the productive pastoral economy, since that economy was inherently unstable. Kürsat-Ahlers (1996b:30–31) is most concise in describing the usual conception of the limitations of the steppe economy. He lists the following limitations: unpredictable ecological downturn destroys herds to such a point that accumulation of surplus is impossible; spatially extensive pastoralism hinders the intensification of production and disperses population; and mobility and the lack of internal coercion mechanisms leads to problems of fission. Accordingly, most of these models view steppe states as being supported only by ideology, raiding, and continual redistribution of prestige items (Bold 2001:125; Kradin 2008b), a formula that works, but not over long time periods (e.g., Wright 2006:309–311). The more than 300-year persistence of the Xiongnu state, including its various reorganizations, argues against such a conception.

An alternative way to approach this problem of the steppe economy is to pose the question of whether the instability of pastoralism might itself have facilitated the regional political process. Archaeological studies of ancient pastoral economies in Mongolia and Kazakhstan have provided strong evidence that these subsistence systems, far from being rigid, over-specialized economies, were particularly good at modulating and adjusting to suit conditions (Honeychurch and Amartuvshin 2007; Frachetti 2008). This conception also explains how and why pastoralism was an advantageous approach to subsistence across the environmental variability found in eastern Eurasia.

Archaeologists have documented a long history of experience with this form of production prior to Xiongnu emergence. Steppe peoples had deeply ingrained cultural knowledges and techniques with regard to animals, mobility, productive risk, and diversifying resources. Multiresource production included varieties of herding, as well as production and use of agricultural and wild products and the knowledge and technology needed to vary degrees of dependence on these investments as local conditions necessitated. Multiple resources could be combined along a wide continuum ranging from an even mixture of subsistence products to specialization in any single component when regional economic and political conditions were supportive. Good examples of specialization seen in the historical record are horse herding and fur hunting for exchange to China.

Also important were modes of social interaction and relationship that supported, diversified, and ensured reliable production through social insurance strategies such as sharing of resources, assistance in times of need, stock dispersion, and allowance of geographic movement. Varying corporate scales at which production might be mutually pursued created repeating "modes" of local, subregional, and regional social configurations that could take form in response to good or bad productive conditions. In short, archaeology has shown that the steppe economy was itself unstable and flexible as an adaptation to an unpredictable and risk-prone productive setting, as many pastoral economies in the Old World seem to have been (Salzman 2004; Humphrey and Sneath 1999:305; Cribb 1991:23–24).

POLITICS, PASTORALISM, AND SOCIAL RE-SCALING

The social and political environment contributed substantially to the conditions that pastoral groups monitored in making productive decisions. Changes in the political environment could prompt different configurations of pastoralism, most notably in the way different geographical scales of movement were arranged, delimited, or expanded. During the nineteenth century when Mongolia was integrated into the Manchurian Qing Empire (AD 1644–1911), the organizational problem of controlling a mobile population was addressed by creating a series of progressively smaller administrative units that constrained both movement and association (Bold 2001:99–106). As suggested above, a somewhat similar situation may have characterized the pre-Xiongnu landscape of small-scale Early Iron Age polities. The beginnings of social differentiation and hereditary inequality between 3,000 and 3,500 years ago initiated a process of political territoriality that archaeologists are just beginning to document (Frohlich et al. 2009).

Though surveys in different regions will test this hypothesis, the result seems to have been the rise of small-scale polities linked by exchange alliances for the procurement of the resources needed to structure local relationships and attract followers (Honeychurch et al. 2011). Jeep reconnaissance across large swathes of Mongolia have shown discrete concentrations of monumental and mortuary activity during this period, separated by intervening buffer zones having no contemporary sites whatsoever (Honeychurch et al. 2007:10–11; Houle 2009). In some areas, for example the Baga Gazaryn Chuluu site of the Middle Gobi desert, major centers of settlements, monuments, and cemeteries were bounded by outlying monument clusters placed at equal distances to the east and west, perhaps as boundary markers (Honeychurch and Amartuvshin 2009). These preliminary observations suggest that with increasing political activity, and perhaps competition over network access and resources, territory became politicized and the maintenance of boundaries became routine.

Similar to the Manchurian period, these fixed boundaries delimited opportunities for doing what is best for mobile pastoralism over the long term, that is, scale-based modulation in the face of changing conditions. If steppe herders of the initial Xiongnu period needed incentive to think in a different way about the new and expanding political community, then conversion from small-scale, compartmentalized, and competitive politics to the politics of integration and geographic expansiveness may have helped. Ethnohistorical research on Mongolian nomadic pastoralism and political systems during the nineteenth and twentieth centuries demonstrates clear productive benefits for commoners and elite alike under larger-scale regional integration (Humphrey and Sneath 1999:292–296). The first rulers of many ethnohistoric states made available new or improved subsistence resources for their populations, which tied commoners closely to central authority. This often disrupted the power of local elites and made commoners directly dependent on central rulership. In the same way, geographical re-scaling under Maodun's polity may have transformed pastoral production and simultaneously undercut the position of preexisting local aristocracies.

Steppe producers would likely have recognized several potential benefits for participating in the Xiongnu political community. These included increased mobility ranges that were best for stock optimization and surplus production, flexible access to wider varieties of pasture and water resources in times of emergency, and greater social and political stability making productive conditions more predictable. In addition to making possible direct advantages to participant communities through increasing productive options, ranges, and flexibility, a fourth benefit would have been recognizable not long after networks of exchange, border trade, tribute extraction, and systematic raiding had been constituted within the early state. Such activities were again directly dependent on the increased scale and integration across the regional polity and would have enabled novel systems of convertibility between surplus animals, material goods, commodities, labor (especially military labor), and political prestige and influence.

Convertibility of value is an attractive option for commoner and elite pastoral producers since animals surpluses readily accrue during a series of good seasons but even more rapidly disappear during seasonal downturns (Cribb 1991:23–24). The ability to readily translate animals into other forms of value allows for the capture and storage of surpluses that are otherwise fleeting. This provides an even greater latitude and flexibility to the already diverse modulations and adjustments traditionally practiced in steppe production and provides added insurance against the risks of uncertain and unpredictable environments. It creates methods for elite accumulation of animal wealth and the attachment of client labor to manage large elite herds in return for use of basic subsistence products (Humphrey and Sneath 1999:223–227). This system, known as the "saun" system as practiced in Central Asia (Khazanov 1994:155; Kradin 2008a) has analogs across the Old World and is well known as the basis for elite economic stratification among such groups as the Tuareg of North Africa (Sáenz 1991).

This model for transformations of steppe production based on re-scaling of a formerly compartmentalized productive landscape is hypothetical. It does offer a testable explanation of the conditions that, in addition to regional instability and changes in belief, may have guided decision making among steppe communities 2,200 years ago. These decisions led steppe groups to participate in a new political order and tolerate asymmetric regional rulership, at least initially. The tools for testing these ideas against archaeological data are just now being applied in Mongolia. In addition to much-needed regional survey, excavation, and dating, the analysis of strontium and oxygen isotopes in animal bones, when matched to isotopic signatures in local geology, can tell us where animals spent their initial years and how far afield they were herded in comparison to the place of death and deposition. Such analysis will be critical for determining whether a rescaling of pastoral productive space did in fact occur during the early polity phase.

STATECRAFT AND SUSTAINABILITY

While public belief and perceived productive advantage encouraged participation in the Xiongnu political order, it is also important to remember that commoner decisions were made within the context of a highly militarized state. Coercion, threat of coercion, reorganization, as well as continued military expansion all influenced political participation. Ensuring that commoners continued to enact the relationships that defined political community required techniques that would outlast the initial decades of state formation. Such techniques would have allowed for the generational time periods required to transform active thinking about political participation to a more passive accommodation of political order. With time and the persistence of a political system, countless acts of individual and group compliance produced a habitual culture of statehood.

To stabilize state relationships over time, the problem of competing local aristocracies or subordinates who could lead factions and establish competing authority had to be effectively diminished. These problems were especially pressing in the case of a geographically extensive polity in which the means for resistance (i.e., horses and bows), were commonly held and routes of access to politically significant external goods, resources, and alliances were far from the state center (Fletcher 1986:14). Competition with preexisting aristocracy and internal factions was always a problem for rulers in archaic states and empires, a good example being Han Dynasty China where military factions quickly allied with the Xiongnu state in opposition to central Chinese rulership (Chang 2007:142).

Actions by Xiongnu rulers attempted to disenfranchise or co-opt similar competition within their own territory. Researchers have long maintained that among nomadic peoples, central leadership could rarely overcome the direct control of local, territorial aristocracy and prevent subgroups from factioning or evading the imposition of political authority. Therefore, regional steppe politics was thought to have been consensual and confederated by necessity and not based on central integration of local territories. While confederation was certainly one form of polity (Sneath 2006:3–4), a wide variety of organizational forms have been documented among eastern steppe nomads, and these demonstrate significant diversity in centralized integration, polity size, and diachronic stability (Di Cosmo 1999).

Recognizable in Sima Qian's history of the Xiongnu state are a number of organizational techniques that very likely disrupted the authority of local power holders in favor of central rulership and diminished the risk of factional challenge. These were not foolproof but were part of the negotiation of power relations within the state between different established groups and interests. The workings of such techniques must be discussed in more detail elsewhere, but some examples are a decimal-based system of military-administrative organization; permanent elite guard units under central control; and a nascent administrative hierarchy composed of hereditary and nonhereditary positions that provided some degree of oversight in outlying areas. The degree to which these arrangements empowered central authority is debated among anthropologists and historians, though similar techniques figure prominently in the ethnohistories of other agro-pastoral states (e.g., Deflem 1999; Sidky 1996).

THE SPATIAL POLITICS OF MOBILITY

Archaeological research gives evidence for an additional set of techniques that reinforced centralized control across the eastern steppe region. The first thirty years of the Xiongnu polity was marked by a tremendous growth in geographic extent, and therefore interrelationships between politics, economics, and geography were key to maintaining state affairs. Three main spheres of activity were significant during this period of expansion: (a) the creation of long-distance access to external materials, ideas, and resources through exchange and tribute; (b) the capability to mobilize and deploy organized military force rapidly over long distances; and (c) the scalar expansion and enhancement of the indigenous multiresource productive economy. Each of these sets of activities played a fundamental role in the initial Xiongnu state under Maodun, and all were entirely dependent on the logistics of movement across the steppe landscape. The ability to monitor, encourage, discourage, or restrict movement of a population within a mobile society constitutes a substantial source of power (Lattimore 1940:67). Spatial politics is the strategic manipulation of a sociospatial landscape for political ends and was practiced in a wide variety of ways by both nomadic and sedentary populations.

An ethnohistorical example of spatial politics from the Kalāt Khanate (seventeenth century), a large agro-pastoral polity of western Pakistan, demonstrates how central rulership can influence movement through a territory for political objectives. Mountainous terrain and a strongly embedded local aristocracy created circumstances in which central rulership could not militarily coerce or easily access many areas within the khanate. However, a major source of income for local aristocracy was taxation of trade caravans that used their passes, and caravan drivers received itinerary information from administrative officials of the khan. The khan actively rewarded and punished subordinate elite by directing caravans through or away from their respective areas, giving him substantial indirect leverage over local aristocracy (Swidler 1972:119).

The degree of spatial management practiced by Xiongnu elite was significantly greater at both the local and polity-wide scales, though the political principle was the same. For example, according to historical sources, the geographical organization of the Xiongnu polity was divided into three regions—western and eastern sections, and a central region having the seat of political power (Watson 1993:137). This tripartite spatial structure can be recognized in the archaeological record of Xiongnu mortuary and settlement sites when these are mapped (Honeychurch and Amartuvshin 2009). Control over information and communication was an important source of support for central authority (Fried 1967: 236) and since these were transport dependent, tripartite political geography facilitated control by channeling any interaction between eastern and western flanks through the central district. This geographical arrangement also discouraged large-scale military challenge from either flank given the potential overwhelming response from combined forces of the center and the opposite flank.

The Xiongnu central region included the Orkhon, Selenge, and Tuul river systems, and is delineated by clusters of mortuary and settlement sites that are among the largest, most complex, and the oldest of the Xiongnu archaeological record, so far. In addition to acting as an organizational wedge between the outer flanks of the Xiongnu state, the central district had geographic characteristics that were likely selected and exploited for political ends. Climate and topography have made this area one of the most productive regions in Mongolia, while river basins and intermountain valleys delimit corridors of movement and create opportunities for monitoring access and use (Honeychurch and Amartuvshin 2009). If long-distance north-south and east-west movements are considered, then based on topography this district forms a macroregional junction where major pathways intersect (Honeychurch and Amartuvshin 2006: 270). Given these characteristics, it is not surprising that over the 2,000 years following the decline of the Xiongnu state, every major steppe empire sought to capture this "centralizing" heartland as critical for sustaining large-scale politics (Allsen 1996:126–128).

Steppe rulers, themselves socialized within the surrounding mobile culture and traditions, understood well the difficulties of monitoring a mobile setting from a fixed geographical point. Historical accounts of mobile elite courts, dating as early as the *Shiji*, give evidence that one strategy for managing a mobile population was for elites to be mobile as well (Kürsat-Ahlers 1996b:34). In such a setting, the walled centers mentioned above assumed the role of impressive points of tether rather than permanent residences. While a walled site may be an important area for seasonal activities and public events, the true political "center" circulated along with the elite retinue, including administrators, military accompaniment, reconnaissance scouts, craft specialists, grain and beverage storage, and herd animals. What amounted to an expansive moving city, maintained oversight within large tracts of steppe lands by way of its presence and the possibility of its presence (Honeychurch and Amartuvshin 2007).

A smaller-scale version of spatial politics played out at the local level as well, and served to embed the agenda of regional leadership into commoner lifeways. A multiyear pedestrian survey carried out in the Egiin Gol valley of Mongolia posed the question of how valley organization transformed as the Xiongnu polity emerged (Honeychurch et al. 2007). Survey results argue for extensive changes in both spatial and economic organization. In comparison to the Early Iron Age period, Xiongnu seasonal habitation sites were substantially larger and appear in the exposed main valley instead of protected side valleys. Ethnographic, faunal, botanical, and mortuary evidence all suggest that Xiongnu people occupied Egiin Gol during warm weather seasons, and may have spent winters at campsites in neighboring valleys. Subject to further survey, this suggests an expansion of local territories and mobility ranges that disrupted the authority of local leaders and reduced cohesion of territorial groups. Finally, the two largest habitation sites in the valley are both four hectares in size, have artifacts similar to those found in elite burials, and were located at opposite ends of the valley near the main areas of entrance and exit, suggesting a strategy of spatial control on local transit.

Strategic manipulation of the sociospatial landscape was one way that Xiongnu elite combined and intermanaged different sources of political power within this expansive territory. The monitoring of movement at local, regional, and interregional scales not only affected the capability of any party to organize militarily but also helped to ensure that long-distance alliances, exchange, and tribute were not interrupted or commandeered. However, these spatial politics also created effective control over pastoral production. Pastoral subsistence depended on animals, pasture, water, and protected winter camps, but access to and the integration of these components depended entirely on mobility. If indeed the initial re-scaling of the Xiongnu polity transformed the spatial latitude of steppe pastoralism, as I have argued, then the political manipulation of movement through these newly opened spaces constituted a form of unequal access to the basic resources of steppe livelihood. This would have been a further inducement for cooperation with the regional political order (Fried 1967:186).

THE UNFOLDING OF A XIONGNU POLITICS OF THOUGHT

Archaic states were dynamic collectives that varied over time and space. They involved corporate and kin relations in diverse ways, were dependent on horizontal as well as vertical forms of organization, and were less directly hegemonic and more negotiated than many have thought. Pathways to statehood were made up of sequential events but were fundamentally nonlinear in that every change unfolded with reference to information and precedent across a range of social, spatial, and time scales. This contingent unfolding was always historically and locationally contextualized, such that no two sequences ever transpired in the same way. However, as anthropologists have long observed, there are underlying similarities between pathways to statehood (Fried 1967: 236). The Xiongnu case-study shows the primary importance of understanding a unique historical and cultural context as the only way to recognize underlying similarities.

Evidence from archaeological and textual sources argues for the Xiongnu state as a vast political community constructed from multiple layers of strategy, response, and contingency. Though I have emphasized elite statecraft, nonelites, political factions, and corporate groups all sought to promote their agendas, continued existence, and security. The negotiation of political community shows that central rulers were not supreme political architects as much as one interest group among others, having asymmetric advantages of wealth and resources, but also having to constantly bolster and secure those advantages. The steppe discourse, in particular, demanded the sharing of wealth and power since the military service rendered by nonelites was ultimately essential for the projection of external authority and the safeguarding of internal order.

My main question has been why would herding groups, fully capable of remaining independent, participate in a large-scale organization that was founded upon such inequality and social stratification? The answer is not at all as straightforward as managerial or coercive models would make it seem (Roscoe 2000:113–115), but rather the answer must be found in the mixture of history and precedent, local conditions, perceived futures, and associated actions on the part of commoners and leaders alike. The Xiongnu state was a particular kind of arena that supported multiscale and multiactor negotiations and these negotiations pertained to how people and groups in the broader community decided to engage with each other day after day. The state, as a decision-making process, was grounded in techniques that encouraged people to enact relationships with designated others in patterned and predictable ways over long periods of time.

A focus on the first few decades of Xiongnu statehood and changes in the frameworks for decision making shows the importance of these time increments in state formation. Destabilization, warfare, and uncertainty may have initially favored compliance with the new state order. Somewhat later in this sequence, the availability of new forms of production and wealth conversion may have further contributed to commoner participation. Within the first decade of Xiongnu organization, broad-based compliance empowered the uppermost leadership to deploy resources, information, and coercion in the building of local and regional techniques for making continued compliance more probable.

Relative to how people think, assess, and make decisions, this intervening time was a critical factor. Within thirty years, people appraised the advantages and disadvantages of participating in an asymmetric political order by radically different criteria. While initially the polity facilitated some benefits, especially in an unstable and risky environment, the persistence of political relationships also facilitated a public culture of statehood through the socialization of individuals born and bred within the stratified order. In public, "thinking the state" became normal and "thinking against the state" became aberrant, even though there may have been little genuine congruency between private ways of thought and public political order (cf. Smith 2001). Inurement, while not representing de facto acceptance in any way, tilted the scale of probability in favor of the existing political order. Members of the Xiongnu political community became more and less favorably disposed to rulership depending on events and immediate conditions. While their reservations could not often have been outwardly expressed, private thought always held the seeds of public rebellion and state collapse.

REFERENCES CITED

Allard, Francis, and Diimaajav Erdenebaatar. 2005. "Khirigsuurs: Ritual and Mobility in the Bronze Age of Mongolia." *Antiquity* 79: 547–563.

Allsen, Thomas. 1996. "Spiritual Geography and Political Legitimacy in the Eastern Steppe." In *Ideology and the Formation of Early States*, edited by H. J. M. Claessen and J. G. Osten, 116–135. Leiden: E. J. Brill.

Barfield, Thomas. 2001. "The Shadow Empires: Imperial State Formation along the Chinese-Nomad Frontier." In *Empires: Perspectives from Archaeology and History*, edited by S. E. Alcock, T. N. D'Altroy, K. D. Morrison, and C. M. Sinopoli, 10–41. Cambridge: Cambridge University Press.

Barnes, Gina. 1986. "Jiehao, Tonghao: Peer Relations in East Asia." In *Peer Polity Interaction*, edited by C. Renfrew and J. Cherry, 79–92. Cambridge: Cambridge University Press.

———. 2007. *State Formation in Japan: Emergence of a Fourth-Century Ruling Elite*. London: Routledge.

Batsaikhan, Zagd. 2003. *Khunnu: Arkheologi, ugsaatny zui, tuukh* [*The Xiongnu: Archaeology, Ethnography, and History*]. Ulaanbaatar: Mongolian National University.

Bold, Bat-Ochir. 2001. *Mongolian Nomadic Society: A Reconstruction of the Medieval History of Mongolia*. Richmond, VA: Curzon Press.

Chang, Chun-shu. 2007. *The Rise of the Chinese Empire: Nation, State, and Imperialism in Early China, ca. 1600 BC–AD 8*. Ann Arbor: University of Michigan Press.

Chang, Claudia. 1993. "Pastoral Transhumance in the Southern Balkans as a Social Ideology: Ethnoarchaeological Research in Northern Greece." *American Anthropologist* 95(3): 687–703.

Chugunov, K. V., H. Parzinger, and A. Nagler. 2004. "Chronology and Cultural Affinity of the Kurgan Arzhan–2 Complex According to Archaeological Data." In *Impact of the Environment on Human Migration in Eurasia*, edited E. M. Scott, A. Yu. Alekseev, and G. Zaitsevaeds, 1–7. Dordrecht: Kluwer Academic Publishers.

Cribb, Roger. 1991. *Nomads in Archaeology*. Cambridge: Cambridge University Press.

Davydova, A. V. 1995. *Ivolginskii arkheologicheskii kompleks: Ivolginskoe gorodishche* [*The Ivolga Archaeological Complex: Ivolga Settlement*]. Saint Petersburg: AziatIKA.

Deflem, Mathieu. 1999. "Warfare, Political Leadership, and State Formation: The Case of the Zulu Kingdom 1808–1879." *Ethnology* 38(4): 371–391.

Derevianko, A. P., and V. I. Molodin. 2000. *Fenomen altaiskikh mumii* [*Phenomenon of the Altai Mummies*]. Novosibirsk: Institut of Arkheologii i Etnografii SO RAN.

Di Cosmo, Nicola. 1994. "Ancient Inner Asian Nomads: Their Economic Basis and Its Significance in Chinese History." *Journal of Asian Studies* 53(4): 1092–1126.

———. 1999. "State Formation and Periodization in Inner Asian History." *Journal of World History* 10: 1–40.

———. 2002. *Ancient China and Its Enemies: The Rise of Nomadic Power in East Asian History*. Cambridge: Cambridge University Press.

Ecsedy, H. 1972. "Tribe and Tribal Society in the Sixth Century Turk Empire." *Acta Orientalia Academiae Scientarium Hungaricae* 25: 245–262.

Flannery, Kent. 1999. "Process and Agency in Early State Formation." *Cambridge Archaeological Journal* 9(1): 3–21.

Fletcher, Joseph. 1986. "The Mongols: Ecological and Social Perspectives." *Harvard Journal of Asiatic Studies* 46: 11–50.

Frachetti, Michael. 2008. "Variability and Dynamic Landscapes of Mobile Pastoralism in Ethnography and Prehistory." In *The Archaeology of Mobility: Nomads in the Old and in the New World*, edited by H. Barnard and W. Wendrich, 366–396. Los Angeles: Costen Institute.

Fried, Morton. 1967. *The Evolution of Political Society*. New York: Random House.

Frohlich, Bruno, T. Amgalantugs, J. Littleton, D. Hunt, J. Hinton, and K. Goler. 2009. "Bronze Age Burial Mounds in the Hovsgol Aimag, Mongolia." In *Current Archaeology in Mongolia*, edited by J. Bemmann, H. Parzinger, E. Pohl, and D. Tseveendorzh, 99–115. Bonn: Rheinische Friedrich-Wilhelms-Universität.

Honey, David. 1992. "Stripping off Felt and Fur: An Essay on Nomadic Sinification." *Papers on Inner Asia*, no. 21. Bloomington, IN: Research Institute for Inner Asian Studies.

Honeychurch, William. 2004. "Inner Asian Warriors and Khans: A Regional Spatial Analysis of Nomadic Political Organization and Interaction." PhD dissertation, University of Michigan, Ann Arbor.

Honeychurch, William, and Chunag Amartuvshin. 2006. "States on Horseback: The Rise of Inner Asian Confederations and Empires." In *Archaeology of Asia*, edited by Miriam Stark, 255–278. Malden, MA: Blackwell.

Honeychurch, William, and Chunag Amartuvshin. 2007. "Hinterlands, Urban Centers, and Mobile Settings: The 'New' Old World Archaeology from the Eurasian Steppe." *Asian Perspectives* 46(1): 36–64.

———. 2011. "Timescapes from the Past: An Archaeogeography of Mongolia." In *Mapping Mongolia*, edited by Paula Sabloff, 195–219. Philadelphia: University of Pennsylvania Press.

Honeychurch, William, Albert Nelson, and Chunag Amartuvshin. 2007. "Death and Social Process among the Ancient Xiongnu of Mongolia." In *Xiongnu: The First Empire of the Steppes*, edited by Eunjeong Chang, 134–153. Seoul: National Museum of Korea.

Honeychurch, William, and Joshua Wright. 2008. "Asia North and Central: Prehistoric Cultures of the Steppes, Deserts, and Forests." In *Encyclopedia of Archaeology*, edited by Deborah Pearsall, 517–532. London: Elsevier Publishing.

Honeychurch, William, Joshua Wright, and Chunag Amartuvshin. 2009. "Re-Writing Monumental Landscapes as Inner Asian Political Process." In *Monuments, Metals, and Mobility: Trajectories of Complexity in the Late Prehistory of the Eurasian Steppe*, edited by B. Hanks and K. Linduff, 330–357. Cambridge: Cambridge University Press.

Houle, Jean-Luc. 2009. "Socially Integrative Facilities and the Emergence of Societal Complexity on the Mongolian Steppe." In *Monuments, Metals, and Mobility: Trajectories of Complexity in the Late Prehistory of the Eurasian Steppe*, edited by B. Hanks and K. Linduff, 358–377. Cambridge: Cambridge University Press.

Humphrey, Caroline, and David Sneath. 1999. *The End of Nomadism: Society, State and the Environment in Inner Asia*. Durham, NC: Duke University Press.

Irons, William. 1979. "Political Stratification among Pastoral Nomads." In *Pastoral Production and Society*, 361–374. New York: Cambridge University Press.

Karugire, Samwiri. 1971. *A History of the Kingdom of Nkore in Western Uganda to 1896*. Oxford: Clarendon Press.

Keyser-Tracqui, C., E. Crubezy, and B. Ludes. 2003. "Nuclear and Mitochondrial DNA Analysis of a 2,000-Year-Old Necropolis in the Egyin Gol Valley of Mongolia." *American Journal of Human Genetics* 73: 247–260.

Khazanov, Anatoly. 1994. *Nomads and the Outside World*. Madison: University of Wisconsin Press.

———. 2001. "Nomads in the History of the Sedentary World." In *Nomads in the Sedentary World*, edited by A. Khazanov and A. Wink, 1–23. London: Curzon Press.

Kradin, Nikolay. 2008a. "Early State Theory and the Evolution of Pastoral Nomads." *Social Evolution and History* 7(1): 107–130.

————. 2008b. "Structure of Power in Nomadic Empires of Inner Asia: Anthropological Approach." In *Hierarchy and Power in the History of Civilizations: Ancient and Medieval Cultures*, edited by L. Grinin, D. Beliaev, and A. Korotayev, 98–124. Moscow: KomKniga.

Kürsat-Ahlers, Elçin. 1996a. "The Role and Contents of Ideology in the Early Nomadic Empires of the Eurasian Steppes." In *Ideology and the Formation of Early States*, edited by H. J. M. Claessen and J. G. Osten, 137–152. Leiden: E. J. Brill.

————. 1996b. "Aspects of State Formation Processes among the Ancient Eurasian Nomads." In *The Evolution of Nomadic Herding Civilizations in the Northern European Steppes: The Tools of Archaeology and History Compared*, edited by G. Afanase'ev, S. Cleuziou, J. Lukacs, and M. Tosi, 25–48. Forlì: A.B.A.C.O.

Lattimore, Owen. 1940 [1992]. *Inner Asian Frontiers of China*. Oxford: Oxford University Press.

Lindner, Rudi. 1982. "What Was a Nomadic Tribe?" *Comparative Studies in Society and History* 24: 689–711.

Miniaev, Sergei. 1985. "K probleme proiskhozhdeniia siunnu [The Problem of the Origins of the Xiongnu]." *Information Bulletin of the Association for the Study of the Cultures of Central Asia* 9: 70–78.

Miniaev, S., and L. Sakharovskaia. 2002. "Soprovoditel'nye zakhoroheniia 'tsarskogo' kompleksa No. 7 v mogil'nike Tsaram [Accompanying Burials of Royal Complex No. 7 at the Tsaram Cemetery]." *Arkheologicheskie Vesti* 9: 86–118.

————. 2007. "Elitnyi kompleks zakhoronenii Siunnu v padi Tsaram [An Elite Burial Complex of the Xiongnu in the Tsaram Basin]." *Rossiiskaia Arkheologiia* 1: 194–210.

Mori, Masao. 1950. "Kyodo no Kokka-sono yobiteki kosatsu [A Preliminary Study of the State of the Hsiung-nu]." *Shigaku Zasshi* 59(5): 1–21.

Nelson, Russell, Chunag Amartuvshin, and William Honeychurch. 2009. "A Gobi Mortuary Site through Time: Bioarchaeology at Baga Mongol, Baga Gazaryn Chuluu." In *Current Archaeology in Mongolia*, edited by Ernst Pohl, 565–578. Bonn: Rheinische Friedrich-Wilhelms-Universität.

Pauketat, Timothy. 2001. "Politicization and Community in the Pre-Columbian Mississippi Valley." In *The Archaeology of Communities*, edited by M. Canuto and J. Yaeger, 16–43. London: Routledge.

Pousaz, Nicole, Denis Ramseyer, and Turbat Tsagaan. 2007. "Mission archéologique helvético-mongole à Boroo Gol, Mongolie: campagne de fouilles." *SLSA Jahresbericht* 2007: 219–232.

Rogers, Daniel J. 1990. *Objects of Change: The Archaeology and History of Arikara Contact with Europeans*. Washington, DC: Smithsonian Institution Press.

————. 2007. "The Contingencies of State Formation in Eastern Inner Asia." *Asian Perspectives* 46(2): 249–274.

Roscoe, Paul. 2000. "Costs, Benefits, Typologies, and Power: The Evolution of Political Hierarchy." In *Hierarchies in Action: Cui Bono*, edited by M. Diehl, 113–133. Carbondale, IL: Center for Archaeological Investigations.

Sáenz, Candelario. 1991. "Lords of the Waste: Predation, Pastoral Production, and the Process of Stratification among the Eastern Twaregs." In *Chiefdoms: Power, Economy, and Ideology*, edited by T. Earle, 100–118. Cambridge: Cambridge University Press.

Salzman, Philip. 1999. "Is Inequality Universal?" *Current Anthropology* 40(1): 31–61.

———. 2004. *Pastoralists: Equality, Hierarchy, and the State*. Boulder, CO: Westview Press.

Schortman, E., P. Urban, and M. Ausec. 2001. "Politics with Style: Identity Formation in Prehispanic Southeastern Mesoamerica." *American Anthropologist* 103(2): 312–330.

Shelach, Gideon. 2009a. "Violence on the Frontiers? Sources of Power and Socio-Political Change at the Easternmost Parts of the Eurasian Steppes during the Early First Millennium BCE." In *Monuments, Metals, and Mobility: Trajectories of Complexity in the Late Prehistory of the Eurasian Steppe*, edited by B. Hanks and K. Linduff, 241–271. Cambridge: Cambridge University Press.

———. 2009b. *Prehistoric Societies on the Northern Frontiers of China: Archaeological Perspectives on Identity Formation and Economic Change during the First Millennium BC*. London: Equinox.

Sidky, Homayun. 1996. *Irrigation and State Formation in Hunza: The Anthropology of a Hydraulic Kingdom*. Lanham, MD: University Press of America.

Sinor, Denis. 1990. "The Establishment and Dissolution of the Türk Empire." In *The Cambridge History of Early Inner Asia*, edited by David Sinor, 285–316. Cambridge: Cambridge University Press.

Smith, Adam T. 2001. "The Limitations of Doxa: Agency and Subjectivity from an Archaeological Point of View." *Journal of Social Archaeology* 1(2): 155–171.

Sneath, David. 2006. "Introduction-Imperial Statecraft: Arts of Power on the Steppe." In *Imperial Statecraft: Political Forms and Techniques of Governance in Inner Asia, Sixth-Twentieth Centuries*, edited by D. Sneath, 1–22. Bellingham: CEAS, Western Washington University.

Swidler, Nina. 1972. "The Development of the Kalat Khanate." In *Perspectives on Nomadism*, edited by W. Irons and N. Dyson-Hudson, 115–121. Leiden: E. J. Brill.

Torbat, Ts., D. Batsukh, T. Batbayar, N. Bayarkhuu, Kh. Jordana, and P. Giscard. 2007. "Baga Turgenii gol-VI Pazyrykiin ueiin tsogtsolboryn arkheologi, paleo-antropologiin sudalgaa [Archaeology and Paleoanthropological Research at a Pazyryk Period Complex, Baga Tureg River-VI Site)." *Arkheologiin Sudlal* 4(24): 188–215.

Tseveendorj, D., V. Molodin, G. Parzinger, M. Bayarsaikhan, and G. Lkhundev. 2007. "Mongol Altain monkh tsevdgiin bulshny sudalgaa (Research on Permafrost Burials in the Mongolian Altai)." *Arkheologiin Sudlal* 4(24): 167–187.

Tsybiktarov, A. D. 2003. "Central Asia in the Bronze and Early Iron Ages: Problems of Ethno-Cultural History of Mongolia and the Southern Trans-Baikal Region in the Middle 2nd to Early 1st Millennia BC." *Archaeology, Ethnology, and Anthropology of Eurasia* 13(1): 80–97.

Watson, Burton. 1993. *Records of the Grand Historian of China: Han Dynasty II.* New York: Columbia University Press.

Weber, Max. 1978. *Economy and Society: An Outline of Interpretive Sociology.* Edited by G. Roth and C. Wittich. Berkeley: University of California Press.

Wright, Henry. 2006. "Early State Dynamics as Political Experiment." *Journal of Anthropological Research* 62(3): 305–319.

Wu, En. 1990. "Lun Xiongnu kaogu yanjiu zhong de jige wenti [Some Questions on the Archaeological Study of the Xiongnu]." *Kaogu Xuebao* 4: 409–437.

Yamada, Nobuo. 1982. "The Formation of the Hsiung-nu Nomadic State." *Acta Orientalia* 36: 575–582.

Yü, Ying-shih. 1990. "The Hsiung-nu." In *The Cambridge History of Early Inner Asia,* edited by David Sinor, 118–149. Cambridge: Cambridge University Press.

THREE

Dividing Land and Creating Class

The Development of a Landlord-Tenant Political Economy in Medieval Iceland

DOUGLAS BOLENDER

INTRODUCTION

Structured inequalities in the production and distribution of surplus labor are not unique to the modern world. For much of the world the archaeological record is the only means to access the emergence of class relations. In contexts with historical documentation, the archaeological record provides information on the real distribution of people and productive resources to compare with the written, and inherently consciously constructed, accounts of class. From this perspective archaeology can fulfill two critical roles in the study of class beyond the simple opportunity to study class in the prehistoric world. First, following the tradition of E. P. Thompson, is the historicity of class formation: class is best understood as a pattern of relations that emerge through time and evolving social practice. The second is a product of the material nature of the archaeological record that highlights the twofold nature of class relations: those based in the structural position of people in relation to the means of production and the actual relations between those people and how those relations constitute their experience and actions.

Class, in the classical capitalist sense of a defining principal of political economy based in the control over capital infrastructure and negotiated wage labor of an alienated proletariat, does not appear in Iceland until the nineteenth century (Magnússon 1985). Instead, classes were formed in relation to access to farmland and control over farmstead labor, resulting in two primary social axes of class relationships: within the farming household and among households. Within the household, class was manifest as differences between farmers, who had rights to land and production through direct ownership or leases, and subordinate household workers in the form of hired hands or slaves who exchanged labor for wages or subsistence. Among households, farmers could be classed as tenants or landowners depending on whether they owned the land they farmed or possibly additional properties.

Landowning and tenant farmers had similar legal standing in Icelandic society, and the principal legal class division was not between landowners and tenants but between those with access to productive land, landowners and tenants alike, and those without access to land: the destitute, invalids, and household laborers. However, tenants held short leases, contracted for one year at a time, and moves were frequent (Bolender 2006; Brynjólfsson 1983). If a household failed to meet rents, failed to maintain the farm to the satisfaction of the landlord, or even if the landlord simply favored another household, the tenant would be evicted from the property at the end of the term and forced to find a new farmstead. Successful tenant farmers often searched aggressively for new leases on a better farm or for a better lease on their present farm (Gunnlaugsson 1988).

Within the household a tenant farmer had the same authority as a landed farmer in regard to subordinate household labor. Tenant farmers and landowning aristocrats ostensibly shared many of the same social rights and responsibilities but clearly did not have the same access to resources or security. Such distinctions could be particularly marked between tenants and their landlords or between tenant or small freeholders and wealthy aristocrats who owned multiple properties.

The complex intersection of social status among farmers and within households was matched by equally complex categories of farmstead properties. The basic property was the legal or taxable farmstead. These farms invariably included a home field, meadows, and pastureland. Legal farms could be subdivided resulting in an additional class of farm, the dependent farm (*hjáleigur*). These dependent farms could not be sold separately and continued to be included in the tax value of the main farmstead property. Dependent farms were often a durable part of the farming landscape, appearing first in the eleventh century and often continuing as subproperties for hundreds of years. Dependent properties could, and often did, exist on tenant farmsteads. When this happened, they paid separate rents to the landlord as well as having set obligations, a portion of the overall farm value, on tax and tithe dues. Thus, many dependent farms functioned in essentially the same manner as other tenant properties.

Dependent farms did not always have full access to farmstead lands. Some only included the farm buildings and a small home field in the property (Pálsson 2001). Access to meadows for gathering additional hay and pastureland were negotiated through the main farmstead, often in exchange for labor obligations at harvest time. This was not always the case but it demonstrates the distinct, and potentially lower, economic opportunities for households on dependent farmsteads. To complicate the situation further, some farmsteads held usufruct rights outside of their immediate lands. Common extrafarmstead rights included stranding, both driftwood and whales, along beaches; eiderdown and egg collection on coasts and islands; and the right to woodlands and peat cutting for fuel.

There was no official difference in the status of a legal farm that was rented versus one that was owner occupied. Every legal farm retained its status as a distinct property and productive unit even when it was owned, and these properties were almost never consolidated into single farm properties. There was a sharp division between the land that a landlord lived on and worked and other farms such that these did not become single properties. The durable identity of the individual farmstead property contributed to the remarkable stability of the settlement system in Iceland. Abandoned farms often retained their distinct identity in land inventories long after they were last occupied.

The multiple categories of labor and farmstead land intersected to create a complex array of social statues and properties. Household formation and marriage were dependent on access to farmland. As many scholars have noted, the Icelandic householding system restricted the formation of new households to those able to gain access to a farm (Gunnarsson 1980; Gunnlaugsson 1988; Vasey 1996). This meant that the availability of farmsteads was the greatest factor restricting marriage and the formation of new households. Ultimately the two axes of social differentiation, those within the households between farmers and dependent labor and those among farmers between tenants and landlords, resulted in three social classes each with distinct places in society: the landowning aristocracy, tenant farmers, and dependent laborers.

At the top of the social hierarchy was the landowning aristocracy, a small minority of the population. The aristocracy owned their own farms and in many cases enjoyed rents from additional properties. In most cases landowners did not form a distinct legal class from other farmers, but households with their own land and additional income from other properties were fundamentally different from other farming households as they were not dependent entirely on their own productive efforts for subsistence. Landowners were also set apart as properties could be transferred from generation to generation. Tenant farmers held a similar legal status to landowners, whether they were on legal or dependent farmsteads, but had insecure rights to land and additional obligations on household production to supply rents. By the eighteenth century, tenant rights to land were quite weak, and children were rarely assured leases on their parents' farms. Beneath farmers, either landowners or tenants, was domestic labor. Individuals without access to land contracted annual labor agreements with existing households. Dependent labor had limited legal status outside of the household. Laborers were free to arrange new contracts each year with their existing household or move to another, but wages were generally low, effectively little more than subsistence and clothes (Gunnarsson 1983).

THE DEVELOPMENT OF CLASS IN ICELAND

Much of what we know about the origins of class in Iceland is based on medieval and modern sources. Medieval land documentation for Iceland is not comprehensive—we know far more about ecclesiastical estates than secular landholdings—but it is clear that the widespread institution of tenancy extends back until at least the late thirteenth and fourteenth centuries. This was a transformative moment in Iceland's history when the formerly independent farmers and chieftains of Iceland ceded authority to the Norwegian king. The loss of political independence by Icelandic farmers and elite families resulted in a new system of political authority that created a social division between farmer and landowning aristocrat (Sigurðsson 1995). At the same time, the Catholic Church gained control over many estates that previously had only been nominally church lands. This division was supported by an increasing accumulation of land held by the church and aristocracy and the replacement of independent smallholding with tenancy as the dominant institution of farming.

The picture of class relations in Iceland prior to the late thirteenth century is complicated by the nature of the historical sources. There is only limited direct documentary material on landholding; instead, most information about the early history of Iceland is preserved in the sagas. Sagas come in two main categories, both composed primarily in thirteenth and fourteenth centuries: the Family Sagas (Íslendingasögur), which describe the first settlement of Iceland and the following century, and the Contemporary Sagas (Sturlungasögur), which describe the rise of elite families in the late twelfth century and the increasing interregional conflict that ultimately resulted in the submission of Iceland to the authority of the Norwegian crown in AD 1262.

The sagas provide a basic narrative of early Icelandic history beginning with the initial settlement of the island in the second half of the ninth century by Norse colonists from Scandinavia and the northern British Isles. By all accounts the first Icelanders imported a highly stratified household structure to Iceland. This included landowning farmers and their families, subordinate labor attached to the household, and slaves. Titles of authority, chieftain-priest (góði), were also imported to Iceland and apparently given real distinction with the formation of the Icelandic assembly (alþingi) in AD 930; however, there is no evidence that these positions of authority were supported by institutions that endowed them with real power. The ready availability of land at the settlement seems to have limited control over labor outside of the household (Bolender et al. 2008; Smith 1995).

WHAT THE HISTORICAL SOURCES DO NOT TELL US

The origins of land inequality in Iceland are not well understood. The sagas vividly describe the settlement and early history of Iceland, including the political dynamics and open conflicts that emerged as farmers attempted to maintain or extend their own authority and power. The main problem with using the saga sources for the earliest period is the introduction of anachronism. The sagas were written in a later period of Iceland's history, during the thirteenth and fourteenth century at the end of the Icelandic

Commonwealth and after its incorporation into the Norwegian monarchy. The authors of the sagas were aware that the circumstances of early Iceland were different from the contemporary world around them, but it is impossible, based on the textual evidence alone, to determine how accurate these accounts of early Iceland are (Ólason 1998).

The gap between the recorded history found in the sagas and the reality of early Icelandic society is bridgeable only by the archaeological record. Friðriksson and Vésteinsson (2003) have called for the cautious use of the history and a concentration on building regional archaeological projects to address the fundamental issues of settlement patterns and economic production at farmsteads. In other words, traditional economically and politically focused anthropological archaeology supplemented with potential insights on social dynamics from the literary record (see Durrenberger 1992).

The call for a regionally based archaeology of settlement is not as easily realized as issued. Much of the archaeological research in Iceland has focused on the early period of Iceland's history, producing a number of household excavations (Vésteinsson 2004). Nonetheless, there are serious limitations to this best witnessed period in the archaeological record. For most of the twentieth century, excavations were conducted more to confirm or illustrate elements of the sagas than challenge our assumptions or expand our knowledge of the period (Friðriksson 1994). Excavations have primarily focused on domestic buildings and have rarely examined all of the buildings on a single farmstead, although there are some valuable exceptions (Berson 2002; Eldjárn 1949). Site choice has often been opportunistic, based on its state of preservation, previous work at the site, or its relevance to the sagas. Historically, there has been little consideration given to the representiveness of the sites chosen for excavation and how they relate to the range of sites in any region or the relationships among neighboring farmsteads. The result, despite a relatively large number of Viking Age and early excavations, is a series of disarticulate windows into the past with little systematic information on the relationships among farmsteads (Vésteinsson 2004).

In the absence of systematic regional coverage, archaeologists have often turned to the sagas, especially *The Book of Settlements* (Pálsson and Edwards 1972) and the later *Jarðabók* of Árni Magnússon and Páll Vídalín (1930) to reconstruct the social dynamics of farm establishment (Smith and Parsons 1989; Vésteinsson 1998; Vésteinsson et al. 2002). The anachronisms inherent in this method are highly problematic and largely acknowledged by the scholars employing these approaches (Friðriksson and Vésteinsson 2003). Using later systematic inventories like the *Jarðabók* to interpret the settlement and subsequent processes of land division introduces an additional problem to that of anachronism: synchronism. These sources do not provide reliable data on the order of farm establishment. Beginning with a hierarchical landscape does not allow us to examine the development of these inequalities as a dynamic process and results in a tendency to see both a densely settled and hierarchical landscape as a product of a single settlement process and not a series of developments.

The geology and nature of the material record in Iceland present their own obstacles to regional archaeology. Large portions of Iceland have already been covered by stage one documentary review and pedestrian survey, especially in northeast and southwest of Iceland where systematic efforts have inventoried entire districts (Friðriksson 2002; Stefánsdóttir 2003a, 2003b). These surveys, while useful for many purposes, do little to resolve issues of the settlement and initial divisions of land as they do not identify buried buildings not recorded in the documentary record and do not provide establishment dates for the early periods of history.

LAND CLAIM AND DIVISION PATTERNS IN THE VIKING AGE

The limited textual evidence for the settlement and Viking Age forces any discussion of changing property and class relations to the archaeological record. It is difficult to identify property ownership in the archaeological record. It is equally difficult to reconstruct the flow of goods from tenant to landlord farm because most rents were in the form of perishable farm products that do not preserve well; for example, wool, cheeses, butter, and leather goods. Animal skeletal remains can show evidence for separate production and consumption sites, and significant work has been done on the movement of cod (McGovern et al. 2006, 2007). Unfortunately most of the movement of cod is from coastal farms to inland farms and may have more to do with geographically based exchange networks than landlord-tenant relations.

Alternatively we can examine the history of the farmsteads themselves. Evidence for household size, property claims, land division, and unequal relations among groups is best found in changing settlement patterns. A

standard methodology in regional archaeology, the systematic identification and dating of early farmsteads in Iceland has proved problematic
largely due to the absence of surface remains—ceramics, lithics, and archi-
tectural remains—commonly used to identify and date sites in more traditional archaeological settings (Smith and Parsons 1989; Vésteinsson 1998;
Vésteinsson et al. 2002). The remarkable continuity in site location typical
of many Icelandic farms exacerbates the problems as the earliest occupational phases of sites may be buried under meters of later occupation or
erased by modern plowed fields (Steinberg and Bolender 2005).

Recent work by the Skagafjörður Archaeological Settlement Survey
(SASS) in northern Iceland documents the process of land claim, farmstead
division, and the first appearance of a new class of subordinate farmsteads
in the late ninth through eleventh centuries (Bolender 2006, 2007; Bolender
et al. 2008; Steinberg and Bolender 2005). In many cases these subordinate
farmsteads were likely produced by the subdivision of existing farmstead
properties, like the historically identified dependent farmstead (hjáleigur),
and are the first evidence we have for landlord-tenant relations in Iceland.

The survey was conducted in the Langholt region of Skagafjörður in
northern Iceland. It is a small area, roughly 4 by 12 kilometers, and currently comprised of approximately twenty farmsteads. Occupation is concentrated on the eastern side of a long north-south running hill in a strip of
productive agricultural land between low wetlands to the east and higher
pastureland to the west. Langholt represents a tiny fraction of Iceland, and
the development of land tenure relations apparent there may not be the
same in other parts of Iceland, but there is some evidence that the general
chronology and patterns evident there may represent dynamics beyond the
local.

SETTLEMENT PATTERNS AND THE EMERGENCE OF A TENANT CLASS

Based on systematic survey data from the Langholt region, three distinct
stages of farmstead establishment are apparent, each reflecting the landowning elite's control over productive land and, after the initial settlement,
dictating the terms of subsequent farmstead establishment: (1) an initial,
sparse settlement with large, independent farmsteads; (2) the later division
of property into additional independent farmsteads; and (3) the subdivision
of existing farmstead properties creating a new class of smaller, subordinate

farms likely to be the first tenant farms in Iceland (Bolender et al. 2008; Steinberg and Bolender 2005).

On the timing of the initial settlement of Iceland, the archaeological record generally conforms to the historical sources. The first farmsteads appear in the second half of the ninth century, after the fall of the AD 871±2 *landnám* tephra layer (Grönvold et al. 1995). In the Langholt region, there are two settlement period farms: Reynistaður to the north and Stóra-Seyla to the south. During the settlement, land was readily available, and farmsteads could be established with minimal consideration of neighboring farmers. Land may have continued to be available for some time after the arrival of the first settlers, and there seems to have been little resistance to the establishment of new farmsteads; the sagas suggest that first settlers claimed areas far larger than they could have used (cf. Pálsson and Edwards 1972). The availability of land and difficulty of exerting control over other farms would have favored large properties and complex servant- and slave-owning households as the principal means of increasing production. Households would have been the locus of social stratification, from slave to chieftain.

By the second half of the tenth century, productive lands were under the control of specific households as lawfully recognized farmstead property. According to the historical sources, immigration to the island ceased in AD 930 when the land was said to be "fully settled" and all productive lands claimed (Þorgilsson 1930). Afterwards, new farmsteads could only be established by dividing an existing farmstead property. These new farmsteads were widely dispersed and had many of the same characteristics of the initial farmsteads. The implication that a later division of the initial land claims produced a second generation of farms matches well with the archaeological material in Langholt, where a number of additional farms were established after the historical settlement period (ca. AD 879–930).

The new farmsteads are generally large, as measured by the area of structural remains and middens, and there is little evidence, in the archaeological record at least, that these farms were subordinate to the earlier settlement farmsteads. Ostensibly they were established on lands claimed by the original settlers—the secondary farms are all within the boundaries of historically identified settlement claims—but property boundaries may have been less defined than they were in later periods. The most likely candidates for establishing the new farmsteads are members of the landholding families who already held rights to the land and its inheritance, although the sagas also relate instances of land sales (often under coercion) for this period. Land division would have put pressure on extensive farm production as the landscape filled in and pasturelands became smaller and closer together. At the same time, the increasing proximity of farmlands would have encouraged a more concrete and definite system of property ownership.

The result of land division was a tessellation of the farming landscape as all available agricultural land was under the control of some household or another. Systems of relict farm boundary walls identified in the northeast of Iceland dating to the late tenth–twelfth centuries indicate that this division of the landscape was a matter of general agreement among landowning farmers as the walls share common boundaries between farms (Einarsson et al. 2002). A network of local and regional assemblies also provided a judicial forum for farmers to air disputes regarding property claims and violations. However, it is important to note that this seemingly complete propertization of the landscape remained localized. Each household was responsible for the preservation of its own land claims as there was no state entity that could enforce them.

The simplest interpretation of the settlement pattern in Langholt is that the institution of tenancy simply did not exist during the settlement. This reduces the set of institutionalized relations of inequality during the settlement to those contained within the household, between landowner and dependent laborers and slaves. This is not to characterize the interhousehold social landscape as one of universal equality. There can be little doubt that there were significant differences in the wealth, social standing, productive resources (in land and labor), and blunt power among settler households. Archaeological excavations have demonstrated a diversity of early farmsteads, large and small, situated in relation to varying resources: the sea, productive lowlands, and highlands. The sagas indicate that titles were imported with their owners to Iceland as well and that this special status—chief (goði)— played in an instrumental role in the early assembly systems established to resolve disputes among farmers and that the advocacy they provided was a potential source of wealth and power (Byock 1988). Nonetheless, direct control over other households' production does not appear to have been a part of the settlement landscape. Without tenants and the accumulation of tenant properties, the status differences among settlement period landowners were less than in later periods when chieftains controlled extended family resources and the wealth of multiple estates (Sigurðsson 1989; Þorláksson 1989).

Around the transition between the tenth and eleventh centuries, there is a major change in both the location and size of new farmsteads representing a new and distinct class of properties. At the beginning of the century, the surveyed area had six farmsteads. During the eleventh century at least four (and possibly eight or more) new farms were established, roughly doubling the number of farms in the region. These new farms are located on lands neighboring the earlier farmsteads. At least one new farm appears in the immediate vicinity of each earlier independent farmstead. The property boundaries of these Viking Age farmsteads are not recorded in historical sources, but the new farms are all located within the land that would hypothetically belong to an existing farm rather than the interstitial areas between existing farms.

The late farmsteads are also relatively small. The area of structures and middens associated with these new farmsteads is significantly smaller than the early farms. Medieval historical records, albeit from well after the time that the farms were established, show that many of the new small farms were subordinate to the principal farms. Many are identified as dependent farms (hjáleigur). In Iceland, while an independent property can be bought and thus become a tenant farm, it is extremely unusual for a previously independent farm to become a subfarm. In the rare instances this happened, it was often after the farms had been abandoned for substantial periods of time and then later reestablished by the new landowning farmstead. Excavations at these farms show no evidence of any break in occupation at the farms during the Viking Age or medieval period, and it seems unlikely that these farms were anything other than subfarms from the time they were first established. When systematic records of farm value become available in the late seventeenth century, all of these farms are of lesser value than the earlier, neighboring farms (Lárusson 1967; Magnússon and Vídalín 1930). It is clear that the farms established during the eleventh century represent a new dynamic of land division. Does the appearance of a new class of subfarms equal the formation of a new class of tenant householders?

DIVIDING LAND AND MAKING CLASS

In the years 2001–2007 the Skagafjörður Archaeological Settlement Survey documented a change in local settlement patterns and the establishment of a new class of farmstead—the hjáleiga—and a new set of labor relations in the Langholt region of northern Iceland. The eleventh century saw other changes: the abandonment of some highland farms (Sveinbjarnardóttir 1992) and the conversion to Christianity in Iceland. The appearance of a new class of farmstead is, of course, not synonymous with the creation of a new class of farmer. While it is reasonable to suggest that the appearance of these new subfarms is associated with the introduction of tenancy in general and a new form of dependency, it cannot be demonstrated that tenancy did not exist in pre-eleventh-century Iceland. The real question is, why were these new subfarms created and what was the relationship between the newly formed households and the preexisting farmers?

I have argued along with John Steinberg and E. Paul Durrenberger that the mostly likely source of the new subfarm households would have been from dependent labor within the earlier farmsteads that subdivided their own land to make the new farmsteads (Bolender et al. 2008). Resituating some household labor on tenant farmsteads would have expanded the productive capacity of the farm by creating new home fields and farmstead infrastructure. It also would have lowered the costs of maintaining large labor pools within the household while still affording landowners a means of benefiting in the form of rents. The establishment of landlord-tenant relationships of production constitutes a substitution of one form of labor control for another: the augmentation of direct control over household labor with the substitution of control over property as an indirect means of control over labor (and production). In this process, landowners managed to fundamentally change the nature of control over surplus labor through the fetishism in space, "making social relations between people appear as relations between places or spaces" (Harvey 1982:338n). In doing so they also managed to fundamentally alter their ability to expand the potential scope of the political economy by incorporating extrahousehold labor into the household economy. How effective was this strategy to expand household production, and what effects did it have on Icelandic society in general?

The reorganization of land and labor appears as a common strategy in the eleventh century in the Langholt region, and there is some evidence that this pattern may be seen in other parts of Iceland around the same time. However, these developments are, in fact, localized: a matter of strategic decisions on the part of individual household heads who reorganized land and labor within their own properties. This must have imparted a new set of relationships with subtenant farmers, regardless of whether they came from existing dependent labor within the household. These localized changes probably contributed to altered production possibilities at subdivided and now landlord farmsteads—the potential of higher production and the support of a larger population on the estate (Bolender et al. 2008)—that undoubtedly had consequences for the broader political economy and the dynamics among independent freeholders. But there is only limited evidence for the general spread of landlord-tenant relationships as a dominant mode of production or as the basis of a political economy. Instead the political economy appears to have remained rooted in political networks of dominant families and independent farmer supporters.

Here the real issue is the degree to which property subdivision constituted a reorganization of society, the introduction of class relations, or was little more than a spatial reorganization of household production. At issue is the social independence of tenant householders, how they operated as social individuals, the degree to which tenant farming became a broader principal of production, whether previously independent properties became tenanted, and the degree to which landholding becomes a principle of social power beyond the local subdivided estate.

The saga literature contains many stories of freed slaves that became dependent tenant farmers. In most cases the ties between former slaves and landowners remained strong. In the volatile world of the sagas, property disputes were common occurrences, and small farmers lacking strong support networks were especially susceptible to aggression of neighbors. In such a world, dependent tenants would have limited social networks (as they are coming from a class without social standing), and former masters and landowners represented the most obvious source of support. Regardless of the historicity of the saga accounts, they are illustrative of real dynamics between landowners and tenants. These dynamics would have reinforced the continued alignment of shared interests between landowner and tenant, a situation that complicates the development of class identity and the opportunities for common organization among disenfranchised people.

Did tenant farmers, especially the initial generation of dependent tenant farmers holding subfarms on landlord estates—possibly former members of the landholder's household—have their own social identity? It seems unlikely that landowners would have taken the risk of placing either former household dependents or outsiders on their own estates if they did not feel assured in the fidelity of those tenants. The lifeless material of the archaeological record offers limited insight into the consciousness of past actors. Nonetheless, we do not necessarily have to apprehend a specific consciousness to see it operating. In fact, the highly patterned nature of most archaeological data places a necessary threshold on the social significance of individual agents, identities, and thought: those that manifest as socially significant structures tend to be preserved; those that are idiosyncratic are often lost. The patterns of behavior preserved in the archaeological record are, in their very nature, representative of not just individual consciousness but of widely held positions that were socially enacted on a broad scale. The individual thought may be lost, but not the actions it engendered. When did landlord-tenant relations become the fundamental organizing principle of the Icelandic political economy?

THE LIMITATIONS OF SETTLEMENT PATTERN ANALYSES AND THE STUDY OF CLASS

Viking Age Iceland provides an unusual historical case in which the initial formation of a landlord-tenant class division coincided with the creation of new household categories and new farmsteads. Settlement pattern analysis deals principally with the relative size, distribution, and chronology of sites within a given locality. In the instance that new and distinct patterns of settlement mark—in fact constitute—the emergence of new social institutions, we can infer the emergence and nature of class distinctions from the location, size, and timing of new farmsteads.

The internal complexity of Norse households remains largely invisible in settlement patterns. Based on analogy drawn from the saga literature and early modern historical sources, we can suggest that the smaller tenant households lacked the numbers of subordinate laborers, the slaves and attached workers, described for the larger farmsteads. Perhaps the social distance between tenant farmers, possibly former slaves themselves, and any subordinate household labor was less than that between landowning farmers, their families, and household slaves at the big farms, but this inference is not supported by the archaeology itself. In fact, it is difficult to locate the complex, hierarchically organized Norse households described in the sagas within the excavated longhouses and their communal halls. The archaeological record provides little evidence for the presence of, let alone the distinctions among, landowning family members, servants, and slaves (Milek 2006). Within the walls of those Viking longhouses it is difficult to see individuals or classes. In the pre-Christian Viking Age, the best archaeological evidence for internal household class distinctions comes not from the settlement patterns or household excavations but rather from the burial practices. Inhumations are biased in favor of older males and are too few in number to represent the full adult population of a farmstead occupied for multiple generations (Eldjárn and Friðriksson 2000). It is likely that these burials represent landowners and their families and that burial practices indicate the class distinctions within the living households (Bolender 2007).

The difficulties archaeologists face in reconstructing internal class distinctions from household excavations and settlement patterns extend to the problem of identifying status changes at existing farmsteads. It is uncertain how much farmstead property was tenant land during the medieval period, but land alienation in the twelfth and thirteenth centuries was not as great as in later periods and certainly significantly less than the 95 percent documented at the end of the seventeenth century (Lárusson 1967). As the church became a major landowner, the aristocracy also increased its landholdings, at the expense of independent farmers. The accumulation of land in the hands of the church and aristocracy can be documented to some extent through the sagas and documentary record. In the twelfth century properties belonging to the major chiefly families amounted to around 300 hundreds in land value, or the equivalent of approximately fifteen farmsteads. The great chieftains of the thirteenth century may have owned around seventy farms (Sigurðsson 1999).

The fourteenth century in Iceland saw a massive expansion in land alienation and the accumulation of property by the church and secular elite. Iceland officially ceded authority to the Norwegian king in AD 1262, resulting in a realignment of aristocratic power from local constituencies of independent farmers to the crown (Sigurðsson 1995). At the end of the thirteenth century the church successfully gained control of many of the largest estates that had nominally been donated to the church but had in fact remained the properties of secular families. Major church institutions— the bishoprics seated in the north and south of the country, monasteries, and parish churches—grew in size and owned dozens and even hundreds of farmsteads (Júlíusson 1995). The expanded landholdings by the church were matched by that of the new secular aristocracy. In 1430, Loftur

Guttormsson, the governor of the north and west of Iceland, had properties in excess of 4,300 hundreds or as many as 215 farmsteads (Sigurðsson 1995), an amount rivaling the bishoprics and much larger than the great families of the previous age.

Settlement patterns are virtually silent regarding the massive expansion of land alienation and tenant households in the fourteenth century. For the most part these transformations in the status of individual households and the accumulation of land holdings by the church and secular elite did not result in the creation of new farmstead properties. After the twelfth century there are, in fact, no major changes in the Langholt settlement pattern until the twentieth century, when the mechanization of agricultural production revolutionized farming practices throughout Iceland and resulted in new land use patterns and farmstead reorganization (Ashwell 1963). After the initial subdivision of farm properties in the eleventh century, the majority of farmsteads were in place, and there is little evidence for further changes in property boundaries or the location of agricultural fields (Bolender 2006). Even the location of the farmhouses was stable, resulting in the creation of small mounds as old turf and garbage accumulated under and around occupation sites over the years. Thus the transformation of a society dominated by independent freeholders to a highly stratified society with a small landowning aristocracy and a large class of tenant farmers is all but invisible in the archaeological settlement pattern.

This is where the archaeological record continues to bury its secrets. While it is a relatively simple, if intensive, process to systematically identify a settlement history and document gross changes in the status of new farms, their proximity to existing farms, the size of those farms on a rough scale, and find in them the prehistory of later medieval land documentation, it is difficult to discern status changes at existing farmsteads. Not the creation of new dependent farmsteads but rather the shift from once-independent freeholder to dependent tenant farmer. Evidence for this lies, in most cases, under a millennium of accumulated occupational deposits. What do the early *hjáleigur* look like? Can we see not just the farm status but the household that goes with it? This is where the issues of class and consciousness lie—in the decisions of those farmers: are landlord and tenant households constituted differently? Do they make different production choices or have different opportunities from larger, landholding or landlord households?

REFERENCES CITED

Ashwell, I. Y. 1963. "Recent Changes in the Pattern of Farming in Iceland." *Canadian Geographer* 7(4):174–180.

Berson, Bruno. 2002. "A Contribution to the Study of the Medieval Icelandic Farm: The Byres." *Archaeological Islandica* 2: 34–60.

Bolender, Douglas. 2006. "The Creation of a Propertied Landscape: Land Tenure and Intensification in Medieval Iceland." PhD dissertation, Northwestern University.

————. 2007. "House, Land, and Labor in a Frontier Landscape: The Norse Colonization of Iceland." In *The Durable House: Architecture, Ancestors, and Origins*, edited by R. A. Beck, 400–421, vol. 33. Carbondale: Center for Archaeological Investigations Southern Illinois University Carbondale.

Bolender, Douglas J., John M. Steinberg, and E. Paul Durrenberger. 2008. "Unsettled Landscapes: Settlement Patterns and the Development of Social Inequality in Northern Iceland." In *Economies and the Transformation of Landscape*, edited by C. A. Pool and L. Cliggett. Monographs in Economic Anthropology: Society for Economic Anthropology. Lanham, MD: Altamira.

Brynjólfsson, Erlingur. 1983. "Bagi er oft bú sitt að flytja." *Cand.mag.*, University of Iceland.

Byock, Jesse. 1988. *Medieval Iceland: Society, Sagas, and Power*. Los Angeles: University of California Press.

Durrenberger, E. Paul. 1992. *The Dynamics of Medieval Iceland: Political Economy and Literature*. Iowa City: University of Iowa Press.

Einarsson, Árni, Oddgeir Hansson, and Orri Vésteinsson. 2002. "An Extensive System of Medieval Earthworks in Northeast Iceland." *Archaeological Islandica* 2:61–73.

Eldjárn, Kristján. 1949. "Eyðibyggð á Hrunamannaafrétti." *Árbók hins íslenzka fornleifafélags* 1943–48:1–43.

Eldjárn, Kristján, and Adolf Friðriksson. 2000. *Kuml og haugfé úr heiðnum sið á Íslandi*. Reykjavík: Mál og Menning.

Friðriksson, Adolf. 1994. *Sagas and Popular Antiquarianism in Icelandic Archaeology*. Aldershot: Avebury.

————, ed. 2002. *Fornleifastofnun Íslands Annual Report 2002*. Reykjavík: Fornleifastofnun Íslands.

Friðriksson, Adolf, and Orri Vésteinsson. 2003. "Creating a Past: A Historiography of the Settlement of Iceland." In *Contact, Continuity, and Collapse: The Norse Colonization of the North Atlantic*, edited by J. Barrett, 139–161. Studies in the Early Middle Ages. Turnhout, Belgium: Brepols.

Grönvold, K., N. Óskarsson, S. J. Johnsen, J. B. Clausen, C. U. Hammer, G. Bard, and E. Bard. 1995. "Ash Layers from Iceland in the Greenland GRIP Ice Core Correlated with Oceanic and Land Sediments." *Earth and Planetary Science Letters* 135: 149–155.

Gunnarsson, Gísli. 1980. *Fertility and Nuptiality in Iceland's Demographic History.* Lund: Meddlelande från Ekonomisk-Historiska Institutionen, Lund Universitet.

———. 1983. "Monopoly Trade and Economic Stagnation. Studies in the Foreign Trade of Iceland 1602–1787." PhD dissertation, University of Lund.

Gunnlaugsson, Gísli Ágúst. 1988. *Family and Household in Iceland 1801–1930: Studies in the Relationship between Demographic and Socio-Economic Development, Social Legislation and Family and Household Structures.* Uppsala: University of Uppsala (Almqvist & Wiksell International, Stockholm).

Harvey, David. 1982. *The Limits to Capital.* Chicago: University of Chicago Press.

Júlíusson, Árni Daniel. 1995. "Bónder i pestens tid: landbrug, godsdrift og social konflikt in Senmiddelaldernes Icelandske Bondesamfund." PhD dissertation, University of Copenhagen.

Lárusson, Björn. 1967. *The Old Icelandic Land Registers.* Lund: C. W. K. Gleerup.

Magnússon, Árni, and Páll Vídalín. 1930. *Járðabók Árna Magnússonar og Páls Vidalíns I-XIII.* Copenhagen: Hið íslenska fræðafélag.

Magnússon, Magnús S. 1985. *Iceland in Transition: Labour and Socio-Economic Change before 1940.* Volume XLV. Lund: University of Lund.

McGovern, Thomas H., S. Perdikaris, A. Einarsson, and J. Sidel. 2006. "Coastal Connections, Local Fishing, and Sustainable Egg Harvesting: Patterns of Viking Age Inland Wild Resource Use in Mývatn District, Northern Iceland." *Environmental Archaeology* 11(1): 187–206.

McGovern, Thomas H., O. Vésteinsson, A. Fridriksson, M. Church, I. Lawson, I. A. Simpson, A. Einarsson, A. Dugmore, G. Cook, S. Perdikaris, K. Edwards, A. M. Thomsom, W. P. Adderley, A. Newton, G. Lucas, and O. Aldred. 2007. "Landscapes of Settlement in Northern Iceland: Historical Ecology of Human Impact and Climate Fluctuation on the Millennial Scale." *American Anthropologist* 109(1): 27–51.

Milek, Karen. 2006. "Houses and Households in Early Icelandic Society: Geoarchaeology and the Interpretation of Social Space." PhD dissertation, University of Cambridge.

Ólason, Vésteinn. 1998. *Dialogues with the Viking Age: Narration and Representation in the Sagas of the Icelanders.* Reykjavík: Heimskringla.

Pálsson, Hermann, and Paul Edwards. 1972. *The Book of Settlements: Landnámabók. Translated, with introduction and notes.* Translated by H. Pálsson and P. Edwards. Manitoba: University of Manitoba Press.

Pálsson, Hjalti. 2001. *Byggðasaga Skagafjarðar: II Bindi Staðarhreppur-Seyluhreppur.* Sauðárkróki, Iceland: Sögufélag Skagafirðinga.

Sigurðsson, Jon Viðar. 1989. *Frá Goðorðum til Ríkja.* Reykjavik: Menningarsjóður.

————. 1995. "The Icelandic Aristocracy after the Fall of the Free State." *Scandinavian Journal of History* 20(3): 153–166.

————. 1999. *Chieftains and Power in the Icelandic Commonwealth*. Odense: Odense University Press.

Smith, Kevin P. 1995. "Landnám: The Settlement of Iceland in Archaeological and Historical Perspective." *World Archaeology* 26(3): 319–346.

Smith, Kevin P., and Jeffery R. Parsons. 1989. "Regional Archaeological Research in Iceland: Potentials and Possibilities." In *The Anthropology of Iceland*, edited by E. P. Durrenberger and G. Pálsson, 179–202. Iowa City: University of Iowa Press.

Stefánsdóttir, Agnes. 2003a. *Fornleifaskráning 1980–2001 ritskrá*. Gutenberg: Þjóðminjasafn Íslands and Fornleifavernd Ríkisins.

————. 2003b. *Útgefnar skýrslur um fornleifaskráningu 2002 auk nokkurra skýrsla frá 2001 sem vantaði í fyrri ritaskrá*. Reykjavík: Fornleifavernd Ríkisins.

Steinberg, John, and Douglas Bolender. 2005. "Rannsóknir á búsetuminjum í Skagafirði (Settlement pattern analysis in Skagafjörður)." *Árbók hins íslenzka fornleifafélags* 2002–2003: 107–130.

Sveinbjarnardóttir, Guðrún. 1992. *Farm Abandonment in Medieval and Post-Medieval Iceland: An Interdisciplinary Study*. Oxford: Oxbow Press.

Þorgilsson, Ari. 1930. *The Book of the Icelanders [Íslendingabók]*. Translated by H. Hermannsson. Volume 20. Ithaca, NY: Cornell University Library.

Þorláksson, Helgi. 1989. *Gamlar Götur og Goðavald*. Reykjavik: Sagnfræðistofnun Háskóla Íslands.

Vasey, Daniel E. 1996. "Premodern and Modern Constructions of Population Regimes." In *Images of Contemporary Iceland: Everyday Lives and Global Contexts*, edited by G. Pálsson and E. P. Durrenberger, 149–170. Iowa City: University of Iowa Press.

Vésteinsson, Orri. 1998. "Patterns of Settlement in Iceland: A Study in Prehistory." *Saga Book (Viking Society of Northern Research)* 25(1): 1–29.

————. 2004. "Icelandic Farmhouse Excavations: Field Methods and Site Choices." *Archaeological Islandica* 3: 71–100.

Vésteinsson, Orri, Thomas McGovern, and Christian Keller. 2002. "Enduring Impacts: Social and Environmental Aspects of Viking Age Settlement in Iceland and Greenland." *Archaeological Islandica* 2: 98–136.

Fried's Evolutionary Model, Social Stratification, and the Nuosu in Southwest China

ANN   MAXWELL   HILL

INTRODUCTION

Social stratification in Nuosu societies in southwest China has a long history extending back to the Ming Dynasty (1368–1644), if not earlier, documented in Chinese chronicles.[1] Although often treated by historians and ethnologists as a single, bounded society with unique characteristics relative to other ethnic groups, including the Han Chinese themselves, the Nuosu communities in the area of the Da Liangshan (Great Cold Mountains) in southwestern Sichuan historically have shown considerable variation, especially in areas where the Nuosu have lived in close proximity to other ethnic groups. Here I compare two Nuosu areas on the periphery of Da Liangshan. While Da Liangshan is often called the Nuosu "core" area because of their overwhelming predominance in the population, the periphery has been dubbed the Lesser Cold Mountains, or in Mandarin Chinese, Xiao Liangshan. Nuosu communities in Xiao Liangshan were more frequently affected by interactions with other peoples, including state agents and populations from China's interior, than Nuosu in the so-called core area. My purpose in resorting to comparison of two areas in Xiao Liangshan is to show through ethnographic detail how local conditions differentially affected stratification in Nuosu communities and coincidently to put to rest the romantic trope of the "independent" Lolo (an earlier name for the Nuosu) popularized by Western travelers to Da Liangshan in the nineteenth and twentieth centuries (Li Lie 2006: 61–62).[2] A second concern is to use the two examples of Nuosu stratification to reexamine Fried's contention in his early work on political evolution that stratified societies without states were inherently unstable and therefore ephemeral (Fried 1967).

Fried's view that nonstate stratified societies are short lived is easily refuted, not only from the longevity in the historical record of Nuosu societies, but also from more recent studies of stratified societies (Rousseau 1990; Johnson and Earle 2000). While modern states tend to lay claim to long genealogies of nationhood, stratified societies, too, we now know, can persist for centuries without the formation of a centralized political system. Examples abound in Polynesia, including the Hawaiian Islands, the Middle East, Melanesia, and Southeast Asia. The question of the intrinsic instability of nonstate stratified societies is more complicated, not least because Fried was not very specific about what he meant by *instability*. He seems to assume the inevitability of a "revolution from below" (my term), as access to resources is increasingly restricted by elites, and kinship begins to fail as both ideology and structure under conditions of population expansion (Fried 1967: 186–187, 196–204).

A question anthropologists consider relevant to the stability of stratified societies is their proximity to states. Ever since Leach's work on the Kachin in the China-Burma border area, scholars have been aware that ethnic groups cannot be productively studied as bounded isolates (Leach 1954). Their relations with adjacent polities and communities contribute to their social forms and identities. In Fried's model, some stratified societies are "secondary" formations (meaning not pristine) affected in complex, subtle ways by nearby states (Fried 1967: 198–199) and inevitably absorbed by them. More recent studies of this relationship see the state as engaged in continual efforts to convert nonstate space into legible, taxable domains (Scott 1998, especially 183–191). There is also the view that the "tribal" zone at the edge of empire sustained high levels of violence, not because the people there were inherently violent, but because indigenous societies were disrupted by the intrusion of the state, or its agents and technologies

(Ferguson and Whitehead 1992). These newer accounts of frontier politics, whether focused on traditional empires, colonies, or the modern nation-state, all tell more of the story from the periphery rather than the center. Local people, knowledge, and institutions are at the heart of these recent accounts, demonstrating that peripheral peoples—in Fried's sense, merely secondary phenomena relative to the state—were far from passive recipients of state initiatives. Their capacity for confounding the predatory intrusions of the state speaks to the ethnographic case at hand, where the Nuosu in Southwest China were often predatory in their own right.

In fact, when I describe Nuosu raids for captives or their antagonistic relations with local Han Chinese, I seem to be confirming the worst-case scenario of war in the tribal zone in response to state intrusions. Furthermore, Fried's confidence in the greater efficiency of the state as a political form in enabling the absorption of less-powerful, less-centralized peripheral groups is, in the final analysis, justified. The autonomy of the "independent" Lolo was finished by the early 1960s, when the last of the Nuosu "bandits" were captured or killed, and all of Liangshan was put on the path to land reform under Chinese socialism. But during the period I focus on, roughly 1850–1950 when historical records are the richest and China's transition from empire to republic begins to reverberate on its periphery, Nuosu societies in both areas that I compare here were expanding and pushing out the Han Chinese and other ethnic groups. During this period, they encountered increasing pressures, direct and indirect, from the presence of Han populations—as soldiers, settlers, opium traders, and bureaucrats. These pressures notwithstanding, Nuosu stratification did not implode. On the contrary, without the perspective provided by hindsight, there was no basis for predicting that the Nuosu would be the losers in conflicts with the Han, nor was it clear that Nuosu society, in comparison with the disruptions experienced by the Chinese in this period, was less stable than China proper.

THE TWO CASES: NINGLANG AND LEIBO IN XIAO LIANGSHAN

The first case, with which I am more familiar, is known to me from extensive fieldwork in China's Yunnan Province and related historical sources. The area of my fieldwork, mainly centered around Ninglang Yi Autonomous County in Yunnan's northwest, is now locally known as Xiao Liangshan. Xiao Liangshan in these parts also includes some counties across the border in Sichuan with substantial Nuosu populations. Xiao Liangshan in north-western Yunnan was settled over several centuries, as Nuosu populations from Da Liangshan migrated south and west. The reasons for these migrations is not very clear, although the Ninglang Nuosu attribute it to feuding that propelled combatants into new territory (see Du Yuting 1984: 1–3 for details on feuding from his interviews with local Nuosu and from my fieldwork interviews below).

The Ninglang case is in marked contrast to an older frontier roughly to the east of Da Liangshan, also called Xiao Liangshan, where the Nuosu have lived for so long that they are considered indigenous people. The second case comes from this older frontier, in particular the part centered around Leibo County in Sichuan. In 2009, I did a month's fieldwork in the county of Leibo along the Jinsha River (Golden Sands River), but am more familiar with Leibo from historical sources.[3]

For the sake of clarity, I refer to the first case as Ninglang and the second, as Leibo. Both are in areas known in the Chinese ethnographic literature on minorities as Xiao Liangshan, obviously a convention for naming the rugged terrain peripheral to the Da Liangshan core area; however, the historical experience of the Nuosu populations on these two frontiers is rather different. Thus, instead of assuming that there is a general model of Nuosu stratification derived from the Da Liangshan core area that has replicated itself in Xiao Liangshan, I want the specifics of each case to illustrate some of the variation, and its sources, among people who call themselves Nuosu. After presenting the cases, I discuss some of the similarities and differences, in the process suggesting what might account for them.

Ninglang: A Multiethnic Zone

Over 200 years ago, the ancestors of the present Nuosu population in Ninglang Yi Autonomous County began leaving Da Liangshan and headed west to settle at altitudes generally above 2,200 meters. In the process, they took land claimed by indigenous groups living at lower elevations, such as the Moso or Pumi, or opened fields on marginal land barely fit for agriculture but suitable for grazing. Generally speaking, the migrants were familiar with high-altitude, shifting cultivation for growing buckwheat, turnips, potatoes and other cold-weather crops and tended to open fields above high valley plateaus. They also raised sheep, goats, chickens, and some cattle and horses, within a frugal system that included enclosed fields and house-barns to maximize manure collection and livestock security.

Older informants say they left Da Liangshan because of feuds. As I have indicated above, the underlying basis for the feuding that drove out Nuosu from the core area to the periphery of Da Liangshan is unclear. However, one source does make clear that some Nuosu in what is now Ninglang County fled from exploitative aristocrats who threatened the livelihood of families under their protection. Crop failures were another reason (see Liu Yumin 1986). And there were cases of slaves captured in Da Liangshan who were sold to masters in the newly settled part of Xiao Liangshan.

Not surprisingly, the aristocrats among the Nuosu, called *nuo* in the Nuosu language and Black Yi (*hei yi*) in Chinese, were seldom the leaders of these migrations into new territory; they tended to come later, when pioneer Nuosu families and lineages felt the need for them. One ethnographic source reported that local Nuosu sent people back to Da Liangshan to persuade aristocrats to come home with them to their new communities, saying that without their lords, they were like "a head without a hat" (Liu Yumin 1986: 208). A less-sentimental read on the situation is that they needed the protection of some in the aristocratic stratum, so they would not be forcibly returned to their old overlords, also aristocrats, in Da Liangshan (Liu Yumin 1986: 208).

Who were the *nuo* deemed so important to society? Informants in Ninglang County told me that in their experience, their society had always been stratified into four levels, often translated from the Mandarin term, *dengji*, as "castes." At the top were the *nuo*. They belonged to patrilineages with the longest genealogies, some traceable to one of the original founding ancestors of the Nuosu. Another Nuosu way of putting this is that these lineages had the "hardest bones," a term indicating that their blood lines were pure and uncorrupted by marriage to people outside the *nuo* group. The second ranked group was the *qunuo* or *quhuo*. These were Nuosu commoners, almost always affiliated with particular *nuo* lineages in varying degrees of subordination and dependence. The *qunuo* were usually the largest strata numerically in Nuosu society; some of their genealogies included people who were slaves way back in the depths of origins of their kin groups; hence, *qunuo* were not as purely Nuosu as the *nuo*. Below the *qunuo* were two strata that were commonly recent captives or their direct descendents brought in from outside Nuosu territory during raids, *mgapjie* and *gaxi*. In general, the *mgapjie* were married couples who worked directly for their owners but had separate houses and fields given them by their masters. On the lowest rung were the *gaxi*, who were unmarried house slaves, often newly captured, or the sons and daughters of the *mgapjie* obliged to work for the households of their *nuo* or *qunuo* masters.

Although the economic underpinnings of ranked groups—tribute, rents, and labor owed to those with primordial claims to land and status—was extirpated by the Chinese Communist government in a process beginning in 1956, the Nuosu in Ninglang continue up to the present to practice endogamy within their ranked groups. Their pervasive system of stratification and the phenomenon of slave holding has led orthodox Marxist scholars in China, using the Stalinist-derived model of social evolution, to classify the pre–1956 Nuosu as a slave society. While there are many nuanced interpretations among Chinese scholars of exactly what this means in the Nuosu case, the label of slave society continues to be used and in fact is naturalized among the Nuosu themselves (see Harrell and Fan's translations of different views of Nuosu slave society among China's scholars, 2003; and Hill 2001 for a Western interpretation).

Although I will say more about slavery in this essay, at this point it is important to note that in Ninglang, Nuosu society was not dependent on slave labor for its subsistence. Slaves did not labor on large plantations producing for markets. Furthermore, there was no slave marketplace in the sense we're familiar with from the US South. Nor were slaves sold outside Liangshan, with the exception of a few, usually Han Chinese, who were ransomed. Slaves were exchanged among the Nuosu, some as soon as they were brought in, others when their masters needed cash. Slaves in effect were prestige goods, although admittedly their labor was most important to *nuo* families, whose men were thought to be above the necessity for field labor.

Nuosu lineages on the Ninglang Xiao Liangshan frontier feuded, although not for the reasons Fried suggests in his discussion of the instability of stratified societies—deprivation and unequal access to basic resources cast as a sort of "revolution from below" (Fried 1967: 185–190). Nuosu informants' stories indicated that the proximate reasons for feuds were theft, homicide, incest, brides who refused their arranged marriages, runaway slaves, and a host of other provocations. Natural allies were patrilineal kin, lineages with a history of intermarriage, and, to a lesser extent, *nuo* and their *qunuo* dependents.

Nuo lineages tended to feud with one another rather than unite against other strata; the same could be said of the *qunuo*. Feuds were settled through mediation and ultimately compensation, but enmities could last for generations after the settlement. Furthermore, there is general agreement that opium production, primarily for Han consumption, grew in the 1920s and led to more guns and more conflict throughout Xiao Liangshan, in turn increasing the likelihood that the Nuosu would take captives from neighboring ethnic groups. Another consequence of opium production was overall enhancement of the power of the local *nuo*, who were more likely than others to have contacts with Han merchants and Nationalist Chinese army units occasionally stationed near Nuosu territories; this meant easier access than other Nuosu to guns and the opium market (Du Yuting 1984: 20).

Yet opium was never produced on such a scale that required a large labor force of slaves or others, and most Nuosu even at the height of the trade in opium and guns were subsistence farmers (see Du Yuting 1984 and Hill 2001 for more detailed evidence). As I have noted elsewhere, in Ninglang rents and tribute were relatively low; there was plenty of land, and family livelihood depended a great deal on labor power (Hill 2004: 683). According to eye witnesses in the early 1940s and shortly before land reform, most Nuosu worked unremittingly hard (Winnington 1959: 57; Tseng Chao-lun 1956: 12). Few but the *nuo*, estimated to comprise about 4 percent of the population, could escape the drudge labor required to produce a living out of poor mountain soils (Du Yuting 1984: 18).

But precisely because land was so plentiful, the *nuo* and other slave owners were constrained in their urge to exploit their underlings, slave or commoner. As was likely the case in migrations out of the core area, families fled masters or overlords who were too exploitative or too cruel. Why revolt when you could walk away? The fact that slaves were often married in arrangements dictated by their masters and required to farm their own land is another indication that the *nuo* had no interest in amassing a large, dependent labor force. Most people were expected to support themselves by dint of their own hard work.[4]

The Nuosu were latecomers to Ninglang, lived at the highest altitudes, and did not intermarry with local Naxi, Moso (Naze), Pumi and other ethnic groups indigenous to this part of Xiao Liangshan. However, they did not exist in an economic or political vacuum. Long before opium became a local commodity, for example, the Nuosu traded with others for salt, important not as a condiment but as a necessity for their livestock. My impression is that salt was brought into the uplands of Xiao Liangshan by the Nuosu themselves, who traveled in small groups back to salt wells in Sichuan or in the twentieth century to local salt sellers in adjacent valley market towns. In a few areas there were Nuosu blacksmiths and silversmiths, but it seems that most iron implements and silver ornaments were imported from other Nuosu areas.

Face-to-face contact with local ethnic groups whom they occasionally raided for captives, such as the Han and Pumi, was not an everyday occurrence but not uncommon, either. Nuosu territory in Xiao Liangshan, from the time of the arrival of the first migrants in the eighteenth century until the twentieth century, was theoretically under the governance of a local *tusi* appointed by the Chinese/Manchu court.

The *tusi* were hereditary, indigenous officials in a special system for control of imperial China's borders in the southwest. This kind of border governance had its origins in the Yuan Dynasty (1206–1368) as a consequence of the Mongol conquest in this area in 1253, but was not really systematized until the Ming (1368–1644). The two local *tusi*, one in Yongning and the other at Xinyingpan, are both regarded by the Nuosu as Moso, although they tend to use one term (*Ozzu*) to refer to both Moso and Pumi (see Shih 2010: 40–51 for evidence of the Pumi identity of the Yongning *tusi*). The significant point is that the first Nuosu who moved from Da Liangshan to what is now Ninglang had to pay the local *tusi* or local families for rights to land.

The land tenure picture from the beginning of Nuosu arrival in Ninglang was complicated. There were tenancy arrangements between *tusi* and incoming Nuosu that were inheritable and transferable. Some of these arrangements lasted until the 1950s in the form of symbolic tribute, but most attenuated in the 1920s coincident with the decline in the *tusi*'s influence and the rise of the *nuo* to become the most powerful group in the area. Suffice it to say that some Nuosu paid for usufruct rights to land in virtual perpetuity; others, for example heirs and slaves, were granted usufruct rights by their fathers or masters.

Tenancy arrangements were separate from the traditional, genealogy-based stratification system, sometimes resulting in *nuo* renting land from *qunuo*, even though the *qunuo* might still owe hereditary tribute to his *nuo* superior. And, more to our point here, tenancy seemed to be a major nexus of relations between different ethnic groups in Ninglang. Not all Nuosu farmed Nuosu land, and some Nuoso had Han or Pumi tenants. However, as I have already noted, by and large, neither rents nor tribute were too onerous. It made no sense to squeeze productive laborers in the groups below you, whether your traditional dependents or your tenants, because you, the recipient, would lose "income" and risk forcing your underlings to leave for another, more accommodating, superior (see Du Yuting 1984: 16–19).

Nuosu relations with the Pumi, Moso, and other indigenous groups living on the slopes below them is difficult to discern from the traditional sources written in Chinese. Moreover, in interviews, older Nuosu informants were rather resistant to questions about other ethnic groups besides the Han. This was because most had few contacts outside Nuosu society and possibly because in their memory, their relations with local Pumi and Moso were rather fraught with tensions linked to the feuding, raiding, and periodic alliances with the Han that characterized Ninglang beginning in the 1920s. Fortunately, Ma Erzi, a prolific Nuosu scholar born in Sichuan's Yanyuan County just to the north of Ninglang whose Chinese name is Mgebbu Lunzyi, has written one of the few accounts that discusses everyday relations between the Nuosu and, in this case, the Pumi (*Ozzu*) (Mgebbu Lunzyi 2003). Ma Erzi's grandfather was born in 1897, and his land adjoined the territory of several Pumi families; in fact, the grandfather purchased his first piece of farmland from the Pumi. The Pumi, fearing the Nuosu, who dominated this multiethnic area, actively courted the locally prominent Nuosu as insurance against raids, not so often directed against themselves as their Han tenants (Mgebbu Lunzyi 2003: 137). Nuosu, including Ma Erzi's grandfather, were invited to Pumi New Year and other celebrations.

The Pumi also arranged for many of their children to be the "dry sons" of Nuosu leaders, who gave them Nousu names. The custom of "dry children," a Han practice, is somewhat like the Mexican comadre/copadre godparent institution, and is a way of cementing relations between two families. When Ma Erzi's grandfather, who himself spoke very little Chinese, saw the advantages of speaking Chinese and using the abacus, he found a teacher from among the Nuosu's Han captives for his sons and other local boys. The group of students included one Pumi boy.

The kinds of cross-cultural relationships described in Ma Erzi's account were more likely to be found between wealthy Nuosu and Pumi families than among poor people. But they provide a glimpse of interethnic relations beyond the focus on *tusi* in Chinese chronicles, and the tendency in all sources, Chinese and English, to reduce intergroup and interpersonal relations on China's ethnically complex frontiers to just those between minorities and the Han and their agents.

Leibo: Nuosu-Han Zone of Contention

The area called Leibo is on the north bank of the Golden Sands (Jinsha) River and by the fourteenth century was a local outpost of the imperial government with a court-appointed Nuosu *tusi* official (Ma Changshou 2006: 17). At this time the vicinity of Leibo on both sides of the river was occupied by the Nuosu. In other words, this part of what is now Sichuan Province was originally an indigenous Nuosu area rather than one recently settled, but Nuosu on the south bank of the Jinsha River probably had more contact with Han (Li Shaoming 1987 [1957]: 3,12). Even earlier, according to local people interviewed in 1937, local Nuosu leaders in this area, called *mahufu yibu* (the Southern Barbarian district of Horse Lake) were recognized by the Mongols as indigenous frontier officials (Ma Changshou 2006). This so-called *tusi* system, briefly described above, was further solidified in successive dynasties, and by the late eighteenth century there were two *tusi* in the vicinity of Leibo, both descendents of *nuo* lineages. Historical records indicate that the two were "subdued" in 1729, which likely reflects the imperial policy of the time aimed at weakening the power of aboriginal officials. As a consequence, one *tusi* line disappeared, but the second *tusi* redeemed himself by quelling a local rebellion. His line continued into the mid-nineteenth century (Huang Lang 1992: 429–430; Li Shaoming 1987 [1957]: 13).

The third Leibo *tusi*, the most powerful, was called Yang in Chinese records. The first of the line officially came to his position in the early nineteenth century because he, too, was instrumental in resolving some local "barbarian" uprisings (Huang Lang 1992: 429); the Yangs (*nuo* in origin but called *nzymo* in recognition of a rank higher than that of the *nuo*) ultimately took over the territory and dependents, both *nuo* and *qunuo*, of the two defunct *tusi* mentioned above. The Yang *nzymo*, Yang Shijin, was said to have recruited Han to settle his territory. This took place in the second half of the 1800s, and was the beginning of substantial Han migrations across the Jinsha River into Nuosu land. As a consequence, Han settlements and a market were created, with Han farmers constructing the dykes and other earthworks necessary for growing irrigated rice. Probably the Han were Yang tenants (Li Shaoming 1987 [1957]: 3, 11–13). This development coincides with a period of extraordinary population growth in southwest China.

From 1700 to 1850, the population of the southwest increased fivefold, "a rate of population growth surpassed during the Qing dynasty only by the upper Yangtze region" (Lee 1982: 720). Most of this increase, according to Lee (742), was a result of migration to the southwest from other regions in China's interior. Toward the end of the Qing dynasty (1616–1911), many of these Han settlers in Leibo, and presumably their descendants, were captured and their land, mostly irrigated fields, taken over by the Nuosu. The raids were led by the *nuo*, with their "rank and file" dependents. By 1921, most of the irrigated areas in Leipo were occupied by the Nuosu or otherwise abandoned (Li Shaoming 1987 [1957]: 3, 5). Local Han henceforth tended to congregate in the Leibo County seat.

After the 1920s, the power of the local Yang *tusi* declined. There were many probable reasons. The first was related to the behavior of the young wife of the last Yang—after the death of her husband, she took up with a man from the *qunuo* stratum. To the Nuosu, this was an abomination. They had strong prohibitions against cross-stratum sexual relations, especially if the relationship was between a *nuo* woman and a man from one of the lower strata. This weakened the traditional status of all *nuo*, but the Yang family in particular was seen as having forfeited its right to traditional obeisance and tribute (Ma Changshou 2006: 20). Second, local Han, descendents by and large of troops sent to the area in the early early Qing (mid-seventeenth century), took advantage of the isolated position of the Yang family to seize their lands without compensation, thereby undercutting the territorial and resource base of the area's most powerful Nuosu family. Third, in this area, as in most Nuosu localities, the *qunuo* vastly outnumbered the *nuo* families, but in Leibo they were especially numerous and were effective in combating the *nuo*, through alliances among themselves, tactical (thus short-lived) relations with *nuo* outside their area, and assistance from Chinese troops beyond the boundaries of Leibo in Yunnan (Li Shaoming 1987[1957]: 51).

Li Shaoming was the first ethnologist to work in Leibo under the new PRC government. He arrived in 1957. What he found was the nearly complete hegemony of the *qunuo*, most of whom were independent of the few remaining *nuo* families. Furthermore, private property was well developed;

the *qunuo* in most areas had the right to buy and sell their land and to pass it to their descendents (Li Shaoming 1987[1957]:33). These families, though, still had *mgapjia* and *gaxi* slaves who were obliged to continue many hereditary services to their masters and whose property rights were relatively restricted. However, the *mgapjie* families had all taken the surnames of their *qunuo* masters and had lineages of their own, a measure of their deeper incorporation into Nuosu society than those of the same rank in Xiao Liangshan.

DISCUSSION

Although the brief sketches above to do not begin to delineate all the dimensions of the difference between the Nuosu of Ninglang and those of Leibo that affected stratification, certain contrasts stand out. For the sake of clarity, for there are multiple subtle differences, I identify them mainly as centering around the power and authority of local *nuo*, Nuosu relations with outsiders, and land tenure. All of these dimensions are interrelated, and all of them are intertwined with differential access to resources. I flesh out some of my points with additional details not necessarily clear in the initial presentation of cases.

In both Ninglang and Leibo, the same categories of social stratification based on genealogical depth, and therefore, the foundation of the *nuo* claim to "harder bones," were widely accepted. But the capacity of the *nuo* stratum in either case to make the most of their ideological superiority waxed and waned. In Yunnan's Ninglang, the *nuo* were not the first families or lineages to arrive from Da Liangshan. According to local informants, the one of the first Nuosu families was the Alu lineage and their descendents who were *qunuo*. As the local story goes, the Alu lineage was soon joined by their former marriage partner lineages in Da Liangshan, and finally a *nuo* lineage. Like later migrants into other parts of Xiao Liangshan, the Alu were said to have "called in" the *nuo*, although the details of the process were not spelled out. As I have indicated above, as much as some Nuosu have expressed the inevitable necessity of *nuo* to Nuosu society, it is also the case that *nuo* were thought of as warriors and protectors who could provide some guarantee of security to their dependents. But when this particular *nuo* family first arrived, their power was for some years eclipsed by the wealth and connections of the Alu lineage and its multiple branches. *Nuo* hegemony in Ninglang Nuosu society, as well as sporadically in lowland Han, Moso, and

Pumi communities, appears to have come into its own only in the 1920s. How did this happen?

Starting in 1924 provincial warlords from Yunnan and Sichuan fought many skirmishes in what was to become Ninglang County in which the Nuosu, usually under *nuo* leadership, became involved. On the coattails of warlord armies, the Nuosu picked up captives and weapons that directly enriched mostly the *nuo*. Over the next several decades, these now-powerful *nuo* were sometimes allies of local provincial army units stationed in the Ninglang; the *nuo* were especially useful as guarantors/escorts for large-scale opium dealers who had a symbiotic relationship with the provincial units of the Nationalist Chinese armies (Guomindang). Surfeited with guns and encountering little opposition but from competing *nuo* with whom they feuded, the Nuosu aristocrats preyed upon lowland Han, Pumi, and Moso farmers, something they had not done to any large extent in the past. Their newfound power, and the havoc they wreaked, overwhelmed the capacity of the old *tusi* to keep order and also resulted in "sales" of his land to newly rich *nuo* (Du Yuting 1984: 6–9). The 1920s, then, were a watershed decade, when the local Moso *tusi* at Xinyingpan, and the Pumi and Moso more generally, lost land and ceded power to the Nuosu *nuo*.

In Leibo, the 1920s marked not only the decline of the Yang *tusi*, but also a concomitant weakening of *nuo* authority overall. Leibo in the nineteenth century was under a Nuosu *tusi*, as we know, and he was rewarded by the Han for keeping local order; that is, fending off Nuosu attacks that threatened the local Leibo administrative town or lowland villages. So in the heyday of the Yang *tusi* in the latter half of the nineteenth century, both *nuo* and *qunuo* in his domains were alike all his subjects. This may have had a leveling effect on differences between the *nuo* and *qunuo* in an area where there were very few *nuo* to begin with (this is Li Shaoming's theory). When the Yang *tusi* began to lose his grip on the Leibo Nuosu, the local *nuo* tried to regain the upper hand. The *qunuo* response was desertion, forming new relations with distant *nuo* to act as their protectors, occasional appeals to Han military hegemons outside Leibo, and forming alliances among their own lineages to chase out or exterminate the *nuo*. When Ma Changshou, a Chinese ethnologist, was in Leibo in 1937, there were very few *nuo* left. Some lived periodically in the county seat and made their living, like some of their wealther *nuo* counterparts in the Ninglang area, as guarantors for Han opium buyers traveling in the mountains outside the town. Robberies and kidnapping continued to make the area a hazard for travelers, but this business of Nuosu predations was not necessarily a *nuo* monopoly. The Nuoso generally were sufficiently fearsome and numerous that Han militias feared venturing out to confront them.

Clearly, Nuoso societies in Ninglang and Leibo were neither isolated nor "independent," the latter a romantic view of the Nuosu popularized by Western travelers to Sichuan in the late nineteenth and early twentieth centuries. And in both cases the Han Chinese—as settlers, soldiers, traders, officials—were categorically the most noisome and threatening to the Nuosu beginning in the mid-Qing dynasty. Historically, the Nuosu in the vicinity of Leibo, however, had had longer and more extensive contact with the Han than the Nuosu migrants to Ninglang. As noted above, the presence of Han settlers around Leibo in the early nineteenth century may reflect the migration of Han to the southwest that gained momentum in the period 1700–1850. In fact, Ma Changshou in 1937 decided against doing further research in Leibo because he found the Nuosu there too assimilated, including the remnants of the Yang family. Moreover, most Nuosu in and around Leibo city were *qunuo* with Han surnames, and the Nuosu-descended population within the city proper, all former slaves of the Yang *tusi*, resembled Han in the manner of their dress and houses. Ma remarks that they gradually had come to no longer recognize themselves as Nuosu (Ma Changshou 2006: 21–24). If these ex-slaves looked Han, Ma is not specific about whether they identified as Han and were accepted as Han by other locals. I doubt it, because having noted this high degree of assimilation of city Nuosu, Ma also discussed at length the history of violent, often homicidal Nuosu-Han relations, a state of affairs during his visit exacerbated by persisting ignorance of the others' language and culture.

Ninglang, unlike Leibo in the late nineteenth and early twentieth centuries, was a multiethnic area. The Nuosu arrived to find Moso, Pumi, and some Han already farming the valleys at low altitudes. Ma Erzi's account of relations between his family and local Moso and Pumi is suggestive of the role of indigenous groups in Ninglang as conduits of Han culture. I have in mind the adoptive relations between families from different ethnic groups described above that mirrored Han practices but would not likely have been known to monolingual, mountain-dwelling Nuosu.

Speaking of language, I also have the impression from fieldwork that older Moso and Pumi people in Ninglang are more likely to speak the Nuosu language (as do some local Han), than the other way around, perhaps reflecting the hegemony of Nuosu in this area since the 1920s. As for the effects of Pumi and Moso on Nuosu stratification, while their own societies were economically stratified and in some areas, slave owning, they served primarily to fill the lower ranks of Nuosu society as captives. The Pumi and Moso in Xiao Liangshan's Ninglang did not feud, possibly because patrilineal descent, an important organizational prerequisite of feuding, was a variable rather than a mainstay in these two populations (see Shih 2001 and Harrell 2001: 193–238 on this complicated question), or possibly because it was counterproductive to feud among themselves in the face of the numerically superior, armed Nuosu. Thus, the Pumi and Moso, and sometimes the Han, were easy prey whose labor and prestige value as captives contributed to the maintenance of Nuosu stratification.

Land tenure presented a rather stark contrast between Ninglang and Leibo. In Ninglang, the *nuo*, comprising only 4 percent of the population (roughly), had rights to about 70 percent of the total land under cultivation (Du Yuting 1984: 18). Some of these rights resembled those of landlord-tenant, others derived from the hereditary status of the *nuo*, and a small portion must have come from *nuo* lands cultivated by family slaves. There was little private property per se.

In the vicinity of Leibo, private property, i.e., property as commodity, was relatively well developed by the 1950s, before land reform was undertaken. The amount of property held, in general, reflected a family's position in the traditional stratification system, although the figures do not reveal individual household size and composition (e.g., to figure out how many people were being fed and how many worked on the land, rough indices of family prosperity) (Li Shaoming 1986: 30–47). Private property in Leibo appeared in areas where the presence and authority of the local *nuo* was eclipsed by the *qunuo*. However, the existence of private property did not transform *qunuo* relations with their field (*mgapjie*) or household (*gaxi*) slaves, nor did it seem to effect the distribution of wealth overall in Nuosu society.

CONCLUSIONS

The longevity of Nuosu stratification, dating back to the fourteenth century, contradicts Fried's assertion that stateless stratified societies are short lived (see Harrell 2001: 85–87 for a review of Chinese sources). The exact nature of Nuosu stratification in those days is not clear in Chinese records, but information from Nuosu oral genealogies and oral histories support the existence of clans, feuding, stratification, and raiding early on. In Fried's view, then, the longevity of Nuosu stratification and, I would add, its changes through time, are things to be explained.

In this comparative essay, for example, the presence of other ethnic groups, most notably the Han, on the periphery of Nuosu areas were important local resources for knowledge, labor, military technology, and access to markets. While the Chinese court periodically appointed or replaced Nuosu *tusi* as their indirect agents, local politics often overwhelmed the imperial system. *Nuo* challenges to the *tusi*, whether Nuosu or identified with other ethnic groups, were a perennial feature of border politics for centuries, a phenomenon seen more clearly in the case of Ninglang. There, *nuo* power, enhanced through relations with Han opium traders and provincial armies, resulted in a system of stratification that more closely resembled stratification in the "core" area than did Nuosu societies in many areas of Leibo.

In the Leibo areas analyzed here, it was the *qunuo* who took advantage of the decline of the *tusi* to break their bonds of obligations to the *nuo*, instead realigning themselves with distant *nuo* who were in many instances only nominal overlords. Relations between *qunuo* and their slaves, however, were left relatively intact. Leibo, like Ninglang, produced opium, but contacts with provincial armies apparently were not as frequent as in Ninglang. Private property in the mid-twentieth century, largely the land holdings of the *qunuo* and a few remnant *nuo* families, also distinguished Leibo from Ninglang. The growth of private property seemed related to the relative absence of the *nuo* and the diminution of their capacity to enforce traditional claims to tribute from land from successive generations of *qunuo* dependents. The opium market may also have been a factor in the prevalence of private property at mid-century. Opium production enhanced the value of land since it was one of the few sources of exchange for salt and silver for the Nuosu. Leibo was also closer to Han markets, generally, than was Ninglang. Han-settled areas were just across the river in Yunnan.

As Nuosu interacted with other local groups, social stratification changed, but did not fundamentally transform in either locality. At least on the periphery of the area where the Nuosu predominated and in spite of internal shifts in the locus of power and control of resources, social stratification was impressively resilient. If to Fried, the strength of the state lies in its capacity to centralize resources, exploit labor, and thereby support armies and a system of differential access to resources, then one might see the strength of Nuosu society in its capacity to fragment and retool social stratification to respond, often combatively, to changes in local conditions.

The real challenge to the ethnographer of the Nuosu is not the question of how societies with no centralized government manage to survive over the long haul. It is rather how to understand patterns in the variations of Nuosu social stratification over space and time, in turn bound up with complex historical processes around the periphery of the Chinese empire and later, Chinese republic. This is a much larger agenda, to which the analysis here is intended to contribute some insights.

Fried's characterization of nonstate, stratified societies as inherently unstable poses a more difficult question. One problem is that empires, not to mention modern nation-states, are hardly immune from instability in the common-sense understanding of the term. Class strife, ethnic conflicts, high levels of violence (both state and nonstate), shifting peripheries, transient populations, etc.—these are all sources of social instability in state formations. But what I think Fried meant was that the form itself—the stratified society—was unstable because its ideology and basis for social order, namely, kinship, was inevitably outstripped by population growth, an internal dynamic in Fried's model of the evolution of the pristine state.

Population growth likely was a factor in the Nuosu migration into Ninglang in the nineteenth century, and perhaps in Leibo's periphery, as well. Seen in this light, Nuosu conflicts with other indigenous people and with the Han, themselves expanding into China's border areas, was an inevitable result. But the Nuosu were not undone by their expansion per se. On the contrary, as I have tried to argue, their stratified societies were remarkably resilient. In a virtual aside about states-in-the-making, Fried notes that a state can "overrun less well-organized neighbors and incorporate them within its own system as an inferior social stratum" (Fried 1967: 232). And this is exactly what happened in 1956.

NOTES

1. The Nuosu today are a subgroup of the officially recognized Yi nationality in the People's Republic of China. They are a diverse group culturally and linguistically,

spread across the provinces of Sichuan, Yunnan, and Guizhou. The Yi number about 8 million. There are probably over 2 million people who call themselves Nuosu. For talking about local frontier populations with historical roots in China's interior and strong feelings of association with Confucian culture, I use the term *Han* because that's the term used by the people narrating the events. Today the Han nationality is the dominant group in the People's Republic of China, and many people talking in *putonghua* (Mandarin Chinese) about the "old days" default to what is a contemporary referent for this dominant population. When speaking Nuosu, Nuosu use their contemporary term for Han, which is *hxiemga*. However, what the Han people living in Xiao Liangshan frontier called themselves and how they self-identified is not clear in the sources I used for this paper.

2. Li Lie has commented extensively on the reasons for seeing the Nuosu as "independent." In the late nineteenth and early twentieth centuries, they were not under the control of China's central government, imperial (ending in 1912) or later, Republican. The Nuosu often had hostile relations with adjacent ethnic groups, who were said to fear kidnapping and plunder at their hands.

3. Thanks to Dickinson College for funding fieldwork in Leibo in November 2009, during my sabbatical. Their support has been generous throughout my fieldwork in Xiao Liangshan, beginning in 1995.

4. There was undoubtedly suffering among the *mgapjie* and *gaxi* in Nuosu society, especially among the latter when first brought into Xiao Liangshan. Marriage improved their lot, as they got their own land and had children recognized as legitimate. Many became thoroughly assimilated into Nuosu society via kinship, taking the name of the master's lineage as their own (See Hill 2001).

REFERENCES CITED

Du Yuting. 1984. "The Slave System of the Yi in Xiao Liangshan (Yunnan Xiao Liangshan Yizu nuli zhidu)." In *Yunnan Xiao Liangshan Yizu shehui lishi diaocha*, edited by Minzu wenti wu zhong congshe Yunnan sheng bianji weiyuanhui, 1–24. Kunming: Yunnan Renmin Chubanshe.

Ferguson, Brian, and Neil Whitehead. 1992. "The Violent Edge of Empire." In *War in the Tribal Zone*, edited by R. Brian Ferguson and Neil L. Whitehead, 1–30. Santa Fe, NM: School of American Research Press.

Fried, Morton. 1967. *The Evolution of Political Society: An Essay in Political Anthropology*. New York: Random House.

Giersch, C. Patterson. 2006. *Asian Borderlands: The Transformation of Qing China's Yunnan Frontier*. Cambridge MA: Harvard University Press.

Harrell, Stevan. 2001. *Ways of Being Ethnic in Southwest China*. Seattle: University of Washington Press.

Harrell, Stevan, and Fan Ke. 2003. Guest Editors' "Introduction" and subsequent articles. *Chinese Sociology and Anthropology* 36(1): 3–93.

Hill, Ann Maxwell. 2001. "Captives, Kin and Slaves in Xiao Liangshan." *Journal of Asian Studies* 60(4): 1033–1050.

———. 2004. "Provocative Behavior: Agency and Feuds in Southwest China." *American Anthropologist* 106(4): 275–286.

Huang Lang. 1992. *China's Tusi System* (Zhongguo tusi zhidu). Kunming: Yunnan Minzu ChubanShe.

Johnson, Allen W., and Timothy Earle. 2000. *The Evolution of Human Societies*. 2nd edition. Stanford, CA: Stanford University Press.

Lee, James. 1982. "Food Supply and Population Growth in Southwest China, 1250–1850." *Journal of Asian Studies* 41(4):711–746.

Leach, E. R. 1954. *Political Systems of Highland Burma*. Boston: Beacon.

Li Lie. 2006. *Yi Studies: Ethnic Imagination and Intellectual Choice* (*Yi xue: Minzu xiangxiang yu xueshu xuanze*). Beijing: Minzu Chubanshe.

Li Shaoming. 1987 [orig. fieldwork report 1957]. "Investigations of 'Independent White Yi' Society in Shangtianba Township, Leibo County, Sichuan Province (Sichuan, Leibo xian, Shangtianba xiang, 'duli bai zu' shehui diaocha)." In *Investigations into the History of Yi Society in Sichuan, Guangxi and Yunnan*, by Guojia Minwei Minzu Wenti Wu Cong Shu zhi Yi, Zhongguo Xiaoshu Minsu Shehui Lishi Diaocha CeLiao Cong Kan., Yunnan Sheng Bianji Zu, 1–55. Kunming: Yunnan Minzu Chubanshe.

Lin Yao Hua. 1961 [1944]. *The Lolo of Liang Shan*. New Haven, CT: Human Relations Areas Files Press.

Liu Yumin. 1986 [orig. fieldwork report 1981]. "Investigations of Yunnan's Zhongdian Yi People (Yunnan Zhongdian Yizu de diaocha)." In *Investigations into the History of Yi Society in Sichuan, Guangxi and Yunnan*, by Guojia Minwei Minzu Wenti Wu Cong Shu zhi Yi, Zhongguo Xiaoshu Minsu Shehui Lishi Diaocha CeLiao Cong Kan., Yunnan Sheng Bianji Zu, 207–219. Kunming: Yunnan Minzu Chubanshe.

Ma Changshou. 2006. *A Report on Investigations of the Liangshan Luo Yi* (*Liangshan Luo Yi kaocha baogao*), vol. 1. Edited by Li Shaoming and Zhou Wenzhou. Chengdu: Ba Shu shu she.

Mgebbu Lunzyi. 2003. "Nuosu and Neighboring Ethnic Groups and Ethnic Relations in the Eyes and Ears of Three Generations of the Mgebbu Clan." Translated by Steven Harrell. *Asian Ethnicity* 4(1): 129–145.

Rousseau, Jerome. 1990. *Central Borneo: Ethnic Identity and Social Life in a Stratified Society*. Oxford: Clarendon Press.

Sahlins, Marshall. 1958. *Social Stratification in Polynesia*. Seattle: American Ethnology Society.

Scott, James C. 1998. *Seeing Like a State: How Certain Schemes to Improve the Human Condition Have Failed*. New Haven, CT: Yale University Press.

Shih, Chuan-kang. 2001. "Genesis of Marriage among the Moso and Empire-Building in Late Imperial China." *Journal of Asian Studies* 60(2): 381–412.

———. 2010. *Quest for Harmony: The Moso Traditions of Sexual Union and Family Life*. Stanford, CA: Stanford University Press.

Tseng Chao-lun. 1956 [1945]. *The Lolo District of Liang-Shan*. Translated by Josette M. Yeu. New Haven, CT: HRAF Press.

Tsing, Anna Lowenhaupt. 1993. *In the Realm of the Diamond Queen: Marginality in an Out-of-the-Way Place*. Princeton, NJ: Princeton University Press.

Winnington, Alan. 1959. *The Slaves of the Cool Mountains: The Ancient Social Conditions and Changes on the Remote South-Western Border of China*. London: Lawrence and Wishart.

Wu Jingzhong. 2001. "*Nzemo* as Seen in Some Yi Classical Books." In *Perspectives on the Yi of Southwest China*, edited by Steven Harrell, 35–48. Berkeley: University of California Press.

Class and Consciousness in the "Antiglobal" South

On Poverty, Climate Change, and the Illusion of Creating Wealth

P A U L   T R A W I C K

INTRODUCTION: WORLDVIEW AND THE ANTICAPITALIST MOVEMENT

The rapid warming of the earth's climate is driven mainly by people's increasing consumption of goods and services of all kinds, including fossil fuels; thus it is a direct result of the kind of "growth" that most economists regard as inherently beneficial to society. The goods being consumed are ultimately finite and scarce, products derived from raw materials and transformed into commodities through inputs of technology, labor, and large amounts of extrasomatic energy. Yet many people, especially relatively affluent individuals living in the "developed" countries, believe that this wealth is potentially limitless, that it is created by humans, and that we can go on producing and consuming it forever. The corrective message that the planet itself, and the poor people of the global South, are now sending out is clear: economic growth of the kind pursued historically is killing us, having become pathological. It must be made to level off, and quickly, shifting the world economy toward providing people with livelihoods that are modest and sustainable, more similar in that sense to the lifestyles prevalent today in the South than to those in the North.

The proliferation of traded goods and services has improved the quality of life for many of the world's people while accommodating a doubling of the human population during the last three decades. Few observers would deny that some of this growth was necessary during such a rapid demographic transition, that it has had positive effects for many people, and that some of its benefits have been shared by us all, such as until recently a significant increase in life expectancy worldwide (Sen 1999; UNMEA 2005). Yet its negative effects and externalized costs are just as evident and becoming increasingly alarming in extreme climatic events such as Hurricane Katrina, whose growing frequency appears to be linked to anthropogenic warming of the seas (Webster et al. 2005), and in technological disasters like the Deepwater Horizon oil spill in the Gulf of Mexico.

These environmental calamities reflect the fact that, from a scientific point of view, economic growth is destructive and has enormous costs, many of which have remained hidden from people in the North until now. This paper argues in support of the claims of increasing numbers of people worldwide, but particularly in the global South, that such growth, seen as a creative and largely benign process, is an illusion. The transformations that lie at the heart of consumerism and drive this growth are essentially destructive, not creative, and to claim otherwise—as wealthy people typically do, especially those in the North—is to deny the physical laws that govern the universe.

The perspectives that have prevailed historically on the two sides of the North-South debate are well defined and have long been diametrically opposed. As the recent climate-change summits in Copenhagen and Cochabamba have shown, the ongoing dispute is about the nature of growth and the fair distribution of its benefits as opposed to its costs. The gap between the two perspectives now shows some signs of narrowing, however, as a nascent consensus seems to be emerging among people in the two hemispheres. As will be explained below, this ongoing convergence may present new possibilities for collective action and for radical change, as it appears to be based on a shared worldview: a closed-system model of the global economy.

According to this perspective, only a limited amount of "good" can be produced in the world under current technological arrangements, and this benefit now comes with a rapidly increasing environmental and opportunity cost. The "game" of global capitalism is not a positive-sum contest in which everyone somehow wins but a zero-sum affair in which one player's gain is increasingly another's loss to absorb. Such a view also implies— against the claims of free-market ideologues and growth theorists every- where—that the vaunted "creation of wealth" is an illusion, the ghost in the proverbial machine. It is a fantasy that keeps people, especially affluent individuals wherever they may live, locked into lifestyles and aspirations that humankind and the biosphere can no longer afford.

The idea that economic growth is beneficial for everyone, a genuine public good, must surely rank as the greatest smoke-and-mirrors trick of all time, as the visionary economist Georgescu-Roegan (1971a, 1971b) observed several decades ago. A great many people seem to have seen through what he called the "conjuring trick," however, especially some indigenous peo- ples of the so-called Fourth World, for example, the Zapatistas of high- land Mexico and the Quechua and Aymara-speaking activists of Ecuador, Bolivia, and Peru who have angrily rejected the conventional growth model of development. They form the heart of an "antiglobalization" move- ment—really an alternative globalization movement that is strongly anti- corporate or anticapitalist—which now unites them with the internet-based phenomenon widely referred to as international civil society. This loose net- work is broadly dispersed but increasingly active politically at a local level as the worldwide groundswell of support for the Zapatistas demonstrated so clearly during the late 1990s and as is evident now in the unprecedented "Occupy Wall Street" movement.

Much has been written by anthropologists and other social scientists about the cultural dimension of this movement, a kind of subaltern society whose members are thought to share a distinctive identity and point of view. But less has been said about the real substance of the matter: the energy and the resources that are at stake in their common struggle against privatiza- tion and corporate dominance of the globe.[1] The central issue appears to be sovereignty in the control of this basic form of wealth, a kind that people cannot create, which is scarce by definition: water, petroleum, natural gas, precious minerals, and other nonrenewable resources, upon whose extrac- tion the entire capitalist economy depends. The goal is to prevent the virtual theft of that scarce "natural capital" under neoliberal mining laws and other privatizing legislation imported from countries in the North and imposed on those of the South. That agenda is hidden, although not particularly well, within the various "free trade" agreements now being signed between developing countries and the United States under the guidance of the IMF and the World Bank.

Such widespread resistance to business as usual is unprecedented, a striking example of class formation at a global level, involving the emergence of a *transnational anticapitalist class* composed of many indigenous elements and allied activist groups (Bircham and Charlton 2002; Callinicos 2003). The vanguard of this movement—people of peasant background who first voted Hugo Chavez and Evo Morales into power and managed to throw corporations like Bechtel and Suez out of their country—seem to present themselves to the world as dispossessed people who are reclaiming their rights to control the aforementioned resources (Olivera and Lewis 2004; Sawyer 2004; Perreault 2006; Spronk and Webber 2007; Bebbington 2009), which they correctly see as a form of common property. The indigenous ancestry that many of them share is clearly not displayed in order to be divisive or exclusive, something worn on their collective sleeve for its own sake; rather, it is the basis of an appeal for a kind of unity among all peoples in support of those communal rights.

It is clear that several steps must be taken in order to slow down the process of climate change and move decisively toward reducing poverty while creating a more equitable and sustainable world. These actions, which complement the goals of the anticapitalist movement (Santos 2003; WSF 2004; Escobar, Sen, and Waterman 2003; Sen et al. 2004; WPCCC 2010), include the following:

1. Reducing drastically, to the point of leveling off, the per-capita consumption of fossil fuels and other nonrenewable resources, particularly in the "developed" countries, in order to limit climate change while increasing the efficiency of energy conversion worldwide;

2. Imposing effective controls over—and taxing fairly—commercial banks and their international flows of finance capital, whose role in the global economy is to increase the concentration of wealth and power among transnational elites and to support excessive consumption by affluent people in general, an effort that denies other segments of the world population the same opportunity;

3. Setting upper limits on market share by corporations, on interest rates, and even on personal income for individuals, in effect establishing a maximum annual wage in each country.

These admittedly radical steps would not involve a centrally planned fine-tuning of the economy but instead merely impose a set of ceilings on basic forms of economic growth, in the name of the common good, thereby creating new channels of redistribution to counter the wealth-concentrating and monopolistic tendencies of an unregulated global market. They are now rather easy to justify scientifically; indeed, the first two have been shown to be imperative for our economic survival (Stern 2007; IPCC 2007; NEF 2008; Jackson 2009; Harvey 2010). And, as we will see below, there is intriguing evidence suggesting that people might actually be able to take them. Recent research on communities built around the management of scarce but essential resources that are held in common—known in the literature as "common-pool" resources (Ostrom 1990)—provides many examples of people acting collectively to impose upper limits on their consumption and to assert just this kind of mutual self-restraint.

The argument presented here is that, if people come to realize that economic growth is a destructive process rather than a creative one, based on the consumption of limited forms of natural wealth that are being rapidly drawn down and made increasingly scarce—both for contemporary Others and for the members of future generations—they will become more willing to undertake such action. The challenges involved are daunting, as we will see, and any effort to scale up existing cooperative institutions to the highest levels of social organization will be fraught with difficulty. But what is most needed, as a necessary if not a sufficient condition for such limits to be imposed, is the adoption of a closed-system view of the world economy. This kind of worldview has been around for a long time, having emerged initially in many peasant societies throughout the world, as we shall see. In academia, it was promoted initially by neoclassical theory in economics—a surprising fact that is no longer widely remembered—and then explored to some extent by the proponents of dependency theory. Today it is given strong support by current knowledge in both the natural and the social sciences, and it appears to be widely embraced within the alternative globalization movement.

ENERGETICS AND "WEALTH CREATION": EXPOSING THE FALSE WORLDVIEW OF THE GLOBAL ELITE

The earth itself forms a well-bounded and closed system that is not capable of physical expansion, that is, one that is permeable to flows of energy and information but not to significant inputs and outputs of matter. Although it is widely thought to be an open system, like the market economy, this view is inaccurate and unsuitable as a guide for human behavior. The only economically significant things crossing Earth's atmospheric boundary—other than satellites and the information they transmit—are enormous flows of solar energy, which are not yet directly harnessed by most people—except, of course, for farmers—in producing, consuming, and carrying out their everyday transactions. Thus the global economy, like the planet itself, is in fact largely closed from a thermodynamic point of view. Certainly it can be said that the planet and the economy together form a closed system, a concept that is paradigmatic within the field of environmental economics (Pearce and Turner 1990; Turner, Pearce, and Bateman 1994; Daley and Farley 2003).

The economy's closure reflects our extremely high degree of reliance on fossil fuels for energy, the innovation that spawned the Industrial Revolution. In the United Kingdom, for example, 88 percent of the total energy consumed by people each day comes from fossil fuels, with the largest portions provided by petroleum and natural gas (IEA 2004). The much bigger economy of the United States is just as dependent on hydrocarbons, which account for 86 percent of its consumption, but it uses up a huge percentage—approximately 25 percent—of the planet's dwindling oil stock.[2] This is to say nothing of petroleum's importance as a raw material in making plastics and other synthetic compounds, artificial materials that form a major component of the built environment in affluent parts of the world and are now the predominant form of waste or trash contaminating both terrestrial and marine ecosystems. At a global level, approximately 80 percent of the total energy used comes from nonrenewable fossil fuels, a figure that varies significantly among countries but has generally shown a dramatic increase, especially in developing nations, during the last few decades. Thus the world economy has become steadily more closed under globalization; yet the extent of hydrocarbon dependence is one of the most significant forms of inequality existing today between "developed" and "developing" countries (Delaney 2005).

The opportunity to purchase and consume the remaining supply of this stored solar energy is clearly a zero-sum game in which one player's gain will be another's loss, a social reality that is a corollary of the closed-system view. This is particularly true if one takes future generations into account, at a time when humanity is rapidly approaching, or has perhaps even already reached, "peak oil" production (IEA 2009). The world is now witnessing the start of another dramatic surge in the price of oil—and a corresponding rise in the price of most other commodities will surely follow—the second that has occurred within the space of only five years. These fluctuations, which are certain to become more frequent as time goes on, make the largely closed nature of the economy increasingly apparent. Yet an open-system view continues to predominate, especially among people in the North, as we will see below.

The First and Second Laws of Thermodynamics (Georgescu-Roegan 1971a, 1971b, 1975) state that in a closed system:[3]

1. Matter and energy are neither created nor destroyed, but merely converted from one form into another; and

2. These conversions lead in one direction only: from highly ordered and low-entropy forms of matter-energy to less-ordered and higher-entropy forms.

Anthropologists and other social scientists have long been familiar with these laws, but attempts to explore their relevance to social and economic life have lately fallen out of favor, after having shown a promising start (White 1943; Adams 1975). Despite the complexity of the entropy concept, the implications are fairly straightforward, at least under current technological arrangements: in a global market where production and distribution are based overwhelmingly on the consumption of fossil fuels and other nonrenewable resources, all economic processes increase entropy (Georgescu-Roegan 1971a, 1971b, 1975), ultimately degrading and thus reducing the amount of low-entropy matter-energy that is available for use on the planet. Driven by the massive consumption of electricity, gas, and petroleum as a kind of basal metabolism, the processes of production, distribution, and consumption lead inevitably toward increasing disorder, producing a build-up of heat and waste and a general reduction in the capacity of energy to do work within the closed global system.

Note that the generalization about entropy is inescapable and would hold regardless of the nature of the energy supply. Indeed, all biological processes are entropic, contrary to what most people think (Schrödinger 1967), including the subset that can be described as economic. The key difference between the two is that life processes, being based on fairly constant and enormous flows of solar energy, are entropic and yet sustainable, at least for the foreseeable future. As for economic processes, the rapid expansion of capitalism—based on the consumption of a finite pool of resources that is bound to diminish rapidly in the end—has ensured that humanity will experience a relatively fast rate of environmental decline. This fossil-fuel-driven entropic process is clearly well underway and is now affecting in some manner nearly all life on the planet.

REAL WEALTH AND VIRTUAL WEALTH: A
SOURCE OF CONCEPTUAL CONFUSION

Economic growth has long been championed by economists as the key to widespread and cumulative enhancements in human well-being, and strongly promoted as an alternative to the redistribution of already-accumulated wealth. Yet, as Stiglitz (2002), Wade (2003), and others have shown, the increasing per-capita consumption of goods and services is only taking place in certain parts of the world and, outside that rather narrow set of developed and newly developing countries, it is generally confined to the privileged classes and the traditional elites.[4]

This profoundly uneven pattern of growth has led to the most skewed distribution of income and resources the world has seen, certainly since the dawn of the industrial age, a pattern that is steadily getting worse. A unique study funded by the United Nations (Davies et al. 2006) recently concluded that the richest 1 percent of the world's people now own approximately 40 percent of the existing assets, and the richest 10 percent own an astonishing 85 percent, while the bottom 50 percent own less than 1 percent of the total available wealth. A staggering amount is now concentrated in so few hands that the per capita distribution cannot be represented graphically on a single printed page in a way that the average person can understand (see Korten 2001:110–112).

People's reaction to this kind of news is instructive and reveals a great deal about their view of the world. When the findings of the UN study were announced in the *Guardian* newspaper in England, Madsen Pirie, an economist who directs the Adam Smith Institute in London, a free-market think-tank, commented on the figures, disagreeing with a statement by Oxfam that the current distribution of wealth is unfair and ought somehow to be corrected:

> The implicit assumption behind this [assertion] is that there is a supply
> of wealth in the world and some people have too much of that supply. In
> fact wealth is a dynamic, it is constantly created. We should not be asking
> who in the past has created wealth and how we can get it off them . . .
> instead the question should be how more and more people could create
> wealth. (*Guardian*, December 6, 2006)

Such references to wealth creation are a kind of category mistake, one that appears frequently today in the press, usually made by financiers and politicians. The errors are ironic at a time when an unprecedented amount of this "created" wealth—that is, virtual wealth in the form of finance capital—has suddenly vanished, inducing a global economic crisis and precipitating the most massive bailout of banks, and of wealthy investors in general, that the world has ever seen. Note that if real wealth—the kind that cannot abruptly disappear—is not constantly created, then the argument against redistributing it by imposing limits on its accumulation and consumption begins to fall apart. Certainly the argument would be greatly weakened if the mysterious creative process lying at the heart of capitalism were shown to be an illusion.

In order to see how the global economy works more clearly from a thermodynamic point of view, the properties of two kinds of wealth must be distinguished, and the common mistake of confusing them by using the concepts interchangeably, as in the above example, must be corrected. Several observers have noted a widespread tendency to do this, evident among experts and nonexperts alike, the first of whom was Nobel laureate Frederick Soddy.

The first form of wealth is *real wealth or productive capital*: material goods such as fossil fuels, other raw materials, technology, and consumer items in general. As both Soddy and Georgescu-Roegen (1971a, 1971b, 1975) observed long ago, these are ultimately finite and can only be produced or made available for consumption through destructive processes that use up available forms of low entropy and, in that sense, gradually run the planet down.

The second form is *virtual wealth and finance capital*[5]: intangible forms of wealth such as stocks, bonds, and derivatives, paper assets that originated in the issuing of credit and debt, and the simultaneous creation of money, by banks. Although people do create such wealth, its value is merely symbolic, potential or virtual—largely imaginary. Essentially consisting of a kind of promissory note on future income, money and other paper assets do not degrade with time or lose their utility or value, like everything else in the universe. On the contrary, they can grow exponentially and increase in value at compound rates of interest, violating the laws of thermodynamics (Soddy 1921, 1926). By reproducing themselves in this way, such virtual assets ultimately act destructively as catalysts that increase the production and consumption of real wealth; thus they accelerate the ongoing process of thermodynamic decline.

THE PHANTOM GROWTH OF VIRTUAL WEALTH

In order to illustrate a basic feature of finance capital and show how the "creation of wealth" works, let us say that someone, either an individual or a corporation, takes out a loan of $1,000 from a bank. The first thing that must be understood is that no money actually changes hands when such credit is given in these transactions; today they merely consist of an exchange of promissory notes, or promises-to-pay with future income or assets, issued by both parties. The interest-bearing note of debt will remain with the bank of origin, to be paid off by the borrower at interest with the cash coming from their future wages or, in the case of a business firm, from future profits. Note that this flow of future income is all that the loan really represents. It has not been created by the lending agreement and would assumedly exist regardless. Nothing substantial has been created except a new creditor/debtor relationship and a corresponding change in the flow of future income, really only that of the debtor.

Meanwhile, the borrowed money or note of credit, if spent as a unit on some investment or on consumption, will end up as a set of electronic digits in an account file in another bank. The bank can then lend most of that fictitious money again at interest—again, without any paper money actually changing hands—issuing more credit and thereby creating more money in a sort of repeating virtual loop (Soddy 1921:24–56, 1926:303–305; Korten 2001:182–185).

This process is widely misunderstood today; people commonly assume that it is the savings of individuals, or their monthly earnings entrusted to banks in personal checking accounts, that is lent and passed on temporarily to other people. In fact only a very small amount comes from that real source; the rest is simply created by the banks out of nothing—and profited on through the charging of interest—when bankers decide to take on a certain amount of risk and to issue credit (Douthwaite 1996; Daley and Farley 2003). The idea that banks actually "lend" money to people in these situations, giving up something that belongs to them, is largely an illusion. It is one that has long been promoted by a transnational capitalist class (Sklair 2000) of extremely wealthy people, who profit from the confusion at the expense of everyone else.

This process of multiplication ultimately generates a huge amount of virtual wealth, all bearing interest, thereby generating the enormous profits that have come to characterize the banking sector in the era of deregulation. Those profits are generally reinvested today, speculatively, within the financial sector, and used in the purchase or sale of various forms of finance capital. Note again that banks do not actually have to turn over any of their own assets in order to make these profits; they only have to promise to pay, if necessary, in the future, thus taking on the risk that the loans will not ultimately be repaid by their debtors, an obligation that is expressed in the banks' promissory notes. Bankers only have to give something up if something eventually goes wrong in the transaction.

In the United States, reserve requirements restrict the amount of the initial loan that can be reloaned to 90 percent, or $900. This ultimately means that, through the continual relending of this shrinking 90 percent, every $1,000 deposited within the banking system today soon multiplies into $10,000 of newly created money, all bearing interest and residing in the electronic accounts of banks (Korten 2001:182–185). This process of "wealth creation" actually drives the printing of money and determines the money supply in most developed countries, through the reserve banking system, a fact that, again, is not widely understood. Paper money itself, the essence of Soddy's virtual wealth, is physically created by banks through the issuing of credit and debt; it represents nothing but the future flows of income promised in ongoing creditor/debtor relationships. Money thus embodies and represents debt; that is one of its primary functions. Many countries, however, have no capital reserve requirements and no reserve banking system, particularly the off-shore tax havens and centers of finance. There the amount of self-reproducing wealth created by banks through the "lending" of money is potentially limitless.

All of this is to say nothing about the banks' practice of selling (also largely unregulated) the debt thus created, the promissory notes on their own future income that people must sign when taking out a loan. In the case of the housing market, the resale of this debt, in the form of "collateralized debt obligations," recently became so extensive that it brought the entire system of global finance to the brink of collapse. The reselling is just as dubious, from a moral point of view, as the right to create money by issuing credit and debt in the first place. We hear a great deal today about the responsibility of debtors to repay loans and avoid bankruptcy, for the benefit of society, but little about the duty of creditors to hold on to the resulting debt and fully absorb the risk they have undertaken so that they can generate profits from it. Bankers today face almost no constraints on their ability to create this virtual wealth, a situation that clearly needs to be changed because the entire financial system has become highly unstable as a result, threatening the future of us all (Radelet and Sachs 1999; Krugman 2008; Stiglitz 2010). Indeed, the system has always been unstable, for that is a part of its inner logic, as we will see below. Deregulation has simply made it more volatile than ever before (Harvey 2010).

This whole phenomenon of modern debt stems from a pivotal political decision, made early in the sixteenth century, to legalize usury, the charging of fixed-rate interest on monetary loans. As a result of that decision—endorsed by Martin Luther and later by John Calvin during the Protestant Reformation, who then forced the pope and other leaders of the Catholic Church to follow along (Hyde 1983:122–140)—a wide array of financial "instruments" based on money and usury were ultimately created.

All of these forms of finance capital were intended to encourage economic activity through investment by providing the owners of such capital with a degree of protection from risk. Until recently most of them—stocks, bonds, options, futures contracts—were catalysts invented to facilitate the investment of real wealth in the production and distribution of manufactured goods, which they did quite well (Hilferding 1910; Kautsky 1911). But they were derived from the unique capacity that money was given to multiply itself and generate profit, without its possessor doing any work other than that involved in "lending" it to someone else. It would be more correct to say that this quasi-magical power—the power to create money out of nothing by agreeing to absorb risk—was given to banks (Soddy 1926; Korten 2001). Indeed, bankers were, until very recently, the only members of society who had this power to create wealth.[6]

Initially, the amount of interest endorsed by the churches and allowed by the emerging secular European states through their central banks was strictly limited, to no more than 5 percent (Hyde 1983:122–140). But such constraints on finance capital were steadily reduced and even eliminated as time went on within the emerging financial system. Up until the deregulation of finance was made complete in the 1990s, all such loans had to be guaranteed with a real-wealth form of collateral of known value—real estate or some other kind of property, along with a steady future income—which could be confiscated or drawn on if the repayments were not made. But that requirement too was ultimately dispensed with as time went on. Today we see the result in the phenomenon of "securitization," the bundling together, by banks, of debt or promises of future cash flows—the most common form are mortgages for the purchase of houses—into tranches that can then be sold on to investors. In the resulting financial "instruments," the collateralized debt obligations, the loans—which are liabilities in accounting terms, promises-to-pay made by the banks on their own future flows of income—are transformed into assets. The only collateral backing up those assets, however—the only real wealth—are the very homes that the loans were issued in order to purchase. Their value ultimately became uncertain in an overexpanded mortgage market now including a great many debtors with no additional assets to back up the loans (the so-called subprime borrowers), thus precipitating the current global crisis.

"Securitization" is an attempt by bankers to remove themselves from exposure to the risk involved in making the initial loans, by passing those liabilities on while still profiting from them as assets. The consequences are now quite evident but still unfolding daily in the global economy for everyone to see. A staggering amount of this "created" wealth and finance capital has simply disappeared, almost overnight, because a massive number of risky loans, which had been sold on to many other investors, thus widely spreading that corresponding risk, could not be repaid. Despite the most massive bailout of banks in history, with funds coming from the public sector in countries throughout the developed world, no one yet knows what the impact on the "real economy" will be, either a severe recession or a second Great Depression (Stiglitz 2010). This situation recently led the editor of one of the world's most prominent financial newspapers, Martin Wolf (2007) of the *Financial Times* in London, to say of the banking system: "No industry has a comparable talent for privatizing gains and socializing losses."

The lifelong servicing of personal debt through continual payments to agents in the financial, insurance, and real estate sectors of the economy has in the view of some analysts become the "new road to serfdom" (Hudson 2006; Toussant 2003; Hannan 2010), which people today tend to embark on without even thinking about it. A permanent relationship of dependency on finance capitalists for credit seems to be widely accepted as somehow natural, or certainly necessary for modern life. This personal relationship may help to explain people's complacency about the bailouts, which have suddenly created enormous national deficits that have effectively mortgaged the future of hundreds of millions of people. Note that this situation is analogous, if not homologous, to the paralyzing debt servitude that people in "Third World" countries experienced during the 1970s through the 1990s, a legacy of economic dependency that has not gone away. Instead, it has arguably become the defining feature of global economic life. This common or shared experience may have the potential to help unite people on both sides of the ongoing North/South debate, making it more of a conversation.

Prior to the decision to allow fixed-rate interest on loans, most of the world's people, and most of its great religions, considered the practice of usury to be exploitative and inherently sinful. The Christian Bible emphatically supports this view, as do the Jewish Torah and the Muslim Qur'an. The creation of virtual wealth continued to be widely seen as morally problematic thereafter, as it still is today, especially by Muslims, who see it as constituting a form of social violence (Hyde 1983). The poorest people in the world—peasants, subsistence farmers who are in a marginal position with respect to the market economy—tend to have a similar view. Peasants, when they first become ensnared in debt in the process of becoming more integrated into the cash economy—whereupon they have to become more concerned with making a profit—often portray such monetized relationships as involving a kind of Faustian pact with the devil (Taussig 1980; Nash 2007). Given the magnitude of the crisis that the creation of virtual wealth has induced today around the globe, and the real possibility that such periodic crises will now be allowed to continue (Volcker 2010; Harvey 2010), these negative perceptions seem to have been to some degree accurate ones expressing a reasonable fear about the future.

The expansion of the financial markets during the last thirty years created a rising tide of optimism in global society that has now abruptly turned the other way. That sudden change, brought on by the crisis and the ongoing "credit crunch," has effectively called into question certain secular myths that are the central fictions supporting the culture of overconsumption that predominates today in the North. These myths include such neo-liberal notions as "a rising tide lifts all boats." Tides go down as well as up, as we have now all seen illustrated again so dramatically, and without this oscillation there would of course be no tides at all. Today, rising economic tides are driven mainly by the rapid creation and transfer of money and finance capital, paper assets whose value, as we have seen, lies in little more than promised future income and underlying creditor/debtor relationships.

Although people are slowly awakening to this reality, there is as yet no sign of it affecting another pervasive idea, strongly promoted today by reality TV shows, that we can all somehow become rich and famous in a world potentially consisting of winners with no losers. Such bits of conventional wisdom are appealing because they promote a "positive-sum" or open-system view of the market economy, the view (strongly promoted by free-market economists) that the world consists of an expanding "pie" of wealth. Such financial folklore rests on the axiom that wealth is created by people, so that our decisions about spending it up or consuming it, especially the necessary and seemingly innocuous form of money, appear not to have any third-party effects, any opportunity costs or resulting losses in quality of life that are borne by someone else. That belief is simply false, as Daley and Farley, two founders of the relatively new field of ecological economics, note in discussing the concept of virtual wealth and other insights presented in the visionary work of Frederick Soddy:

> [T]his undisciplined, imaginary magnitude was used as a symbol and counter for real wealth, which has an irreducible physical dimension, and cannot be created or annihilated. Money is a problem precisely because it leads us to think that wealth behaves like its symbol, money; that because it is possible for a few people to live on interest, it is possible for all to do so; that because money can be used to buy land, and land can yield a permanent revenue, therefore money can yield a permanent revenue. (Daley and Farley 2003:255)

Finance capital has multiplied exponentially during the last three decades, as it has been almost entirely freed of all regulation, taking on some new and very obscure forms (derivatives are the best example, of which collateralized debt obligations are one type). Such virtual wealth has come to dwarf the economy of real wealth or productive capital during this short period, today being, according to one conservative estimate, about four or five times as large as the GDP (Bond 2003; IMF 2004). Every day approximately two trillion dollars of this finance capital—$2,000 billion of stocks, bonds, futures, etc.—are traded speculatively by investment banks, corporations, and individuals. As Daley and Farley (2003:257) have noted, this indicates that the buying and selling of paper assets and currencies is now more than twenty times greater in size than exchanges in the real economy.

The illusion of creating wealth thus became a kind of reality long ago; but it remains a conjuring trick based on imagined or potential values and the continual relending of previously loaned money, as well as the sale of much of the resulting debt, all underwritten by the future labor of real people, in a kind of global pyramid scheme (Krugman 2008). The endless generation and accumulation of such imagined wealth, and the periodic financial crises that result, are driven by a strange combination of personal insecurity and greed. Those of us who are heavily in debt contribute to this false growth by living on credit beyond our means.

Other than household mortgages, a form of debt that today is widely regarded as a necessity, at least in the global North, credit cards provide the best illustration. By the year 2006 the amount of debt sustained by people through the use of these cards (again, primarily in the North) had exploded, reaching an average of $12,000 per person in the United States, while in the United Kingdom it stood at £7,700 per person, having risen by 52 percent during the previous five years (www.in2perspective.com/nr/2006/06). On the other hand, those of us who are fortunate enough to have savings end up being money lenders. We either put those savings into some kind of investment ourselves, in effect lending it and turning it into finance capital, or, if we take out a savings account or put it into a pension plan, the end result is the same.

Unless we take special precautions, we join in the collective fever to always seek the highest interest rate, dividend, or other kind of return. Inevitably, the bubble of bogus value must burst periodically as a result of this essentially parasitic and largely imaginary growth, and the rising tide must fall again (as instability in the value of the Euro now threatens to show once more) taking the real economy down with it (Radelet and Sachs 1999; Perez 2003; Harvey 2010; Volcker 2010). Yet the fallacy persists, in part due to widespread confusion about the nature of created wealth, that speculation and accumulation somehow increase the overall amount of well-being available to people in the world and thereby benefit us all.

"CREATIVE DESTRUCTION": THE PRODUCTION OF REAL WEALTH

Real wealth, unlike its virtual counterpart, is arguably something that human beings cannot create. As a category it consists of forms of matter-energy that are finite and subject to nature's laws: raw materials, natural resources, and exosomatic energy (both fossil and renewable forms), as well as the material artifacts, tools, and goods that people produce through manufacturing and the use of technology (Georgescu-Roegen 1971a, 1971b). Services, on the other hand, or human labor in the many forms that it takes, have exchange value or wealth potential—inherently also possessing what economists call "use value"—since they too can be exchanged for, or converted into, real wealth through the artificial medium of money. But they too are limited in availability and, in a closed economy where petroleum literally drives almost everything that moves or grows, are subject to those same laws.

In such an economy, real wealth or productive capital is either transferred from one person to another, converted into a different form, or ultimately consumed, leading in any case to a gradual build-up of heat, waste, and disorder on the planet. Such wealth is scarce and limited in terms of supply, created through production processes that are, in net terms, ultimately destructive of order. Its "creation" is thus an illusory and self-contradictory concept, an oxymoron of the highest order. Perhaps, then, it would be best if, when talking about wealth, we dispense with the metaphor of creating it.

In a world characterized by runaway growth in population, and based on the increasing consumption of finite, nonrenewable resources, the more we squander such limited wealth and the more of the world's resources we consume individually every day, the faster the ongoing environmental decline and the bigger and more disruptive of our lives the problems of poverty and global warming will become. All of the seemingly creative economic activities we engage in require raw materials and huge amounts of fossil fuels (stored solar energy), and all of them consume and degrade an enormous amount of that matter-energy, gradually running the planet down. As Georgescu-Roegen (1971b:80) pointed out, like Soddy (1926) before him, "In entropy terms, the cost of any biological or economic enterprise is always greater than the product . . . any such activity necessarily results in a deficit." This, rather than the fictions of wealth creation, the rising economic tide, and the self-regulating market, is what science—both natural science and social science—now tells us. In the real world, and in the "real economy," the creation of wealth is an inherently destructive process.

Agribusiness, strangely enough, provides the best illustration of these points. In the United States and other developed countries, spectacular yields per hectare are achieved by virtually pumping petroleum products into the ground or the air-tractor fuel, petrochemical fertilizers, and insecticides, while rapidly eroding the topsoil and mining the groundwater stored in underlying aquifers. From a scientific point of view, such creation-through-destruction is quite emblematic of economic growth as we now define it. The efficiency of the US food production system, as measured by its energy input-to-output ratio, is shockingly low and utterly unsustainable. For every kilocalorie of food energy that people in America consume today, ten kcal of petroleum-derived energy are consumed and made unavailable for use in the future (Pimentel 1993; Giampietro and Pimentel 1993, 1994). A large part of this consists of fuel for tractors and other equipment to replace human labor in the cultivation process, but the greatest amount is expended after the food leaves the farm.

In the short space of fifty years, this basic distortion of agriculture by agribusiness has progressed to such an extent that fossil-fuel inputs now constitute approximately 60 percent of the total energy used in food production, while the solar energy harnessed through photosynthesis accounts for only 40 percent. Since agriculture is the sector of the economy that is tied most directly to solar energy capture—the process upon which the food chain and the whole web of life depend—there can be no clearer illustration of the fact that economic growth as we have chosen to define it historically is destructive, and that the global economy does form a largely closed system. Efficiency figures for other sectors of the economy would have to be far worse in comparison.

Admittedly, growth for feeding, housing, and clothing a rapidly expanding world population could only have been achieved by generating a great amount of credit and investment, and creating a large amount of virtual wealth. These assets based on promissory notes can be a means of redistributing real wealth, of combining limited resources in new ways, and of putting those resources to new productive uses. But such growth is not sustainable. Nor does it all come down to a kind of casino game played only by the very rich and driven almost entirely by their greed, although that is an appropriate analogy for much of what goes on today in the financial markets (Strange 1998). Again, most of us buy into and support the game by living on credit beyond our means, by aspiring continually to have more "goods" and to enjoy "the good life," whose faddish trappings are forever changing, or by wanting to become wealthy. To take the analogy further, the game would be a different one without our active support, if we refused to see it any longer as the only one in town.

Therein lies the potential power we have to influence the world through the financial markets, to shape the decisions being made daily on our behalf in the global "futures trade," especially through purchases made on credit and through the investment of our pension funds. Our power, and our obligation to poor people throughout the world and to coming generations, lies in our choice of lifestyle, in how much of the future—how much real wealth—we decide to spend up and consume every day, rather than to leave behind.

THE CLOSED-SYSTEM VIEW: DEPENDENCY THEORY, NEOCLASSICAL ECONOMICS, AND THE IMAGE OF LIMITED GOOD

One of the first anthropologists to employ the concept of worldview was George Foster (1965), who spoke of a general "cognitive orientation" that guides people in their behavior and is shaped by a set of axioms or presuppositions about the world and how it works. Pointing out that we are not necessarily conscious of our worldview or able to say much about it, since the presuppositions are culturally inherited, Foster argued that people in peasant societies share a distinctive model of reality, one profoundly shaped by their material poverty, whose central axiom he called the "image of limited good."

According to this hypothesized folk understanding, there is only a limited amount of "good" in the world; thus any good that one person acquires and enjoys comes at the expense of someone else, denying them of that same chance. Foster insisted that peasants see their local worlds as closed systems and that they apply this simple idea to everything desirable in life: access to resources like land, water, and labor; the opportunity to earn money and enhance one's social status; the enjoyment of less tangible things like a sense of honor and prestige, or even parental love. Peasants, he said, lack any power to increase the quantities of these that are available, so that any such "good," "like land, is seen as inherent in nature, there to be divided and re-divided, if necessary, but not to be augmented" (Foster 1965:296). Consequently, their subsistence-oriented village societies feature norms that discourage any effort to acquire more goods, and thus to draw attention to oneself, or to do anything else that might threaten the stability of established social relationships, which are based on the sharing of a prevailing scarcity. Peasants are highly individualistic, Foster claimed, yet averse to nearly all forms of risk; fearful, envious, and reluctant to show what they have; and generally lacking in any motivation to change.

Foster's argument was rightly criticized for being tautological and providing a rationale for contradictory kinds of behavior, as well as for lacking scientific rigor (e.g., Kaplan and Saler 1966). As he himself noted, a closed-system worldview could, theoretically, just as easily sustain strong leadership and lead to widespread cooperation as it could promote envy and jealousy among individuals. Yet his snapshots of peasant life from countries throughout the world only seemed to illustrate the latter negative qualities. His work soon faded from view, partly as a result, but it was not forgotten. As one of the earliest attempts to consider the behavioral implications of a closed-system worldview, his work on the idea of limited good was destined to be revived.

The most prominent anthropologist who has done this recently is June Nash (2007), who uses the concept as a central theme in discussing her years of experience with Maya people affiliated with the Zapatista movement in Chiapas in highland Mexico, her previous experience working with tin miners in Bolivia, and an intervening period of study of Mandalese rice cultivators in Burma. For her, the idea of limited good is indispensable in accounting for the remarkable resilience of these people and the rural peasant societies of which they are a part. The Zapatistas, still one of the most highly visible indigenous peoples on the world stage, are known for extraordinary forms of leadership and cooperation that extend across lines of gender, age, and other social divisions, as well as for the practice of direct democracy. Nash portrays their ongoing struggle for autonomy and self-defense in the militarized zone of Chiapas, like other similar confrontations occurring today in different parts of the global South, as a conflict between two distinct ways of seeing the world: the "notion of limited good" and the "specter of the unlimited good." And there is no doubt about which of the two worldviews she considers more accurate as a depiction of physical and social reality:

> The growing awareness of the finite nature of the good has transformed
> the expectations of unlimited possibilities into a specter of paradise
> lost for growing multitudes of impoverished people . . . Those whose
> response is to declare war on all who compete for control of diminishing
> oil, water, minerals and other resources are beginning to encounter resis-
> tance from social movements that seek to reinforce international cov-
> enants on the environment and the rights of the poor. I hope to rescue
> Foster's insights on the peasant worldview and what that may offer for
> those concerned with a sustainable future for world populations. (Nash
> 2007:36)

There is an academic version of this general way of viewing the world, a school of thought in political economy known as *dependency theory*. It originated in Latin America and, despite rumors to the contrary, it too is alive today in the global South, though perhaps also in need of some rejuvenation. The classic formulations of Cardoso, Frank, Amin, Petras and others, published in the 1960s and 1970s, pointed to the disadvantageous position shared by most people in the "underdeveloped" countries lying at the periphery of the world system, with its historically derived division of labor. Their arguments focused on the "unequal terms of exchange" that result from this structural marginality, which have persisted largely unchanged through time. These constraints have supposedly hindered people in the developing countries by keeping real wealth, in the form of primary products—minerals, fossil fuels, other raw materials, and agricultural produce—and the profits resulting from their exportation flowing out of the periphery and accumulating in hands of people in the core countries. The essence of the *dependistas'* argument has always been that the "game" of global capitalism is fixed, the deck "stacked" in terms of a fixed division of labor and exploitative terms of trade, and the net sum basically zero, or winners-take-nearly-all.

According to this argument, the vast majority of the profits generated by the investment of foreign capital in developing countries—initially for the extraction of primary products and, more recently, for the assembly of low-cost consumer items in sweatshops—have always been repatriated by foreign capitalists to the metropolitan or core countries where they live, and often then put into offshore bank accounts in order to avoid taxes. The rest have been exported by the allies of foreign capital (complicit national elites) into foreign bank accounts, and then either used to finance consumption or reinvested, usually in speculative enterprises. The end result in either case has been the "development of underdevelopment" (Escobar 1995), the gradual enrichment of people in the North at the expense of those in the South, where the profits resulting from international trade would otherwise have been invested or spent.

Nearly all of the recent critiques of globalization coming out of political economy lend support to this view in terms of their gloomy prediction of no significant structural movement, and no substantial long-term economic growth for the vast majority of people in the South (George 2000). The critiques seem to agree that even if capital does begin to accumulate again and concentrate in a new center (Arrighi 1994), as seems to be happening today in Asia (Perez 2003), most of Latin America and Africa will be left out of this process (Petras and Veltmayer 2001; O'Hara 2004). Perhaps the most significant recent revision of dependency theory is that of Surin (1998), which focuses specifically on global movements of finance capital for investment, rather than on productive capital and the profits resulting from it, as the earlier formulations did. His analysis is similarly pessimistic and reveals an even greater degree of polarization within the global economy than earlier versions.

Today, finance capital is penetrating slowly and selectively into just a few peripheral nations, yet is by far the predominant form being invested in the world as a percentage of Direct Foreign Investment (FDI). This foreign capital is being invested mainly for speculation by hedge funds in "instruments" like derivatives and futures contracts, rather than in facilities for manufacturing and producing real wealth (Bond 2003). Such speculative investment is actually "crowding out," or competitively discouraging, the investment of domestic capital in all the poorer countries except for a few favored nations, that is, those that did not have to follow the orthodox policies imposed by the Washington Consensus in the past (China, India, and Brazil are the prime examples.)

The conclusion reached in all the newer versions of dependency theory is that most of the countries of the South have no prospects for significant advancement within the current global system.[7] The capital accumulation now taking place in the world is said to be concentrating in fewer and fewer hands and occurring at the expense of the majority of people in the developing world. It has even been suggested that governments in the southern hemisphere should consider "decoupling" their economies as much as possible and moving toward a more self-reliant strategy for development, particularly in the domain of food production (Taylor 1991; Barkin 1998; Bello et al. 2000). Many South Americans will be struck by the fact that this is precisely the kind of "economic nationalist" path pursued by governments throughout Latin America during the 1960s and 1970s, by popular leaders such as Allende, Roldos, Torrijos, and Velasco, until they were deposed or even assassinated, allegedly with US government support (Perkins 2004).

Dependency theory continues to be influential in Latin America and other parts of the global South, but its star has faded somewhat in recent years. The body of work basically overlooks the crucial role of energy and, despite the strong focus on primary products and raw materials, it does not actually portray the global economy as a closed system. Perhaps its impact has diminished with time for these very reasons. The irony is that a renewal of sorts could easily have come about long ago, inspired by an unlikely source: neoclassical economic theory, the origin of "neoliberalism," the promoting of "free trade" and "free markets."

Although it is not widely known outside the academic discipline, the canonical versions of neoclassical theory of the nineteenth century were based on a general equilibrium model, which depicted the economy as a closed system governed by the laws of Newtonian mechanics as well as the newly discovered First Law of Thermodynamics. The global economy was said to be a closed system in which economic value or utility was conserved, even as value was converted from one form to another through production and exchange. Beinhocker notes some of the implications in a recent overview of the history of the discipline:

> Traditional economics typically portrays value as a fixed quantity that is converted from one form to another . . . New wealth isn't actually created; rather, the world begins with a finite set of resources that are allocated among producers, who in turn create a finite set of commodities that are allocated among consumers. One can allocate that wealth in ways that are more or less efficient, just as one can burn a lump of coal in ways that are more or less efficient, but in general equilibrium models the economy can't create new wealth any more than a lump of coal can reproduce. This emphasis on a fixed pie of wealth caused the English economist Lionel Robbins in 1935 to famously call economics the "science of scarcity." (2005:67)

One would never know this today, mainly because neoclassical theory was abruptly wedded, in a kind of forced marriage, to growth theory beginning in the 1950s, as Beinhocker goes on to explain. Unfortunately, that awkward synthesis completely changed the theory as a way of representing the physical and social world. The "fixed pie" was replaced with the "expanding pie" view that, assumedly, was more consistent with the political agenda of most economists, or at least those of the ascendant Chicago School, the famous shapers of the Washington Consensus.

According to the version of events handed down in the lore of the discipline, the basic elements of the original theory were somehow discovered—quite independently and at roughly the same time—by several prominent thinkers of the mid-nineteenth century: Walras, Jevons, Ricardo, Pareto, and others. Mirowski (1984:8), however, has shown that those elements were simply borrowed or copied directly from physics: "neo-classical economic theory was appropriated wholesale from mid-19th century physics; utility was redefined so as to be identical with energy." If value was to be equated in the social world with energy, then that value, according to the newly discovered First Law, had to be conserved somehow in economic transactions. And so the theory emerged.

Both Mirowski and Beinhocker criticize early economists for this unacknowledged borrowing, and for inappropriate use of what is, for them, only a loosely fitting metaphor: value as a kind of social energy. Yet they also chide later neoclassical theorists for having basically ignored the Second Law, the entropy law. Mirowski (1991:88–98) casts doubt on the relevance of both laws to economics, rightly noting that energy itself became a highly problematic concept in twentieth-century physics due to revolutionary developments in cosmology and in quantum mechanics, the sciences of the very large and the very small. There is, he observes, real doubt among physicists today about whether energy is conserved at either of those levels, a doubt they do not often share with outsiders.

Mirowski is quick to point out that "utility" is ultimately a subjective and social phenomenon that cannot simply be reduced to energy, as Georgescu-Roegen (1971a, 1971b, 1975) emphatically showed. But he seems to overreact in suggesting that economists today should abandon energetics altogether. Energy expenditure may not entirely explain the creation of value, but it is certainly necessary for the production of all real wealth, as he is well aware. What would the implications of the Second Law have been for neoclassical theory as originally formulated, since the Second Law was not widely understood, even by physicists, until the latter part of the nineteenth century? Mirowski implies that there would have been none of any interest.

The Second Law states that in a closed system, energy, although conserved in absolute quantity, inevitably undergoes a qualitative change, especially as it is harnessed to do work. Only a certain amount of the total energy present in a system can do this: the *available* energy or *free* energy, which degrades as it is harnessed and turned into *bound* energy, thereby becoming unavailable and incapable of doing any further work (Georgescu-Roegen 1971b:76–83). Entropy, as a mathematical measure of the disorder or randomness in the encompassing system, shows this gradual degradation, increasing inexorably with time. The early neoclassical economists, when they appropriated the energy concept, were only dimly aware of the significance of the increasing disorder, which of course gives a direction to time and to history and imparts an irreversibility to human affairs. Thus they equated value with energy in general rather than with *available* or *free* energy, as they probably would have had they been aware of the Second Law.

Regardless of which way they chose to go—with value as energy or with value as free energy—the implications could have been profound, at least for the way that economics represents the economy and the social world. Wealth in the most general sense, or the potential to produce wealth by consuming energy, is said by economists *not* to be created by people since we cannot increase the total amount of low-entropy matter, energy that is available for use on the planet.[8] The Second Law is ultimately incompatible with growth theory, so that its proper appraisal would have prevented the forced marriage referred to earlier, and thus precluded the emergence of today's "expanding pie" worldview.

But had the early economists gone with value as available or free energy, the worldview promoted by the discipline today would have been even more radically transformed. Value would not be said to be conserved as economic processes unfold within the global system, but would instead be seen as undergoing a gradual and inevitable decline, as free energy does. That insight would have strengthened political economy and given dependency theory much greater clarity and force than it has today. The opportunity to produce wealth, and thus the opportunity to prosper, would—according to the theory—be used up gradually within the economy as time goes on; all economic processes would be seen as irreversible in this respect and be said to have this "opportunity cost." Prosperity would perhaps be regarded today as a scarce commodity, achievable by people only during a brief window of time and always capable of being enjoyed by some other people in some other place. Its cost, in terms of the entropy and the general disorder produced, would be capable of being passed on to those same others and externalized, as indeed it commonly is in the form of widespread environmental destruction and a rapidly warming and increasingly unstable global climate.

Economists might therefore have come to portray the economy not as a self-regulating mechanism but as the complex social and historical phenomenon that it is. Some countries would be seen to occupy a privileged position in both space and time, being able to spend up the future that other countries might otherwise have experienced. Certainly our image of wealth would have changed, along with our illusions about creating it and perhaps even our ideas about how that wealth—now correctly seen as a gift of nature or of God, and thus a form of common property—should rightly be distributed. Although he lacked this overall vision, the words of Alfred Marshall, one of the foremost economists of the early twentieth century, nevertheless ring true today:

> Man cannot create material things . . . when he is said to produce material things, he really only produces utilities; or in other words, his efforts and sacrifices result in changing the form or arrangement of matter to adapt it better for the satisfaction of wants. (Marshall 1947:63, cited in Mirowski 1991:290)

EXPANDING PIES AND FIXED PIES: AN ETHNOLOGY OF SUSTAINABILITY AND MUTUAL SELF-RESTRAINT

All of these insights about wealth and capital seem to suggest that the prospects for positive change, based on the adoption of a closed-system view of the global economy, may indeed be greater than they appear at first glance. Worldview is not prominent among the social issues being debated today in academia; but interest is growing rapidly and already there is disagreement over what the implications of adopting a closed-system view might be. The key question is whether such a change would promote, or somehow discourage, more widespread cooperation among people.

A great amount of research on human behavior has now shown, through repeated laboratory experiments and through focused studies done in a wide array of cultures, that people are neither inherently altruistic, as political liberals tend to think, nor inherently selfish, as conservatives tend to think. Obviously they are capable of both kinds of behavior, and the research has shown that both kinds are regularly displayed by significant numbers of people in any enduring social group. On balance, however, the cooperative tendencies of people are stronger than we have been led to believe.

The best generalization that can be made today about humans as a species is that they are "conditional cooperators" and "altruistic punishers," that is, they have a strong tendency to cooperate, provided that others do, and they will punish those who violate the norms of cooperation even when such action comes at a cost to themselves, one that stands little obvious chance of being repaid in the future (Gintis et al. 2005). This inherently sociable portrait—which contrasts so sharply with the competitive selfishness of the "rational self-serving individual" of neoclassical economics—is now known to characterize a significant percentage of people in all societies, although that capacity is clearly not achieved in all situations. The set of behaviors is called *strong reciprocity*.

The evidence to support strong reciprocity is truly overwhelming, but the concept is not a normative one that predicts how most people will behave in a certain kind of social setting. Rather, it is a general schema or model summarizing the way that different types of individuals seem to interact in organized social groups, a "behavioral ecology" that is compatible with a wide variety of cultural norms. In any society, whether large or small, only a minority of individuals will tend to be strong reciprocators, altruistic individuals who obey agreed-upon rules and are willing to sacrifice by punishing wrongdoers in order to make a point and uphold the common good. The majority appear to be opportunists, individuals who choose their behavior carefully in response to the presence or absence of reciprocators, and who do not punish. Entirely capable of cheating in order to benefit themselves, these individuals basically follow the example of others and copy the kind of behavior that seems, at the moment, to "work" and to get the highest payoff or reward (Gintis et al. 2005:22–24).

A great amount of interdisciplinary and cross-cultural research indicates that strong reciprocators are generally numerous enough in any society to be able maintain order through the influence that they periodically exert on conformists by demonstrating their willingness to punish cheaters. They play a crucial role in maintaining social cohesion by convincing the less idealistic majority to follow their example and obey the rules. Both kinds of people will be found in any viable group, but strong reciprocators, at least in theory, are able to ensure that norms are enforced periodically and that cooperativeness prevails among most of the people most of the time.

The problem with such a brief summary is that it gives the impression that cooperation is not generally problematic when of course it is in so many situations, and it suggests that all societies are equally capable of realizing the potential for this kind of outcome. In discussing strong reciprocity and the supporting research, Beinhocker (2005:430) emphasizes the crucial importance of a cultural belief that there are payoffs for such behavior and claims that "societies that believe in a fixed pie of wealth have a difficult time engendering cooperation."

No evidence is given to support the latter assertion. The statement seems to reflect a prejudice that is common among economists today: surely people will only cooperate with each other if they are part of a system that is somehow expanding in terms of total available wealth. That is the main presupposition supporting the false ideology and worldview promoted by contemporary capitalism, as we have seen, a worldview that is sustained by the illusion of creating wealth. The bias may help to explain the discipline's abrupt shift toward growth theory in the 1950s and away from the traditional closed-system view of neoclassical economics. Yet the statement also seems to echo Foster's rather negative and one-sided view of peasants. We have seen that a "zero-sum" or "fixed pie" worldview, which Foster ascribed to peasant societies everywhere, can just as easily support strong leadership and widespread cooperation as it can encourage envy and mutual mistrust. That is the point that Nash makes so strongly in her recent reflections on the Zapatistas. Beinhocker's error is to assume that, in a fixed-pie context where the "good" is seen to be strictly limited, there are no rewards for cooperation. Nothing could be further from the truth, as the ethnographic record clearly shows.

One of the major developments of the last thirty years in anthropology and the other social sciences has been the emergence of a vast literature on the management of "common-property" or "common-pool" resources, forms of natural wealth that belong, not to individuals, but to communities and local groups (NRC 1986; McCay and Acheson 1987; Bromley 1992; Ostrom et al. 1999; Ostrom et al. 2002). A great surge of studies focused on the communal management of resources like pasturelands, forests, fisheries, and water for irrigation, many of them inspired by a desire to refute Hardin's (1968) famous argument in "the tragedy of the commons," a work that has had more influence on policymakers than any other in the history of social science. These analyses reveal the complex dynamics behind many local situations, documenting and explaining many different outcomes, both positive and negative, in people's efforts to cooperate. But on the whole they show that people are quite capable of working together and resolving the "commons dilemma," the supposedly inevitable conflict between the interests of the individual, assumed by Hardin to be entirely selfish, and the cooperative needs of the group.

The ethnographies in each case examine how a fixed pie of natural wealth is shared within one or more user groups, a scarce common-pool resource that is "subtractable" in the sense that one person's use of it comes at the expense of everyone else by reducing the overall amount that is available. The solution, and the key to avoiding a tragic outcome, is for individuals to exert a form of mutual self-restraint, as Hardin himself noted, each limiting their consumption so that the resource can be utilized in a sustainable way that is beneficial for all in the long run. A great number of studies have shown that local resource users are capable, by working together, of devising their own institutions or rules to accomplish this. They do not need to be coerced into doing it by an authoritarian state, one of Hardin's proposed solutions, nor would they benefit from having the resource privatized so that it can be allocated in a more selfish and competitive way by markets, his other proposed solution.

Such positive outcomes are by no means inevitable, for they involve the kind of complex within-group dynamics that are revealed so clearly in the laboratory research on strong reciprocity. But people in common-pool resource situations are often able, through collective action, to create institutions that, along with the constraints imposed by the dynamics of the resource itself, allow strong reciprocity to prevail. These relatively happy outcomes—a kind of "comedy in the commons" (Smith 1984, cited in McCay and Acheson 1987:15)—have been documented in many places throughout the world, and for a wide array of communal resources, but they are especially frequent in the use of water for irrigation.

Again and again in Peru, Mexico, Spain, India, Nepal, and the Philippines, relatively autonomous communities of irrigators—peasants and small farmers in every case—have been shown to share this vital form of "natural capital" in a sustainable way, imposing upper limits on their consumption of a scarce resource upon which the lives and livelihoods of all households depend.[9] This kind of collective action, now known to characterize a great many local hydraulic societies, is an achievement that policy makers, until recently, thought to be impossible, as Hardin argued.

My own research indicates that these local solutions to the commons dilemma often turn out to be the same outcome of a collective agreement. Comparative analysis of data on irrigation systems in various countries, including several in the global South, shows that successful farmer-operated systems are based on the central principle of equity or fairness, which often seems to be defined and achieved in the same way (Trawick 2001a, 2001b, 2002a, 2002b, 2003, 2005, 2008, 2010). The rules require that the scarcity be shared by all users on a single schedule of rotation, in such a way that it affects all land, and all landowners, in the same way and to a similar extent. That achievement is especially significant because the communities are stratified in every case including both "large" landholders and smaller ones, so that like all human societies they contain significant differences in wealth. While irrigation is taking place at a rhythm or pace that is the same for everyone, a basic proportionality is maintained among household water rights, a uniform land-to-water ratio that limits the total volume of water consumed during each distribution round.

A remarkable symmetry is ultimately created, a basic equity that pervades the existing set of rights, the set of corresponding duties, and governs the relationship between rights and duties. The rules in each case require that the contributions of households to yearly maintenance of the canal system in the form of labor, food, money, and other inputs be proportional to the amount of irrigated land that each family has. Because of this pervasive symmetry created by institutions expressing a need and a desire for cooperation, fairness, and mutual self-restraint, I call this type of system "the moral economy of water."

Note that these are not idyllic and homogenous systems, nor are they structurally simple ones. The studied examples range in complexity from small-scale systems operated by a single peasant community to multicommunity systems covering thousands of hectares and requiring the daily coordinated action of tens of thousands of small commercial farmers. They exist today in remote corners of the Andes—the highlands of Ecuador, Peru, and Bolivia—and in the bustling tourist zone of Valencia on the Mediterranean coast of Spain, one of the world's most cosmopolitan cities. The institutions governing them in these cases are hundreds or even thousands of years old and they appear to have emerged independently on different continents, forming the heart of distinct Andean and Islamic hydraulic traditions (Glick 1970; Trawick 2001b, 2005, 2008, 2010).

From a practical point of view, fairness in these contexts has always meant the same thing that it does today: no one person is allowed to accumulate and use so much water that they jeopardize the rights and the livelihood of everyone else. In a context of scarcity, no one may irrigate more often, or use more water, than the prevailing conditions will allow in situations where mutual well-being and the minimization of social conflict are widely shared goals. Similarly, people's duties to give back to the community are proportional to the benefits that they derive from living there and using its resources. The prevailing scarcity creates an incentive to conserve water, but that is reinforced and made strong by the uniform frequency of irrigation, an expression of a collectively chosen rule. Under this arrangement there is a direct and obvious link to the individual farmer between the efficiency and orderliness of water use and the duration of the irrigation cycle. By conserving the resource and obeying the rules, people are maximizing the frequency of water use for themselves and everyone else, responding to a close correspondence between individual self-interest and the common good that cannot be achieved through any other kind of arrangement.[10]

Such collective agreements are possible because the distribution systems are highly transparent, enabling community members to routinely monitor each other's behavior. People can tell through direct observation whether the rules governing the consumption of this basic form of wealth are generally being obeyed. The rules are simple and known to everyone, requiring the unbroken movement of water, canal by canal and field by field, through well-defined and contiguous sectors of irrigated land. Consequently, the stealing of water—the most socially disruptive form of cheating or free-riding that plagues so many irrigation systems throughout the world—is easily detected, reliably punished, and relatively rare. Strong reciprocity prevails.

This kind of equity and transparency may be difficult, at a glance, to envision creating on a global scale through mutually imposed limits on the per-capita consumption of scarce goods like petroleum, other fossil fuels, and the electricity that is derived from them. That, of course, is the main challenge we are facing today at a global level in order to stabilize the climate. The same can be said of the other institutional changes proposed at the start of this essay: the efforts to limit the size of banks and regulate their international flows of finance capital and to impose upper limits on bonuses and executive pay, not just in the financial sector but more generally throughout the corporate world. The latter, if extended to the entire public and private sectors, would amount to a global maximum wage, a limit that is advocated today by growing numbers of people.[11] All of these struggles are now underway, and what is at stake is indeed our mutual survival, as people in the global South have insisted for some time. The forces arrayed against such collective action—economic, political, even military—are formidable and capable of extreme violence, a fact of which southerners need no reminder. But a demand for profound change is increasingly expressed by northerners too and is now a truly global phenomenon. And the limits to growth themselves are by no means impossible to achieve. The evidence from successful farmer-managed irrigation systems of small, medium, and even fairly large scales, which are often governed by highly similar rules, suggests that they might even be achievable by applying a relatively simple set of principles to each macroeconomic problem.

The greatest challenge in any effort to "scale-up" existing cooperative institutions lies in solving the "assurance problem," that is, in creating distribution systems that are transparent and that will enable people to routinely monitor each other's behavior, as Ostrom (1990:42–45) has shown in her groundbreaking work on the management of virtually all kinds of common-property resources. That is the most important step in any effort to cooperate by limiting consumption: assuring people, and in this case ultimately even assuring whole countries, that an agreement will be mutually enforceable and will work. But in the digital age, technology makes it possible to create such transparency on a scale never seen before; that is the great advantage that we now have. Computers and information technology make it possible, at least in theory, to hold each other accountable and to reliably enforce any agreed-upon set of rules at any level of social organization. Local economies can obviously be made more equitable and transparent at the ground level, but these must be nested hierarchically within similar institutions at higher levels, sustaining polycentric governance in the regulation of economies at local, regional, national, and global scales (Ostrom 1990, 1998; Ostrom et al. 1999, 2002; Dolšak and Ostrom 2003; Marshall 2005).

This will not be easy, for the global economy is not just a big irrigation system. Yet there is no reason why the world cannot be made to work like one, and, more importantly, to look like one. Water is, after all, a basic kind of material wealth, like energy, one that is absolutely unique and vital to all economic activity, indeed vital for all life. As any farmer is keenly aware, people cannot create water or destroy it, but they can certainly lose it, waste it, or degrade it to such an extent that it becomes unavailable for use by any-one else. Or, alternatively, they can circulate that limited wealth in an equi-table and sustainable way that is beneficial for all, as farmers commonly do in many places throughout the world. The political will to do this through-out the entire economy is growing rapidly today, and necessity will only add to the mounting pressure as time goes on. But the current groundswell of support, of popular resistance against business as usual, will only become truly global if people widely come to see the world—the physical and social world—in a more similar way.

CONCLUSION: THE WORLD AS A CLOSED SYSTEM

The argument presented throughout this essay is that, if people come to realize that economic growth is a destructive process rather than a creative one, based on the consumption of limited forms of natural wealth that are being rapidly drawn down and made more scarce both for contemporary Others and for the members of future generations, they may become more willing to take action to restrain growth by mutually limiting their con-sumption. The challenges involved in moving humankind toward sustain-ability in this way are daunting, and any effort to scale up existing coopera-tive institutions to the highest levels of social organization will, of course, be fraught with difficulty. But what is most needed, as a necessary if not a sufficient condition, is the adoption of a closed-system view of the world and of the global economy. Also crucial is the abandonment of an idea that lies at the heart of the open-system worldview now seen to be outmoded: the illusion that people create wealth.

The alternative worldview of "limited good" has been around for a long time, for it does accurately depict physical and social reality. It emerged repeatedly, and often independently, in many peasant societies throughout the world, and it has clearly survived among the indigenous peoples of the global South, for many of whom it seems to be traditional. The closed-system view also emerged and flourished briefly in academia, having been promoted initially by neoclassical theory in economics—a fact that is no longer widely remembered—and then was explored by dependency theorists, radical critics whose work is still widely influential in Latin America and other parts of the southern hemisphere. Today it is strongly supported by contemporary knowledge in the natural sciences, based on an understanding—seemingly new but perhaps in fact very old—of how the laws of thermodynamics express themselves as fundamental constraints in human affairs. Although such knowledge is not yet widespread, it may help to explain why the worldview appears to be embraced by growing numbers of people within the alternative globalization movement.

The open-system view long promoted by economists, financiers, and politicians must be replaced with a more realistic one built upon the axiom that the "good" in human affairs is nearly always limited. Today the closed-system worldview, which focuses the mind on everything material that we have in common as the inhabitants of a small and fragile planet, may be destined finally to prevail. It would be foolish to claim, however, that this alternative vision will prove to be a tipping point that unites people all over the world, creating a new class of global citizens who define themselves in terms of their mutual relationship to scarce forms of property that ultimately belong to us all. One could still argue that such a paradigm change, occurring at a global level, might promote and intensify conflict rather than encourage cooperation of the strong reciprocity type, or that it might prove to have no substantial effect on people's behavior. Only time will tell. The safe thing to say, therefore, is that we may soon find out just how important worldview really is.

ACKNOWLEDGMENTS

I wish to express my gratitude to the John D. and Catherine T. MacArthur Foundation for generously supporting the irrigation research discussed in the latter part of this paper. Thanks should rightly go to too many colleagues to list here, but especially to Ellen Messer and Bill Mitchell for their help and encouragement throughout the years, to Richard N. Adams for providing early insight and inspiration, to Jim Harris for insisting that I first put these thoughts down on paper, to Chris Perry and Joe Morris, who read earlier versions and made helpful comments, to Paul Durrenberger for the impulse to see the project through, and to Susan Mitchell, my wife and toughest critic, who always has a hand in anything I write that turns out to be fit to print.

NOTES

1. With a few notable exceptions (e.g., Friedman 1994, 2004; Turner 2004, 2005), anthropological critics of globalization have tended to focus their attention on how globalization is experienced—how it shapes representations and identity— and left examination of the underlying flows of resources, of capital, and even the clash of social classes to political economists and researchers in other disciplines.

2. These figures are for total use of "extrasomatic" energy by individuals and corporations in the world economy; they obviously do not include the solar energy harnessed to produce crops that are ultimately consumed by people as food, nor do they include the solar energy that helps to heat our homes in winter and to make the environment generally warmer and more habitable than it would otherwise be.

3. My usage here conforms to the way these terms are generally used in physics. An *open system* is one whose boundaries are permeable to matter, energy, and information, whereas a *closed system* exchanges energy and information with its environment but not matter. An *isolated system*, such as the universe, is self-contained in all three respects.

4. Wade (2003), Pollin (2003), and others have shown that Bhagwati's (2004) well-known defense of globalization in his reply to Stiglitz is not really valid, since the main "developing" countries that have benefited from globalization, China and India, are doing so because they did not follow the neoliberal formula imposed by the Washington Consensus, which, until very recently, formed the heart of economic globalization.

5. Soddy (1926:202–207) invented the concept of virtual wealth, defining it as the aggregate value of the real assets that the community voluntarily abstains from holding in order to hold money instead, and thus avoid the inconvenience of barter (see Daley and Farley 2003:248). It is an abstract concept, but one largely synonymous with money and with debt, whose relationship to finance capital is more complex than can be explained fully here.

6. Today most transnational corporations seem to function as both commercial and investment banks, arranging the financing through debt of many of the items that their customers purchase. This practice began with the major automobile manufacturers, but has expanded enormously to the point that today it is typical of transnationals in general. As Sklair (2000) and Bond (2003) have noted, such

financing at interest is now a major source of their profits, capital which is then further multiplied by investing it in the financial markets.

7. Some critics might disagree by pointing to the high growth rates now being experienced in several South American countries, which seem to be weathering the current crisis better than the "core" or G8 countries. However, with the sole exception of Brazil—one of the few to have advanced to the "semiperipheral" status of a newly industrialized country—all of the South American nations continue to export mainly primary products and to have virtually no industry, a situation that is unlikely to change. Even Chile, often touted as a success story of neoliberalism, exports mainly minerals, fruits and other produce, wine, and goods like factory-farmed fish. A dependency theorist would say that the resulting increases in the GDP of Chile and other countries mask the fact that the flow of wealth is largely confined to the traditional elites and that these societies are becoming steadily more unequal.

8. We can, of course, learn how to harness available energy more effectively and efficiently, especially solar energy and other renewable forms that are derived from the thermal activity of the sun or from gravity.

9. A large number of studies document positive outcomes in farmer-managed irrigation: for example, Glick 1970, Maass and Anderson 1978; Coward 1979; Siy 1982; Wade 1988; Ostrom 1990, 1992, 1998; Tang 1992; Treacy 1994a, 1994b; Gelles 1994, 2000; Sengupta 1991; Ostrom and Gardner 1993; Lam 1998; Trawick 2001a, 2001b; Palerm and Martínez 2000; Boelens and Davila 1998; and Boelens and Hoogendam 2002. For a debate about how equity is defined in these systems, and how much they all have in common in that respect, see Trawick 2005 and Boelens and Hoogendam 2002.

10. The close correspondence between self-interest and the common good distinguishes the moral economy type of system—at least in my analysis—and makes it possible for exchange to be based on cooperation rather than competition. Competition is basically equivalent to cheating or free-riding, a temptation that is virtually eliminated because of the near-certainty of punishment in a situation marked by a high degree of transparency. This congruence of self-interest and the common good may be achievable—by setting up the right institutions—in other spheres or domains of exchange.

11. The person who has advocated this most strongly is Andrew Simms (2001), head of the New Economics Foundation in London. However, a maximum wage is by no means a novel idea, particularly as a way of dealing with situations of economic emergency. As Susan George (2008) has pointed out (also Korten 2001:62–65,88), the most notorious example was the unification and reorganization of the entire commercial economy, involving strict rationing of both fuel and food, that the Allies achieved and relied on in order to win World War II. That mobilization was financed by a highly progressive tax policy that radically limited and redistributed individual income above a certain level, one that was successfully implemented

in both Great Britain and the United States, apparently with little squabbling and very little cheating or "free-riding."

REFERENCES CITED

Adams, Richard N. 1975. *Energy and Structure*. Austin: University of Texas Press.

Arrighi, Giovanni. 1994. *The Long 20th Century: Money, Power and the Origins of Our Times*. London: Verso.

Barkin, David. 1998. *Wealth, Poverty, and Sustainable Development*. Mexico City: Editorial Jus.

Bebbington, Anthony. 2009. "The New Extraction: Rewriting the Political Ecology of the Andes." *NACLA Report on the Americas* 42: 12–20.

Beinhocker, Eric D. 2005. *The Origin of Wealth: Evolution, Complexity, and the Radical Remaking of Economics*. London: Random House.

Bello, W., K. Malhotra, N. Bullard and M. Mezzera. 2000. "Notes on the Ascendancy and Regulation of Speculative Capital." In *Global Finance: New Thinking on Regulating Speculative Capital Markets*, edited by W. Bello, N. Bullard, and K. Malhotra, 1–26. Dhaka, Bangladesh: New University Press.

Bhagwati, Jadesh. 2004. *In Defense of Globalization*. New York: Oxford University Press.

Bircham, E., and J. Charlton, eds. 2002. *Anti-capitalism: A Guide to the Movement*. London: Bookmarks.

Boelens, Rutgerd, and Glora Davila, eds. 1998. *Searching for Equity: Conceptions of Justice and Equity in Peasant Irrigation*. Assen, The Netherlands: Van Gorcum.

Boelens, Rutgard, and David Hoogendam, eds. 2002. *Water Rights and Empowerment*. Assen, The Netherlands: Van Gorcum.

Bond, Patrick. 2003. "US and Global Economic Volatility: Theoretical, Empirical and Political Considerations." Paper presented to the Empire Seminar, York University, Toronto. University of KwaZulu-Natal School of Development Studies and Centre for Civil Society. http://www.ukzn.ac.za/ccs.

Bromley, David, ed. 1992. *Making the Commons Work: Theory, Practice and Policy*. San Francisco: Institute for Contemporary Studies.

Callinicos, A. 2003. *An Anti-capitalist Manifesto*. Cambridge: Cambridge University Press.

Coward, E. Walter. 1979. "Principles of Social Organization in an Indigenous Irrigation System." *Human Organization* 38(1): 28–36.

Daley, Herman, and Joshua Farley. 2003. *Ecological Economics: Principles and Applications*. New York: Island Press.

Davies, J. B., S. Sandstrom, A. Shorrocks, and E. N. Wolff. 2006. "The World Distribution of Household Wealth." United Nations: Institute for Development Economics Research.

Delaney, David. 2005. *Territory: A Short Introduction*. London: Blackwell.

Dolšak, Nives, and Elinor Ostrom, eds. 2003. *The Commons in the New Millennium: Challenges and Adaptation*. Cambridge, MA: MIT Press.

Douthwaite Richard. 1996. *The Ecology of Money*. Schumacher Briefings No. 4. Devon, UK: Green Books.

Escobar, Arturo. 1995. *Encountering Development: The Making and Unmaking of the Third World*. Princeton, NJ: Princeton University Press.

Escobar, A., J. Sen, and P. Waterman, eds. 2003. *Are Other Worlds Possible? The Past, Present and Futures of the World Social Forum*. New Delhi: Viveka.

Foster, George. 1965. "Peasant Society and the Image of Limited Good." *American Anthropologist* 67(2): 293–315.

Friedman, Jonathan. 1994. *Cultural Identity and Global Process*. London: Sage Publications.

———. 2004. "Champagne Liberals and the New 'Dangerous Classes': Reconfigurations of Class, Identity, and Cultural Production in the Contemporary Global System." In *Globalization: Critical Issues*, edited by Allen Chun, 49–82. New York: Berghahn Books.

Gelles, Paul. 1994. "Channels of Power, Fields of Contention: State Dominance and Community Resistance in the Colca Valley of Peru." In *Irrigation at High Altitudes: The Social Organization of Water Control Systems in the Andes*, edited by W. P. Mitchell and D. Guillet, 233–274. Society for Latin American Anthropology Publication Series, Vol. 12. Washington, DC: American Anthropological Association.

———. 2000. *Water and Power in Highland Peru: The Culture and Politics of Irrigation in an Andean Community*. Rutgers, NJ: Rutgers University Press.

George, Susan. 2000. "A Short History of Neo-Liberalism: Twenty Years of Elite Economics and Emerging Opportunities for Structural Change." In *Global Finance: New Thinking on Regulating Speculative Capital Markets*, edited by W. Bellow, N. Bullard, and K. Mulhotra, 36–41. Dhaka, Bangladesh: New University Press.

———. 2008. "We Must Think Big to Fight Environmental Disaster." Special Report: How Our Economy Is Killing the Earth. *New Scientist Magazine* 2678 (15 October 2008). Available at http://www.zcommunications.org/we-must-think-big-by-susan-george.

Geogescu-Roegen, Nicholas. 1971a. *The Entropy Law and the Economic Process*. Cambridge, MA: Harvard University Press.

———. 1971b. "The Entropy Law and the Economic Problem." In *Valuing the Earth: Economy, Ecology and Ethics*, edited by H. E. Daley and K.E. Townsend, 75–88. Cambridge, MA: MIT Press.

———. 1975. "Selections from 'Energy and Economic Myths.'" *Southern Economic Journal* 41(3). Reprinted in *Valuing the Earth: Economy, Ecology and Ethics*, edited by H. E. Daley and K. E. Townsend, 89–112. Cambridge, MA: MIT Press.

Giampietro, M., and D. Pimentel. 1993. "The Tightening Conflict: Population, Energy Use, and the Ecology of Agriculture." *NPG Forum* (October 1993). Teeneck, NJ: Negative Population Growth Inc.

———. 1994. "Energy Utilization in Agriculture." In *Encyclopedia of Agricultural Science*, edited by C. J. Arntzen and E. M. Ritter, 2: 63–76. San Diego, CA: Academic Press.

Gintis, Herbert, S. Bowles, R. Boyd, and E. Fehr. 2005. *Moral Sentiments and Material Interests: The Foundation of Cooperation in Economic Life*. Cambridge, MA: MIT Press.

Glick, Thomas F. 1970. *Irrigation and Society in Medieval Valencia*. Cambridge, MA: Harvard University Press.

Hannan, Daniel. 2010. *The New Road to Serfdom: A Letter of Warning to America*. New York: Harper.

Hardin, Garret. 1968. "The Tragedy of the Commons." *Science* 162: 1243–1248.

Harvey, David. 2010. *The Enigma of Capital and the Crises of Capitalism*. New York: Profile Books.

Hilferding, Rudolf. 1981 [1910]. *Finance Capital: A Study of the Latest Phase of Capitalist Development*. Edited by Tom Bottomore. London: Routledge and Kegan Paul [1981].

Hudson, Michael. 2006. "The New Road to Serfdom: An Illustrated Guide to the Coming Real Estate Collapse." *Harper's Magazine* (May 2006): 39–46.

Hyde, Lewis. 1983. *The Gift: Imagination and the Erotic Life of Poetry*. New York: Vintage Books.

IEA. 2004. *Key World Energy Statistics*. Paris: International Energy Agency.

———. 2009. *World Energy Outlook*. Paris: International Energy Agency.

IMF. 2004. *Global Financial Stability Report: Market Developments and Issues*. Washington, DC: International Monetary Fund.

IPCC. 2007. *Climate Change 2007: The Physical Science Basis*. Contribution of Working Group 1 to the Fourth Assessment Report of the Intergovernmental Panel on Climate Change. Cambridge: Cambridge University Press.

Jackson, Tim. 2009. *Prosperity without Growth: Economics for a Small Planet*. London: Earthscan.

Kaplan, David, and Benson Saler. 1966. "Foster's 'Image of Limited Good': An Example of Anthropological Explanation." *American Anthropologist* 68(1966): 202–206.

Kautsky, Karl. 1911. *Finance Capital and Crises*. London: Social Democrat.

Korten, David. 2001. *When Corporations Rule the World*. Bloomfield, CT: Kumarian Press.

Krugman, Paul. 2008. *The Return of Depression Economics and the Crisis of 2008*. New York: Penguin Press.

Lam, D. Wai Fung. 1998. *Governing Irrigation Systems in Nepal: Institutions, Infrastructure, and Collective Action*. Oakland, CA: Institute for Contemporary Studies Press.

Maass, Arthur, and L. Anderson. 1978. *And the Desert Shall Rejoice: Conflict, Growth and Justice in Arid Environments.* Cambridge, MA: MIT Press.

Marshall, Graham R. 2005. *Economics for Collaborative Environmental Management: Renegotiating the Commons.* London: Earthscan.

McCay, Bonnie, and James Acheson, eds. 1987. *The Question of the Commons: The Culture and Ecology of Communal Resources.* Tucson: University of Arizona Press.

Mirowski, Philip. 1984. "Physics and the Marginalist Revolution." *Cambridge Journal of Economics* 8:361–379.

———. 1991. *More Heat Than Light: Economics as Social Physics, Physics as Nature's Economics.* Cambridge: Cambridge University Press.

Nash, June. 2007. *Practicing Ethnography in a Globalizing World: An Anthropological Odyssey.* Lanham, MD: Altamira Press.

NEF. 2008. *A Green New Deal.* Written by the Green New Deal Team. New Economics Foundation. London.

NRC. 1986. *Proceedings of the Conference on Common Property Management.* National Research Council. Washington, DC: National Academy Press.

O'Hara, Phillip A. 2004. "A New Transnational Social Structure of Accumulation for Long-Wave Upswing in the World Economy?" *Review of Radical Political Economics* 36(3): 328–335.

Olivera, Oscar, and Tom Lewis. 2004. *Cochabamba: Water War in Bolivia.* Cambridge, MA: South End Press.

Ostrom, Elinor. 1990. *Governing the Commons: The Evolution of Institutions for Collective Action.* New York: Cambridge University Press.

———. 1992. *Crafting Institutions for Self-Governing Irrigation Systems.* San Francisco: Institute for Contemporary Studies Press.

———. 1998. "Reformulating the Commons." In *The Commons Revisited: An Americas Perspective,* edited by J. Burger, R. Norgaard, E. Ostrom, D. Policansky, and B. Goldstein, 1–26. Washington, DC: Island Press.

Ostrom, Elinor, J. Burger, C. Field, R. Norgaard, and D. Policansky. 1999. "Revisiting the Commons: Local Lessons, Global Challenges." *Science* 284(5412): 1–10.

Ostrom, Elinor, T. Dietz, N. Dolšak, P. C. Stern, S. Stonich, and E. U. Weber, eds. 2002. *The Drama of the Commons.* Washington, DC: National Academy Press.

Ostrom, Elinor, and Roy Gardner. 1993. "Coping with Asymmetries in the Commons: Self-Governing Irrigation Systems Can Work." *Journal of Economic Perspectives* 7(4): 93–112.

Palerm, Jacinta, and Tomas Martinez, eds. 2000. *Antología sobre Pequeño Riego,* vol. 2, *Organizaciones Autogestivas.* Mexico City: Plaza y Valdes, S.A.

Pearce, David, and Kerry Turner. 1990. *Economics of Natural Resources and the Environment.* London: Harvester Wheatsheaf.

Perez, Carlotta. 2003. *Technological Revolutions and Financial Capital: The Dynamics of Bubbles and Golden Ages.* Glasgow: Edward Elgar Publishers.

Perkins, John. 2004. *Confessions of an Economic Hit Man*. San Francisco: Berrett-Koehler Press.

Perreault, Thomas. 2006. "From the Guerra de Agua to the Guerra de Gas: Resource Governance, Neoliberalism, and Popular Protest in Bolivia." *Antipode* 38(1): 150–172.

Petras, James, and Henry Veltmayer. 2001. *Globalization Unmasked: Imperialism in the 21st Century*. London: Zed Books.

Pimentel, David. 1993. "Economics and Energetics of Organic and Conventional Farming." *Journal of Agricultural and Environmental Ethics* 6: 53–60.

Pollin, Robert. 2003. *Contours of Dissent: U.S. Economic Fractures and the Landscape of Global Austerity*. London: Verso Press.

Radelet, S., and J. Sachs. 1999. "What Have We Learned, So Far, from the Asian Financial Crisis?" CAER II Discussion Paper 37. Cambridge, MA: Harvard Institute for International Development.

Santos, Boaventura. 2003. "The World Social Forum: Towards a Counter-Hegemonic Globalization (Part One)." Paper Presented at the XXIV International Congress of the Latin American Studies Association, Dallas, Texas, USA, March 27–29, 2003. Available at http://www.choike.org/documentos/wsf_s318_sousa.pdf.

Sawyer, S. 2004. *Crude Chronicles: Indigenous Politics, Multinational Oil, and Neoliberalism in Ecuador*. Durham, NC: Duke University Press.

Schrödinger, Erwin. 1967. *What Is Life?* Cambridge, MA: Cambridge University Press.

Sen, Amartya. 1999. *Development as Freedom*. New York: Anchor Books.

Sen, Jai, A. Anand, A. Escobar, and P. Waterman, eds. 2004. *The World Social Forum: Challenging Empires*. New Delhi: Viveka Foundation. Available at http://www.choike.org/nuevo_eng/informes/1557.html.

Sengupta, Nirmal. 1991. *Managing Common Property: Irrigation in India and the Philippines*. New Delhi: Sage.

Simms, Andrew. 2001. "The Alternative Mansion House Speech: Excess Pay, Corporate Power, and an Environmental War Economy." London: New Economics Foundation.

Siy, R. Y. 1982. *Community Resource Management: Lessons from the Zanjera*. Quezon City: University of the Philippines Press.

Sklair, Leslie. 2000. "The Transnational Capitalist Class and the Discourse of Globalization." *Cambridge Review of International Affairs*. Available at http://www.theglobalsite.ac.uk.

Soddy, Frederick. 1921. *The Role of Money*. London: George Routledge and Sons, Ltd.
———. 1926. *Wealth, Virtual Wealth and Debt*. London: George Allen & Unwin

Spronk, Susan, and Jeffrey Webber. 2007. "Struggles against Accumulation by Dispossession in Bolivia: The Political Ecology of Resource Contention." In *Latin American Perspectives* 34(2): 31–47.

Stern, Nicholas. 2007. *The Economics of Climate Change: The Stern Review*. Cambridge: Cambridge University Press.

Stiglitz, Joseph. 2002. *Globalization and Its Discontents*. New York: W.W. Norton & Company.

———. 2010. *Freefall: Free Markets and the Sinking of the Global Economy*. New York: Allen Lane.

Strange, Susan. 1998. *Mad Money: When Markets Outgrow Governments*. Manchester, UK: Manchester University Press.

Surin, Kenneth. 1998. "Dependency Theory's Reanimation in the Era of Finance Capital." *Cultural Logic* 12. Available at http.//clogic.eserver.org/1-2/1-2index.html.

Tang, Shui Yan. 1992. *Institutions and Collective Action: Self-Governance in Irrigation*. San Francisco: Institute for Contemporary Studies Press.

Taussig, Michael. 1980. *The Devil and Commodity Fetishism in South America*. Chapel Hill: University of North Carolina Press.

Taylor, Lance. 1991. "Economic Openness: Problems to the Century's End." In *Economic Liberalization: No Panacea; The Experiences of Latin America and Asia*, 91–147. Oxford: Oxford University Press.

Toussant, E. 2003. *Your Money or Your Life: The Tyranny of Global Finance*. London: Pluto Press.

Trawick, Paul. 2001a. "Successfully Governing the Commons: Principles of Social Organization in an Andean Irrigation System." *Human Ecology* 291: 1–25.

———. 2001b. "The Moral Economy of Water: Equity and Antiquity in the Andean Commons." *American Anthropologist* 103(2):361–379.

———. 2002a. "The Moral Economy of Water: General Principles for Successfully Governing the Commons." *GAIA: Ecological Perspectives in Science, the Humanities and Economics* 11: 191–194.

———. 2002b. "Trickle-down Theory, Andean Style: Indigenous Practices Provide a Lesson in Sharing." *Natural History* 111(8): 60–65. Available at www.naturalhistorymag.com; October 2002 issue.

———. 2003. *The Struggle for Water in Peru: Comedy and Tragedy in the Andean Commons*. Palo Alto, CA: Stanford University Press.

———. 2005. "Going with the Flow: The State of Contemporary Studies of Water Management in Latin America." *Latin American Research Review* 40(3): 443–456.

———. 2008. "Scarcity, Equity, and Transparency: General Principles for Successfully Governing the Water Commons." In *Mountains: Sources of Water, Sources of Knowledge*, edited by E. Wiegandt. Kluwer Series Advances in Global Change Research, 31: 43–62. Dordrecht, The Netherlands: Springer.

———. 2010. "Encounters with the Moral Economy of Water: General Principles for Successfully Managing the Commons." In *Water Ethics: Foundational Read-*

ings for Students and Professionals, edited by P. Brown and J. J. Schmidt, 155–166. Washington, DC: Island Press.

Treacy, John. 1994a. "Teaching Water: Hydraulic Management and Terracing in Corporaque, the Colca Valley, Peru." In *Irrigation at High Altitudes: The Social Organization of Water Control Systems in the Andes*, edited by W. P. Mitchell and D. Guillet, 99–114. Society for Latin American Anthropology Publication Series, Vol. 12. Washington, DC: American Anthropological Association.

———. 1994b. *Las Chacras de Corporaque: Andeneria y Riego en el Valle del Colca*. Lima: Instituto de Estudios Peruanos.

Turner, Kerry, David Pearce, and Ian Bateman. 1994. *Environmental Economics: An Elementary Introduction*. London: Harvester Wheatsheaf.

Turner, Terence. 2004. "Shifting the Frame from Nation-State to Global Markets: Class and Social Consciousness in the Advanced Capitalist Countries." In *Globalization: Critical Issues*, edited by Allen Chun, 83–119. New York: Berghahn Books.

———. 2005. "Anthropological Activism, Indigenous Peoples and Globalization." In *Human Rights: The Scholar as Activist*, edited by C. Nagengast and C. Velez-Ibanez, 83–119. Alexandria, VA: Society for Applied Anthropology Monograph Series.

UNMEA. 2005. *Millennium Ecosystem Assessment and Human Well-being: Synthesis*. Washington, DC: Island Press.

Volcker, Paul. 2010. "The Time We Have Is Growing Short." *The New York Review of Books* 57(11): 12–14.

Wade, Robert. 1988. *Village Republics: Economic Conditions for Collective Action in South India*. Cambridge: Cambridge University Press.

———. 2003. "Is Globalization Really Reducing Poverty and Inequality?" *World Development* 32(4): 567–589.

Webster, P. J., G. J. Holland, J. A. Curry, and H. R. Chang. 2005. "Changes in Tropical Cyclone Number, Duration, and Intensity in a Warming Environment." *Science* 309(5742): 1844–1846.

White, Leslie. 1943. "Energy and the Evolution of Culture." *American Anthropologist* 43: 335–356.

Wolf, Martin. 2007. "Why Banks Are an Accident Waiting to Happen." *Financial Times*, 27 November 2007.

WPCCC. 2010. People's Agreement of Cochabamba, World People's Conference on Climate Change and the Rights of Mother Earth, April 22, 2010. Cochabamba, Bolivia.

WSF. 2004. *World Social Forum, Charter of Principles*. Mumbai, India, January 16–21. Available at http://www.wsfindia.org/charter.php.

Crash, Collapse, and Catastrophe in Postindustrial North America

D I M I T R A   D O U K A S

THE END OF THE WORLD AS WE KNOW IT—DISASTER SCENARIOS

The world as we know it is soon to end, according to many, possibly most, North Americans. In the early twenty-first century, end-of-the-world discourse has burst forth from the lunatic fringe into excited conversations, face-to-face, from the pulpit, on the Internet, and on late-night talk radio. This paper examines four major disaster scenarios for the class specificity of their constituencies, preoccupations, symbols, prescriptions, and villains, as an arena for the development of class consciousness.

I will discuss briefly the "end of the world as we know it" as a contrast set, then focus in on a vast, largely working-class discourse, the NWO or New World Order, an interlocking web of "conspiracy theories" with countless millions of adherents. Close analysis of message content demonstrates that each of these scenarios registers (if through a glass darkly) a strong analysis of particular class predicaments that, we can speculate, could remain otherwise unspoken in a dominant culture of class denial (Silverman 2007; Durrenberger and Doukas 2008). Together, I'll suggest that examination of the crash, collapse, and catastrophe scenarios of the early twenty-first century can tell us something useful about class "in itself," as Marxians say, and class *for* itself."

This distinction dates to *The Poverty of Philosophy* (1847). Proletarian status, Marx argues, arises from the bourgeoisie acting as a class "for itself," in its own interests. The proletariat started out as peasants with customary claim to land, as Marx tells it. Many would have preferred to stay that way. They became an industrial proletariat through the political domination of industrial capitalists and united to pursue their own interests in opposition to that domination.

> The combination of capital has created for this mass a common situation, common interests. This mass is thus already a class as against capital, but not yet for itself. In the struggle, of which we have noted only a few phases, this mass becomes united, and constitutes itself as a class for itself. (1847 [1999])

Like Durrenberger and Erem's "union consciousness," Marx's class for itself coalesces in, and can be identified by, a sense of "sides" in an oppositional relationship to capital (Durrenberger 1997, 2002). Although it is not a form of class consciousness that classic Marxist analysis predicted (and sought to shape), the NWO scenario, this paper suggests, promotes a sharpening working-class opposition to capital by exposing the abuses of an inaccessible, contemptuous "global elite"—perhaps in anticipation of struggle.

By *scenarios* I mean shared versions of what's going to happen in the near future, that affect how we plan and act in the present. Disaster scenarios are usually "underground" or "backstage" conversations, only rarely surfacing in the public sphere and major media. As a unit of analysis, each scenario represents a cluster of active conversations. Conversational threads stretch across class boundaries, but each scenario anchors to a particular class constituency and embeds particular class interests, because these scenarios project a future "we" must act on to survive.

The model of class-specific disaster scenarios sketched below allows for a "middle class" delimited by sufficient education in the vocabularies of the dominant culture ("formal" education) to decode and participate in conversations that use those vocabularies.[1] By setting the bar at educational attainment, with due respect for the material foundation required for educational attainment, this distinction outlines an *etic* "middle class" with an economic

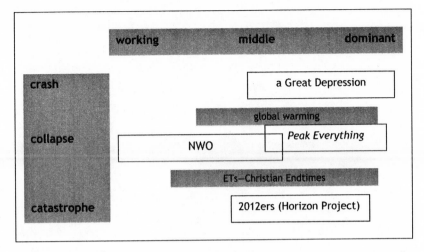

6.1. CLASS AND DISASTER SCENARIOS—A CONTRAST SET

base in largely *cultural* capital.[2] The asset of formal education can materially offset some of the insecurity associated with wage-earner status, and occasionally be parlayed into dominant-class status, but always at the risk of "falling" through the largely cultural middle-class/working-class border.

Emicly, ethnographically, the "middle class" label can be extended even to relatively uneducated ("formally"), underemployed, and unemployed people, and often is in conversations among the "blue-collar middle class" (in filmmaker Michael Moore's helpful phrase). The etic working class represented in this model, then, is basically the one proposed by sociologist Michael Zweig: people who labor (when they can) at the broad bottom of the job market, in nonsupervisory, insecure positions, about 62 percent of the workforce (2002).

A *crash* is disruptive of business as usual, but it is cyclical, a "correction" with a predictable end and a return to "normalcy." A *collapse* is more disruptive, with a less predictable or unpredictable end. A *catastrophe* is largely not survivable, except perhaps by a chosen or fortunate few. We will examine each of these scenarios in turn, with the exceptions of global warming, because it has breached its previous fringe status and entered mainstream public discourse, and the religious and extraterrestrial scenarios, for lack of ethnographic access.

At the dominant-class end of the spectrum are the relatively more visible scenarios of impending global depression and/or US dollar crash, with a primary constituency of people who wish to protect the value of accumulated capital, and Peak Oil, which stretches to include peak soil, peak water, and peak natural gas—in a nutshell, as movement intellectual Richard Heinberg put it, *Peak Everything* (2007). The social and economic collapse scenarios that draw on the facts of Peak Oil include some wealthy folk in their constituencies, but have their largest following in the educated but relatively capital-poor "middle class." Working-class scenarios (and more drastic versions of relatively elite scenarios) are further beneath the cultural surface, communicating today by way of "alternative media." In the early 1990s I was first clued into the New World Order (NWO) "conspiracy theory" by audio cassette, passed from hand to hand like the Ayatollah Khomeini's fiery speeches in revolutionary Iran. In the early years of the twenty-first century the NWO scenario has exploded onto the Internet.[3]

The 9/11 attacks have prompted some scholarly rethinking about so-called conspiracy theories. After 9/11, sociologist Ray Pratt observes, "everyone now knows [that] conspiracies are real"—we have all witnessed "secret treachery" in action (Pratt 2003:256, 260). No recent studies relegate "conspiracy theories" to the lunatic fringe of the society. Sociological or anthropological, studies of millennialism (Clarke 2000), "secular millennialism" (Heard 1999), "apocalyptic culture" (Quinby 1999; Wojcik 1997), and conspiracy theory (Fenster 1999; Stewart and Harding 1999) agree that we are looking at something that "permeates all levels of American society" (Wojcik 1997). Omnipresent in popular culture, anthropologists Stewart and Harding note, is a "deep worry that normality is not normal anymore" (1999:294).

None of these studies, however, deals systematically with class, except to speculate that uneducated and disaffected masses are drawn to "conspiracy theory" as a way to recapture their lost social agency (Stewart and Harding 1999; Pratt 2003; Fenster 1999). This is a cogent observation, particularly for working-class scenarios, but leaves much to be discovered in the *content* of these views. This paper seeks to advance the insights of other social researchers by analyzing the messages and class constituency of current disaster scenarios.

THE DATA

The data examined for this study come from two sources, ethnography and "alternative" media, namely, the Internet and late-night talk radio. Disaster discourse is not a fit topic for the nightly news. "If people knew the truth," a late-night talk radio guest opined, "they would probably pull their money out of the market" (Matt Savinar, *Coast to Coast AM* 11/2/07). Though elites may indeed be motivated to soft-pedal impending crises (see "Crash," below), alternative media, particularly the Internet, have hosted an explosion of disaster scenarios as the cost of Internet access has fallen. Ethnographic sources include many years of fieldwork in the deindustrialized Mohawk River Valley of New York and a year of participant observation with a Peak Oil activist group in Boulder, Colorado.

My interest in disaster scenarios began serendipitously in the process of ethnographic fieldwork in central New York in the early 1990s. One day a local activist passed me a cassette that a friend had passed to her the day before, with the urgent message that I *had to* listen to it and get it right back to her because she had promised it to someone else. The cassette had been recorded by another friend at a local evangelical church the previous weekend. It was a hair-raising secular sermon on the NWO or New World Order, also known as One-World Government. The speaker cited chapter and verse, not of scripture but of executive orders dating from the Nixon administration that amounted to, in the speaker's estimation, a plan for the declaration of martial law in the United States, soon.

This was news to me! The New World Order is a conspiracy theory, certainly, but it is also a visionary scenario of the coming totalitarian United States, when martial law will be declared, democracy crushed, and everyone bar-coded, disarmed, and enslaved. The cassette turned out to be an ethnographic Rosetta Stone, with which I could decode a range of references that I had not been able to understand or process because the scenario *only circulated in working-class venues.*

The use of mass-mediated data requires the additional analytical step of grounding media data in the conditions of their production (Ginsburg, Abu-Lughod, and Larkin 2003). The visible hand of profit seeking introduces a potential for "top-down" manipulation, or social control, as classic anthropological analysis of witchcraft, millennialism, and other cultic/occult phenomena have emphasized (Harris 1974). Clearly disaster sells ads, both on late-night radio and on the Internet, at the cost of an implicit taboo on overtly political speech. The medium constrains the message to nonpolitical speech or covertly political speech. At the same time, however, the low transaction costs of participation on the Web, late-night talk radio, and other alternative media materially allow for the possibility of "bottom-up" self-organization. The nonelite, *not* prime-time scenarios discussed in this paper, though they fill advertisers' pockets, do not necessarily further the project of elite social control. This paper focuses on ideological self-organization for the defense of class interests—arguably class acting *for* itself.

THE CRASH

The elite end of the spectrum is the least accessible to ethnographers (Nader 1972). Elite status buys privacy. While little direct knowledge is available, some can be inferred, for example, from websites that sell services to high-end investors. These typically offer teasers online but save their real advice for the expensive newsletters and "programs" that cyber guests might click into their virtual shopping carts. One web example can stand for several.

Many websites include graphs to communicate the cyclicality of the phenomenon. Officially, good investments and good fiscal policy could still result in a "soft landing" and swift return to normalcy. The dreaded "hard landing," though, appears to be the scenario on which many large investors are acting. The financial activity that has presumably followed the expensive advice has swelled global markets for precious metals and "dollar hedge funds," and spurred the dumping of dollars for euros and yen by international central banks, all consistent with a move by holders of dollar-denominated capital to salvage what they can of its value by getting out of dollars and into something more stable, before it's too late.

Hard or soft, crashes predictably end. They are survivable, though they necessarily leave a large fallout of losers. The message is: do not find yourself among them. Clearly if everyone rushed for liquidity at the same time, most would not find it in a heavily debt-leveraged financial system. A solution on the order of cashing out before the "common herd" perceives the crisis and makes a "run" on the banks could account for the impenetrable economistic jargon in which this example and many others are couched. The unintelligibility of this message to noninitiates is a social practice that enforces a thick class-cultural boundary. Add to this linguistic coding the further expense of gaining access to the details, and a picture emerges of

> ## Currency Majors Technical Analysis
>
> Mon, Oct 29 2007, 05:54 GMT
> **... If you want to receive alerts via email subscribe to the newsletter.**
> **European Session**
> **EUR/USD—Euro Dollar**
> 1,4421. EUR USD is in an uptrend supported by 1H exponential moving averages.
> The volatility is low. Bollinger bands are parallel and form the trend. ForexTrend
> 1H, 4H, daily (Mataf Trend Indicator) is in a bullish configuration. 1H, 4H ForexSto
> (Modified Stochastic) indicate a bullish pressure on EUR USD. The uptrend should
> continue on 1,4500 (80 pips) resistance. We won't take a position. The risk/reward
> ratio is too high to take a position.
>
> http://www.fxstreet.com/technical/analysis-reports/currency-majors-technical-analysis/2007-10-29.html

6.2. Protecting the Value of Accumulated Capital

insider discourse, sealed off against mass scrutiny. The villain of the piece is
the masses, the "mob."

CATASTROPHE—THE 2012ERS

Not mentioned in the recent studies with which I am familiar are the
catastrophic disaster scenarios that converge on ancient Maya calendrical
prophesies. These prophesies (insofar as anyone has really decoded them)
place the end of the world as we know it in the year 2012, the point at
which all thirteen or so nested cycles of Maya time intersect, and end. For
most (not all) 2012ers "the end" will be a great "period of cleansing" that
many will not survive, catastrophic "changes to earth," and a rebirth or
"greater evolution" of humankind (psychic and Doctor of Divinity Evelyn
Paglini, *Coast to Coast AM* 10/26/07). 2012ers mingle in New Age venues,
actual and virtual, an educated middle-class constituency with a sprinkling
of wealthy folk.

One such cosmic catastrophe scenario is the Horizon Project, directed
by a team of engineers who seek to merge science and ancient prophesy,
all available on DVD from their website (http://www.thehorizonproject.
com). Like other 2012 scenarios it is wrapped in the trappings of hard science, complete with brilliant artists' renderings of intergalactic space and
bold-printed text bristling with PhDs.

Our solar system is quickly approaching what scientific research
and ancient records refer to as "The Dark Rift" or "The Galactic
Plain". This will result in increased gravitational influences
upon our solar system; causing global devastation and loss of
life on Earth . . .

http://archive.coasttocoastam.com/gen/page1856.html?theme=light

6.3. THE HORIZON PROJECT

According to these researchers, when the solar system intersects the
Galactic Plane, a *theoretical* plane that bisects our disc-shaped galaxy, predicted increases in gravity and magnetism will flip the earth around in its
inclination to the sun, causing oceans to slosh over mountains as new polar
caps freeze up and a new equator bulges out. When will that happen? 2012.

For most people, this cosmic catastrophe will not be survivable. (Nevertheless, you can buy survival gear on some 2012er websites.) This is a sci-fi
or *scientistic* millennialism without solution or deliverance. Horizon Project
theorists envision an end-of-the-world scenario of such cosmic proportions
that human effort, other than possibly prayer and purification, is futile.
Which part of earth bulges up and which part sinks beneath the waves cannot be predicted. A mass die-off is certain, though a few may live to start
anew. Individuals cannot guarantee their own survival.

2012 scenarios may incorporate Peak Oil and global warming into the
cosmic catastrophes that are their distinctive feature. (Some Peak Oilers
more or less surreptitiously share the kabalistic timetable.) Interestingly,
there is no blame in the 2012er scenario. The cause of the problem is vast
cosmic processes, beyond human comprehension or influence. Horizon
Project cofounder Brent Miller assured the audience of a hugely popular
late-night talk radio show that global warming had nothing to do with
human activity (*Coast to Coast AM* 1/29/07).

COLLAPSE—PEAK OIL

In the Peak Oil scenarios, on the other hand, the excesses of human greed
and consumerism are clearly to blame for the impending collapse. The

Peak Oil discourse dates from the 1950s and the calculations of respected Houston oil geologist M. King Hubbert for the "curve" of oil reserve depletion and the "peak" of US oil production. Production "peaks" when half the oil in a deposit is, as they say in the industry, "recovered" (note the implicit entitlement)—the more oil pumped out, the less pressure in the deposit and, thus, the more pressure needs to be applied mechanically, capital intensively, to extract the remaining oil. At some point recovery becomes impractical, when the energy *in* is equal to or greater than the energy *out*. Some reserves may never be "recovered." The halfway point, then, is an index of steeply climbing "recovery" costs. The US hit peak in 1970, exactly as Hubbert predicted. World oil production, some data suggest, may have peaked in 2006 (http://www.richardheinberg.com/museletter/185). Peak Oil arguments take some advanced education to follow and so have been relatively elite in constituency.[4]

What will happen as the predicted steep rise in the price per barrel of oil hits the gas pumps, furnaces, and stoves of North America? Transportation costs will soar, imports will become unavailable or available only to the wealthy few, and *suburbs will become unlivable*—the topic of many books and documentaries available on Peak Oil websites. Perhaps the largest of these is the Post-Carbon Institute, supporting a large network of local affiliate groups (http://www.postcarbon.org).

The *End of Suburbia* (Greene 2004) preoccupation points, I believe, to the class constituency of this scenario. The Post-Carbon group members I work with are surburbanites or former suburb dwellers, professionals and children of professionals. Many surely share elite interest in protecting the value of their capital, but the solution they propose as activists is a *community* solution, a radical deglobalization and the construction or reconstruction of thriving local economies.

A vibrant Relocalization Network has 170 or so affiliates in North America and globally that sponsor film series, lectures, and Buy Local campaigns, forging partnerships with local governments and chambers of commerce and experimenting with innovative forms of property.[5] Peak Oil is survivable by the *connected*, the prepared, the smart, and the hard working, though a mass "die-off" is part of some Peak Oil scenarios (e.g., http://dieoff.org). Peak Oil scenarios provide "enough blame to go around," but it is directed toward depersonalized villains, the moral weakness of humankind and the inherent limitations of Nature.

The "Mark" of the Beast (666):

6.4. "HUMAN BRANDING."

(Image from http://religion-cults.com/ Secret/Freemasonry/newworld.gif)

Capacitor   Micro Chip

Smart Card Reading

Antenna Coil   Glass Tube

"Micro Chip": Injected under the skin. Size: 1/20 of a grain of rice. Holds 20,000 pages.

COLLAPSE—THE NWO

"The New World Order," anthropologists Stewart and Harding observe, "has become a kind of apocalyptic lingua franca" that crosses the secular/ religious boundary (1999:295). Also running under the banner of One-World Government, the NWO scenario overlaps the End Times scenario of evangelical Christianity. Both secular and religious versions may date to the same root, "isolationist" opposition to the United Nations (and possibly the League of Nations before it) as combinations of the rich to oppress "the common man," a continuing conversation.[6] Christian "dominionist"[7] leader Pat Robertson titled a 1991 book *The New World Order*, and the apocalyptic Left Behind Book Series,[8] in which the Anti-Christ becomes secretary-general of the United Nations, features many NWO staples, including what I think of as the signature preoccupation of the discourse, mandatory identification systems.

On the cassette I heard in the field, the speaker was passionately opposed to the idea of a national identity card, or worse, a barcode tattooed on the forehead, arm, hand, or neck, which he saw as the first step down the slippery slope to tyranny. Barcoding in this scenario is mandatory. Showing your tattoo would be the only way to access the *paperless* money (another signature preoccupation) that people would need to purchase all the necessities of life. In the early years of the twenty-first century, the barcode preoccupation was superseded by a more grisly one, mandatory implantation *in the body* of RFID (radio frequency ID) chips, or "tags"—spychips.com calls it "human branding" (see also nocard.org, softwar.net).

Last year, late at night, I was driving cross-country when I heard the unmistakable strains of NWO on AM talk radio. It was a call-in show with a large audience of truckers and security guards, workers on the graveyard shift, and other insomniacs: *Coast to Coast AM*.[9] The show was created in the 1980s by working-class culture hero Art Bell, who for years ran the whole thing out of his trailer in Pahrump, Nevada. Art provided a forum for NWO theorists, psychics with stock tips, prophets, remote-viewers, cryptobiologists, UFO theorists, and fringe academics. Broadcast in every time zone, every night from 10 PM to 2 AM (Pacific Time), *Coast*, as fans affectionately call it, is now "the most listened to talk show in the world," with a loyal nightly audience of some 16 million people (*Coast* 10/27/07) and a vast echo chamber of blogs and spinoff websites.

I recognized the NWO discourse by the signature opposition to a national identification system. The show has hosted many discussions on the topic of RFID technology and the threat to freedom. According to *Coast* guests, Katherine Albrecht (a PhD candidate in Education) and Liz McIntyre (a former bank examiner), authors of *Spychips: How Major Corporations and Government Plan to Track Your Every Move with RFID* (2006), there are relatively benign applications of RFID technology. Thousands of pet owners have had RFID tags implanted in their four-legged friends, just as RFIDs are now embedded in merchandise of all kinds to simplify inventory taking (*Coast* 10/1/05).

But these are just the beginning, Albrecht and McIntyre argued. They know because they studied US Patent Office applications. They say IBM just patented a device to link customer identities at the checkout counter with merchandise RFIDs in a massive new database, for the purposes of personally targeted marketing. Of course, Albrecht and McIntyre pointed out, all this information can be sold and "data mined" by others for more nefarious purposes. IBM, Albrecht quipped, stands for "I Been Monitored" (*Coast* 10/1/05).

The deeper concern is with the potential implantation of RFID tags in human beings. The authors' homepage features a photo of a California protest against Verichip, an RFID tag the size of a grain of rice, that has already been experimentally implanted, for medical reasons, in soldiers and Alzheimer's patients. Gruesomely, Albrecht and McIntyre found patent applications for a new device that would be implanted deep inside the *organs* of the human body, where it could not be removed. "Human beings essentially become inventory themselves!" Albrecht exclaimed to the *Coast* audience (10/1/05).

On another show Art's guest was Ross Mitchell, a TV news host at the Reno, Nevada, ABC network affiliate. New RFID tags are as small as a piece of dirt, he reported, and no wider than a hair. The military calls it "smart dust," and it has already been used, he said, to capture suspected terrorists. It can be embedded in food or just sprinkled on chairs or on the ground to be picked up on the targets' clothing and shoes. The new technology allows *Them* to go much further than before, Mitchell asserted. Tags can be imbedded in money and credit cards, for example, so retailers would "know how much cash you got in your pocket when you walked into the store" (*Coast* 7/17/06).

Who is *Them*? Who would want to electronically ID every citizen and bring about a One-World Government? "The global elites," of course. The Council on Foreign Relations, the Tri-Lateral Commission, the secretive Bilderberg Group,[10] the Freemasons, all fall under the suspicion of being what many call, ironically, "Illuminati," the mysterious puppeteers who pull the strings of global politics and economics. At the top of this global elite, the ultimate authority and beneficiary—and here today's NWO theorists agree with the consensus of my 1990s fieldwork—are bankers or financiers, euphemistic terms, I would suggest, for the stigmatized "capitalists." Figure 6.5, one of many such diagrams on the Internet, illustrates the proposed hierarchy of the New World Order.

What "the elites" want is nothing less than world domination, according to Texas talk radio host and filmmaker Alex Jones. *They* said in the 1950s, according to Jones's research, that *They* were going to "create a European Union first, *by stealth*" through "trade deals and military agreements." Next will come a North American union, an Asian Union, and an African Union. Then *They* will merge these into a single One-World Government. *They* plan to do it by fanning people's fears, creating artificial scarcities (including Peak Oil) and playing people off each other (Alex Jones, *Coast* 10/27/07).

The current state of the art in NWO theory (at the time of this writing) is probably Jones's documentary film, *Endgame: Blueprint for Global Enslavement* (2007). In it he documents outrage after elite outrage, from warfare for profit and mass sterilizations to the inclusion of mercury in vaccines

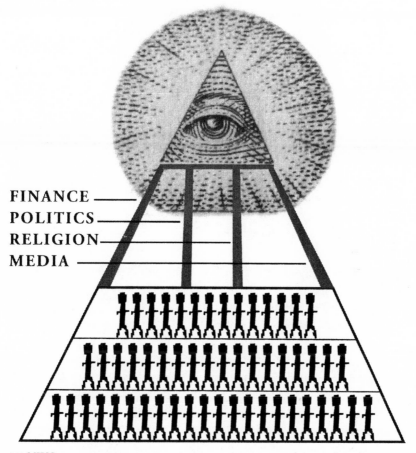

FINANCE
POLITICS
RELIGION
MEDIA

6.5. NWO GLOBAL HIERARCHY. *(Image from http://openyoureyes.web1000.com/web_images/ Illuminati%20Power%20Structure.jpg)*

and viruses in GMO crops—to dumb down and sicken what Jones calls, in one breath, "the middle class," and in the next, "the mass."

Why? Because *They* mean to exterminate us.

Endgame tracks the New World Order concept to a 1900 essay by H. G. Wells, and to Wells's circle of eugenics enthusiasts, including his lover Margaret Sanger and their friend Julian Huxley, Aldous's brother, both sons of T. H. Huxley, cofounder with Francis Galton of the eugenics movement. *They* believe, according to Jones, that *We* are their evolutionary inferiors—*They* say they want to reduce world population by 80 percent (*Coast* 10/27/07)!

Jones's major research for *Endgame* was indeed extensive, finding its way to the public and private documents of the circle around Francis Galton and the Huxleys, and the vast network of organizations and celebrities spawned by the eugenics movement. He has gone back to the primary documents—his audiences are referred to websites where every document he cites is posted or linked to. Jones may leap to connections a professional researcher would not but, *from the perspective of working-class social location*, his findings have a lot of explanatory value for those who must account for the unsettling experience of radical downward mobility.

Jones was a wildly popular guest on *Coast to Coast AM*, promoting *Endgame* shortly after its October 2007 release, his gravelly voice rising in the cadences of a Southern preacher as he recited the liturgy of elite abuses. The evening's host, Ian Punnet, took a skeptical stance. If *They* want to exterminate us and *they* have so much power, he asked Jones, what's holding them back?

They say, Jones replied, that "once they've got that World Government" in place, population control measures will accelerate. *They*'ll make it sound good, he added—they'll say it's all about "balance" and "saving the earth," but it's really "a rationale to exterminate and enslave" (*Coast* 10/27/07).

How does it make sense to exterminate your slaves? Punnet pressed. *They* think, Jones responded, that the world is *"overpopulated"*—*They* don't need that many slaves—everybody who's gone to college, Jones added, has been taught that the world is suffering from a "population crisis" (*Coast* 10/27/07).

"Eugenics is really a war against the middle class," Jones told the *Coast* audience. This "middle class" is the emic one most US citizens claim, but much of Jones's audience, by self-identification and other markers, is the etic working class. Jones only rarely uses class terms, though, preferring heroic descriptors like "the free, dynamic human spirit" (*Coast* 10/27/07) and "the free peoples of the planet" for his audience (infowars.com).

Jones's NWO pitch is antiracist.[11] "Type 'Margaret Sanger blacks' into Google," he advised his *Coast* audience, and you'll find copies of letters in which Sanger calls African Americans "subhuman weeds" and worse (*Coast* 10/27/07). Hitler admired Sanger as she did him, Jones said, but after the war the connection proved embarrassing, and the eugenics movement went underground—not before, Jones claims, the forced sterilization of at least 400,000 "undesirables" in the United States alone. And now, he observed ominously, "these Planned Parenthoods are there in every Hispanic community" (*Coast* 10/27/07).

In the face of *class* extermination, by Jones's logic, all races are linked in a vast nonelite *We*. When the host opened the lines for the call-in segment, multiracial listeners called in to support Jones and the documentary. A Hispanic woman asked Jones with touching sincerity, "What can I do?" Educate yourself, Jones advised, and tell your friends.

What kinds of arms and ammo would Jones recommend? a Texan caller asked. *"The last thing you want to do is get physically violent!"* Jones responded forcefully, because *They* have all the firepower. Jones favors nonviolent resistance, he said, "like Mahatma Gandhi" (*Coast* 10/27/07).

Host Ian Punnet asked Jones what he thought of a recent news story about "evolutionary theorist" Dr. Oliver Curry (a research associate at the London School of Economics) who theorized that the human race would split in two by about the year 3000, into a numerically small, tall, "fair-skinned" elite and a numerically larger, short, "unattractive" worker class that looks like "dwarf goblins."[12] *"The elite already see us as dwarf goblins!"* Jones exclaimed (*Coast* 10/27/07).

Taken together, the pervasive and potent message of *Endgame* is about the contempt of "the elites" for the vast nonelite *Us*. Don't be duped, don't believe them, don't follow them, don't feel any loyalty to them. *They betrayed us*. They *used* us. They are cheating us. At a moral level, the NWO limits personal responsibility for the decades-long epidemic of downward mobility, and appropriately so.

The subtitle of Jones's film, *Blueprint for Global Enslavement*, marks a deeper fear, of being reduced to having nothing, losing the capacity to meet even the most basic needs, and so being enslaved. Identity systems, RFID and barcodes—"human branding" (*Coast* 10/1/05)—symbolize the social status of another's *property*. At the bottom of the economic system, especially for the millions of "redundant workers," slavery, as low as you can go on the scales of dignity and respect, may feel hauntingly near.

Linking bankers and remnant aristocrats, the NWO "global elites" embody a long history of parasitic rulers, so resistance to the NWO becomes the next episode in a long heroic struggle for "liberty." The villains of the NWO scenario are a contemptible few who think they're better than the *We* to whom NWO theorists appeal—they stand over *Us* with arbitrary, life-and-death power, have subverted American democracy to get that power, and are planning to exterminate us! NWO adherents stand opposed to a capital-ist elite, as Marx suggested a working class *for itself* would.

Was the class consciousness of the NWO scenario the product of struggle with capital, as Marx said it would be? Arguably, yes, the long failed struggle against NAFTA and deindustrialization more broadly. NAFTA and the large popular protests against it were the historical context of the fiery NWO sermon that initiated me into the discourse. The labor movement fought deindustrialization for decades, facing arrogant, disloyal dismissal from management strategists bound for the Third World and an even less enfranchised workforce. This may qualify as the kind of struggle with capi-tal that can unite a class in the pursuit of its own interests.

If not armed rebellion, of what does resisting the NWO consist? At this point, as far as I am aware, of speaking out, spreading the word, and *considering options* for civil disobedience. Under consideration in NWO media channels (at this writing) are ways to resist being "chipped" (i.e., car-rying or being implanted with an RFID)—ideally with a camera crew film-ing the whole thing[13]—and ways to fight the implementation of the North American Union, as it is manifesting in the construction of a new (priva-tized) "NAFTA highway" across the United States from Mexico to Canada. The NWO has developed a rhetoric of class opposition, a sense of "sides," but not yet, evidently, organization or a plan of action for itself.

CONCLUSIONS

Through the prism of disaster scenarios, the social production of class con-sciousness can be seen in each class location, as participants reckon with the challenging times they foresee. Classes, at least class fractions, are promot-ing class solidarity and, with the possible exception of the 2012er catastroph-ists, protecting class interests:

- dominant-class scenarios (as far as they are visible) envision the loss of accumulated capital, the basis of class dominance, and prescribe ways to quietly exchange dollar-denominated capital for more stable forms of wealth.

- middle-class scenarios bemoan the excesses of globalization and suburban sprawl, and prescribe the construction or reconstruction of functional local economies.

	working	middle	dominant
future	fascism, enslavement, "depopulation"	excesses of globalization come home to roost	declining capital value
solutions	educate yourself and your friends— resist!	relocalize— disengage from globalization	save it before it's too late
villains	*global elites*	*the cosmos*	*"the mob"/mass*

6.6. DISASTER SCENARIOS AND THE BLAME-GAME

- working-class scenarios envision further looming enslavement and promote antielite solidarity, prescribing disengagement from the thrall of elite lies, and civil disobedience to resist elite impositions.

Adding the *blame-game* dimension—who plays the villain—to the model outlines a landscape of class polarization that may represent a social process of mobilizing class solidarity through mutual exclusivity. For the dominant class, the masses, the "common herd" are the villains who could stampede and ruin their plans. The working class blames "the elites" (the dominant class). A person must be either one or the other, not both. Intriguingly, both middle-class scenarios examined in this paper duck the blame-game entirely, positing a scientistic causality of cosmic coincidence, and opting out of the mutual antagonism of capital and labor. Working class and dominant class blame each other. The "middle," ever elusive, dodges controversy, perhaps politically disengaged, or perhaps, as a two-class model could imply, in fact taking one or the other side.

This is an important question for future research, one that could contribute to longstanding discussion in the social sciences about the nature of class, and particularly about the ontological status of the so-called middle class. Following Durrenberger's lead (Durrenberger and Doukas 2008), it may be possible to quantify middle-class political "neutrality" and/or identification with one or another of the two classes that, empirically, face off in mutual opposition.

The New World Order is, as analysts suggest (above), about disenfranchised people trying to recapture lost social agency. But the working-class constituency for the NWO and related "conspiracy theories" is not *un*educated—it is *self*-educated. Participants make a keen critical analysis of their predicament, within a particular shared "American" vocabulary.

More importantly, *are they* recapturing social agency? Perhaps, if agency is reflected in soaring numbers of participants. The New World Order is a "backstage," even prophetic conversation to which late-night radio and web media are ideally suited. Millions can tune in and share their fears and dreams in virtual community, *anonymously*. How, indeed whether, this far-flung, media-dependent network could move from "virtual" (vicarious?) participation to an actual "resistance" of organization and action is unclear.

Many contributors to this volume have described a measure of social breakdown across the postindustrialized world. Pockets of prosperity are shrinking, and for increasing numbers of people it is difficult to make a bare living in the scorched postindustrialized landscape. This is the kind of context in which social analysts might predict the emergence of crash, collapse, and catastrophe scenarios. The North American data examined for this study suggest that end-of-the-world-as-we-know-it scenarios, encoded in whatever shared vocabularies are available, are likely to embed sharpening cross-class antagonisms, in view of a broadly anticipated near future of increasing scarcity.

NOTES

1. This view is indebted to Ehrenreich (1990) who argues cogently that education is the primary hurdle to be leapt in strategies for the reproduction of middle-class status across generations.

2. My use of the Bourdieu-based social/cultural *capital* metaphor relies on an unconventional but classically Adam Smithian model of capital, probably grounded in then-familiar images of seed corn, not money. Also called "stock," it is the part of this year's production that is not consumed but applied toward next year's production (Smith 1982[1776]). Thus social capital and cultural capital can be seen as "stock" in goodwill and useful knowledge, the fruit of prior social and cultural work.

3. An October 2011 Google search on "New World Order" produced 195 million hits.

4. Peak Oil arguments and their rejection could once have marked a middle class/working class cultural border, with adherents of the NWO scenario rejecting

Peak Oil arguments as yet another "artificial scarcity" of the elites, a position now under reconsideration.

5. Notably Community Supported Agriculture (CSAs), which fund farmers' inputs with the purchase of "shares" in the harvest, and Community Land Trusts (CLTs), which hold affordable housing developments off the real estate market.

6. See, for example, screwtheun.blogspot.com and contenderministries.org.

7. Chris Hedges labels the leadership of the Christian Right as "dominionist" from the Old Testament reference to God giving Man "dominion over all creation" (2006:10).

8. This series of evangelical Christian apocalyptic novels by Tim LaHaye and Jerry B. Jenkins, first published by Tyndale House Publishers in 1995, has now swelled to sixteen titles (http://www.leftbehind.com/, accessed 12/10/07).

9. *Coast to Coast AM* is a property of Premier Networks, a little California company that got big on the popularity of neocon Rush Limbaugh and was acquired by Clear Channel in 1999 (http://www.premiereradio.com/pages/corporate/about.html, accessed 12/10/07).

10. A small (120–130), secretive organization of monarchs and former monarchs, corporate brass, and their bankers that has met annually since the mid-1950s.

11. NWO discourse does harbor racist and anti-Semitic fringes (see, e.g., http://www.natall.com/free-speech/fs9612a.html). It is possible that these sentiments were once more central than they are today.

12. More information about this disturbing story, and Punnet's witty rejoinder, can be found on his blog, http://www.fm1071.com/lol/user/FM107_Ian/blogs (accessed 11/20/07)

13. YouTube, the huge Internet video forum, had a long clip of Alex Jones at the Texas Motor Vehicle Department, being taken off to jail for refusing to be thumb-printed for his drivers license, with multiple video cameras filming the confrontation (http://video.google.com/videoplay?docid=-6423510709336035849&q=%22Alex+Jones%22&total=8260&start=0&num=10&so=0&type=search&plindex=6). This link is currently dead.

REFERENCES CITED

Beck, Ulrich. 1992. *Risk Society: Towards a New Modernity.* New Delhi: Sage.

Clarke, Lee. 2000. "Review: The End of the World as We Might Know It." *Sociological Forum* 15(3): 553–561.

Durrenberger, E. Paul. 1997. "That'll Teach You: Cognition and Practice in a Union Local." *Human Organization* 56(4): 388–392.

———. 2002. "Structure, Thought, and Action: Stewards in Chicago Union Locals." *American Anthropologist* 104(1): 93–105.

Durrenberger, E. Paul, and Dimitra Doukas. 2008. "Gospel of Wealth, Gospel of Work: Hegemony in the U.S. Working Class." *American Anthropologist* 110(2): 214–224.

Ehrenreich, Barbara. 1990. *Fear of Falling: The Inner Life of the Middle Class*. New York: Harper Perennial.

Fenster, Mark. 1999. *Conspiracy Theories: Secrecy and Power in American Culture*. Minneapolis: University of Minnesota Press.

Ginsburg, Faye D., Lila Abu-Lughod, and Brian Larkin. 2003. "Introduction." In *Media Worlds: Anthropology on a New Terrain*. Berkeley: University of California Press.

Greene, Gregory. 2004. *The End of Suburbia: Oil Depletion and the Collapse of The American Dream*. Documentary Film.

Harris, Marvin. 1974. *Cows, Pigs, Wars, and Witches: The Riddles of Culture*. New York: Vintage Books.

Heard, Alex. 1999. *Apocalypse Pretty Soon: Travels in End-Time America*. New York: W. W. Norton.

Hedges, Chris. 2006. *American Fascists: The Christian Right and the War on America*. New York: Free Press.

Heinberg, Richard. 2007. *Peak Everything: Waking Up to the Century of Declines*. Gabriola Island, BC: New Society Publishers.

Marx, Karl. 1955 [1847]. *The Poverty of Philosophy*. Moscow: Progress Publishers.

Nader, Laura. 1972. "Up the Anthropologist—Perspectives Gained from Studying Up." In *Reinventing Anthropology*, edited by Dell H. Hymes, 284–311. New York: Pantheon Books.

Pratt, Ray. 2003. "Review: Theorizing Conspiracy." *Theory and Society* 32(2): 255–271.

Quinby, Lee. 1999. "Virile-Reality: From Armageddon to Viagra." *Signs* 24(4): 1079–1087.

Silverman, Sydel. 2007. "American Anthropology in the Middle Decades: A View from Hollywood." *American Anthropologist* 109(3): 519–528.

Smith, Adam. 1982 [1776]. *The Wealth of Nations*. Books I–III. Edited by Andrew Skinner. Harmondsworth, UK: Penguin Books.

Stewart, Kathleen, and Susan Harding. 1999. "Bad Endings: American Apocalypsis." *Annual Review of Anthropology* 28: 285–310.

Wojcik, Daniel. 1997. *The End of the World as We Know It: Faith, Fatalism, and Apocalypse in America*. New York: New York University Press.

Zweig, Michael. 2002. *The Working Class Majority: America's Best Kept Secret*. Ithaca, NY: ILR Press.

Class and Consciousness

The American Farmer's Daughter

B A R B A R A   J .   D I L L Y

INTRODUCTION

The current focus of empirical analysis of class and class consciousness on the intersecting processes of capitalist relations, historically constituted regional frameworks, and the contexts of lived experiences and understandings (Adams and Gorton 2006; Durrenberger and Erem 1997; Heyman 2007) provides a fruitful framework for examining conceptions of class consciousness for young farm women in American agriculture. Diverse regional commodity markets and transnational dynamics intersect with race, religion, ethnicity, immigration status, and the cultural values that defined gendered divisions of farm family labor to circumscribe young farm women's social and economic realities as well as consciousness of their ability to negotiate opportunities.

Capitalist social systems and economic structures reflect ideologies and practices of inequality that enabled capital to exploit the labor of daughters of farmers in the expansion of American agricultural production for national and global markets. Young farm girls provided a flexible labor force that was essential to the expansion of the frontier, rural economies, and global markets. It can further be argued that their labor was historically more flexible than that of any other farm family member. The daughters of farmers contributed to child care and care of the elderly, sick, or infirm; engaged in household labor; and participated in a highly variable range of cottage craft industries, gardening, livestock care, food production, processing, and marketing. They typically participated in these activities from the age of five and continued with these roles until they married or moved away from the family, or, in some cases, their entire lives.

The daughters of farmers also worked in the fields when necessary and away from home as wage laborers, domestics, or teachers, sending their earnings back to their families. Yet, the cheap, flexible, and often skilled labor of farm daughters was not recognized as such because the romance of the yeoman family farm with its sacred values of honest labor, intimate kinship relations, and rural community self-sufficiency obscured oppressive labor practices and class realities in American agriculture. The yeoman family farm labor system, however, was just one mode of production in a hierarchical labor class structure in American agricultural history.

This paper examines class consciousness and agency from the diverse perspectives of the daughters of American farmers who participated in a variety of production systems through several historical periods to understand the gendered, cultural, regional, and historical contexts that accompanied the transformation of agricultural production from household to commercial modes. It examines the pre–Revolutionary War colonial period, the Federalist period, the Frontier period of the early nineteenth century, the Civil War period, the Populist era, the Depression/New Deal era, and the post-WWII Industrial era. Regional, racial, and ethnic perspectives, although by no means exhaustive, are also examined to identify some of the intersecting conditions of translocal power that shaped economic realities and class identities for diverse groups of people. This paper also supports Deborah Fink's observation that major trends in agricultural demographics point to the effects of class realities and conflict between capitalists, family farmers, and hired farm laborers (1992: 49).

While there is little systematic scholarship that explores how farmers' daughters actually experienced class consciousness and how they incorporated it into their self-identities (Little and Austin 1996:102), this study argues that daughters of farmers exhibited both class consciousness and class agency as they either resisted or augmented the transition from household production to commercial production through their labor roles. And while few would have articulated transnational capitalism and class relations in their consciousness of their circumstances, they clearly understood their own local realities in terms of class.[1] They also certainly understood their realities in terms of gender. Examination of the class realities of farmers' daughters furthers, then, a more sensitive interpretation of the class and gendered effects of farm policies. It identifies those farm policies that strengthened consciousness of class distinction for various groups of farmers, and hence, their daughters, while agreeing with Deborah Fink's argument (1992:10) that agrarian ideologies and farm policies did not recognize gender or class inequalities.

THEORY AND METHODS

Existing oral histories and ethnographic data contributed by historians and anthropologists comprise a large literature base from which to examine the class experiences and consciousness of farmers' daughters. The literature reveals a highly culturally diverse and class-stratified rural America, beginning with the colonial period that becomes increasingly less diverse as agriculture is transformed from household to industrial systems of production. In this study, objective measures of class focus on structural economic inequalities for household or community units such as differential access to land, credit, and market opportunities. Further objective measures of class for young women within household and community units include traditional gendered division of farm and off-farm labor roles and the personal agency to consciously shape control over sexuality, marriage, and educational and social opportunities. The analytic framework of the paper is based on informal comparisons of various historical periods to examine intersecting class processes as changes occurred in the farm and off-farm labor roles for daughters of farmers in the expansion of the global market for agricultural products. While these comparisons are systematic, they are by no means exhaustive.

While it is certainly the case that farm sons as well as daughters could often choose between off-farm wage labor strategies as well as familial and community economic labor roles to negotiate class status, the agency of daughters reveals a much more complex dynamic between class, race, religion, immigration status, and gender as intersecting systems of inequality in American agriculture. Each of these systems intersected in complex and changing contexts in the processes by which farmers' daughters came to understand and negotiate class consciousness in the transformation of local and regional agri-economies into a global commercial economic system.

In each historical period, the class status of the daughters of farmers is first examined from the perspective of their fathers in terms of capital relations. The data show how the class status of the fathers intersects with cultural traditions that define the social status of daughters within the family and the community. While patriarchal authority was initially a significant source of subordination for many young farm women within the family production system, many farmers' daughters realized upward economic and social mobility through the material success of their fathers as land values increased and markets expanded. As the market gradually diminished, patriarchal authority over household production and the labor value of daughters was restructured in terms of the market, offering other opportunities for upward mobility for some farm daughters. The class consciousness of farmers' daughters reflected these realities as well as the range of opportunities available to them by expanding market contexts in the regions in which they lived. This study identifies the conditions under which wage labor did not always offer greater opportunities for upward class mobility to the daughters of farmers. The historical relationship of farmers' daughters to labor roles indicates the class consequences to the social organization of agricultural labor as the market intruded on every aspect of farm family production and consumption.

THE COLONIAL PERIOD

For all of its benefits to religious sects pursuing utopian agendas, colonial agricultural production was developed on and institutionalized a wide range of labor roles and relationships that restricted freedom and opportunity for large numbers of the population based on gender, race, ethnicity, and regional contexts. From its beginning, the colonial agricultural system was part of a global economic system as well as regional, gendered, class, and racial systems.

Slavery and indentured servitude were not only legal, but were the predominant sources of labor for the propertied laborer and planter classes.

These systems further exploited the daughters of even the freed laborers in these systems, as English Common Law defined their labor as the property of their fathers and typically prohibited them from rights to their own property. Further, ideologies of equality within religious utopian communities did not always translate to equal opportunities and freedom for women, restricting them to the traditions of the patriarchy that were also upheld by English Common Law.

The daughters of colonial farmers did experience a more lenient attitude of laws regarding their sexuality, marriage, and labor and property rights in the colonies than was the case in England because there was a relative shortage of women in many areas of the colonies, particularly frontier regions. (Lerner 1969:8). Young women had relatively more social freedom and were held in greater esteem due to their economic contributions and social necessity (8, 12). Especially within religious sects, farmers' daughters acquired a wide range of occupational skills as apprentices necessary to self-sufficient farming households and communities. For them, labor was both a sacred and a civic duty. Still, they did not play determining roles in the social system, participating as dependent family members and not as individuals; their class status reflected that of the men in their families (8).

Despite the relative egalitarian status of European colonial women compared to men, there was a high level of labor exploitation of other racial and ethnic daughters of farmers in American agricultural history. The status of daughters of Native American farmers, who were frequently dispossessed of their land, was lowered from a traditional egalitarian status after European contact. Native women were typically given political status within their tribe to make decisions regarding marriage, divorce, sex, residence, and warfare as well as economic power to distribute agricultural production (Farnham 1997). This ended when Europeans imposed patriarchal authority over Native women, through English Common Law that defined labor rights, religious values that restricted female sexuality, and through cultural change that identified Native men as heads of farming households. Young native farm girls could be hired by European immigrants as cheaply as if they were slaves, and they were treated as such (Street 2004:108).

The emerging American cultural expectations of the relationship between class and women's roles in the farm family were derived from the aristocratic English cultural norms that placed women in the house and not in the fields as early as the seventeenth century (Garkovich and Bokemeier

1988:218). This varied from the peasant experience of most European immigrant women, who were accustomed to field work. Attracted by reports of opportunities to engage in domestic farm labor, female Europeans who immigrated to American during this period hoped to improve their class status by not engaging in fieldwork. This was not always the case, however, for many indentured female laborers worked as field hands, thereby restricting their opportunities to marry into a higher class.

The status of field laborer was also a problem for African-American farm daughters. The labor rights of daughters of African field hands on large plantations were not subordinated by their fathers, but through the institutions of slavery that relegated young African women to the lowest class of farm-working women because they not only worked in the fields along with men but had no rights over marriage choices or their sexuality. Daughters of the planter class, however, enjoyed the highest class as the daughters of large land-holding elites who did not work at all except to supervise their household slaves.

Class consciousness for the daughters of farmers in the colonial period was based primarily on the relations of their race, culture, religion, and immigration status to the dominant social and political groups. This defined their traditional labor roles within their family and community, their sexuality, their marriage opportunities, their relationship to land, and market opportunities for their production. Their role in determining their status was severely limited by these local and transnational processes.

FEDERALIST ERA

After the Revolutionary War, most Americans in the Northern colonies lived in self-sufficient farming neighborhoods where they engaged in a wide range of production of agricultural products and crafts. The daughters of farmers were essential to these diverse production systems. They traded surplus locally and internationally for cloth and other manufactured goods. Plantations in the South were more dependent on international trade because they grew cash crops like rice, indigo, and tobacco. A large number of Northeastern seaport merchants were also dependent on this trade. One of the new American government's first priorities was the protection of the international trade economy based on the export of agricultural products. Other priorities were to establish a system of federal courts to defend the

Constitution and the payment of war debts through taxation. The new government established excise taxes on coffee, tea, wine, and spirits (namely, whiskey). In 1789, a tariff was passed on imports.

These policies were enacted by Secretary of Treasury Alexander Hamilton who sought to centralize the political and economic power of the national government to establish international credit and promote commercial interests. He set up a national bank and rewarded private corporations for investing in the bank. Hamilton and other Federalists sought to preserve trading relationships with Britain and to expand the government bureaucracy to collect taxes. These actions created a class conflict between independent, community-oriented New England farmers and merchants. Farmers were asked to pay taxes to repay the war debt, which was owed to the merchants and other business interests. Because the national economy was depressed, farmers had to go into debt to pay their taxes. When they could not pay, they were taken to debtor's courts and charged legal fees. Some were even sent to prison.

In 1786–1787, Shay's Rebellion in Massachusetts was a farmer-led rebellion in the defense of liberty. Farmers, fearing the loss of all they had fought for in the Revolution, burned down debtor's courts and ran tax collectors out of their communities (Szatmary 1980). Congress tried to hire an army to put down the rebellion, but they couldn't recruit one from among a largely farmer population nor did they have the funds to pay for it. An armed conflict between farmers who defended their life, liberty, and property, and merchants who sought to finance economic expansion ended with many dead and wounded. Lawyers and political leaders joined the merchants with privately funded militias to arrest the farmers and indict them for treason.

In 1790, frontier farmers in Pennsylvania protested the excise tax on distilled spirits, arguing that it did not represent them and that it was unfair to smaller businesses. The tax operated in proportion to the number of people and not to the wealth, which they asserted made it unjust. Farmers refused to pay the tax and rebelled with violence. This time, in 1794, President Washington was able to muster up a militia of 12,950 men that he called to suppress the rebellion.

Issues of taxation made early American farmers very much of a social class as part of a growing divide between rural and urban interests. The daughters of farmers learned well that political and economic power was vested in urban commercial interests in the new nation, not in the local rural citizenry. Daughters also learned that rebellions among yeoman farmers cost them the lives of fathers and potential husbands. They, and their fathers, resigned themselves to the fact that the agricultural sector was called upon to produce more surplus goods for urban and international markets. They also hoped that these expanding markets would bring profits. In response, dutiful and patriotic daughters of yeoman farmers in the North and the South developed a wide range of flexible skills in the production of food, yarn, cloth, and crafts to help support their families to meet the needs of a growing population and to pay taxes. By age fourteen, yeoman daughters of the eighteenth century were employed full time at baking, spinning, weaving, producing cloth, and constructing garments or crafts that they sold at local markets along with other farm produce. They also were hired out as laborers or apprentices for neighbors.

During this period, mercantile interests prevailed in the South where growing cotton became more profitable with the invention of the cotton gin. A new demand for cotton, and hence a new demand for slaves, created an economy ever more dependent on slaves and international markets. The daughters of slaves continued to work as field hands and as domestic servants on large plantations where the daughters of the planter class enjoyed a comfortable life with imported luxury goods. Farm products from the North and the South were exported, and European manufactured goods were imported, through the growing merchant cities of Boston, New York City, Philadelphia, Baltimore, and Charleston.

The structural factors that shaped rural economic circumstances, namely, the concentration of political and economic power in the Eastern marketplaces, grew as the global market for agricultural products also expanded. Yeoman farmers came to depend on the power brokers for credit, protection of their property, and access to markets. And daughters knew their fathers depended on them to help support the household income and to pay taxes and interest on loans.

THE FRONTIER PERIOD

Despite the centralization of urban economic and political power in the American government by the Federalists, Thomas Jefferson's rise to the presidency in 1800 represented a move toward the civil liberties and economic freedom of farmers and a reduction in the power of merchants and elites who controlled the centralized government. Jefferson believed that small-scale landowner farmers should have the power to govern themselves and that their economic interests, not those of the merchants, should be protected by the government. Jefferson argued that farmers and planters should have the right to trade in international markets without the intervention of merchant middlemen. He also advocated landownership for as many people as possible and opposed the national bank, which he feared would promote speculation on agricultural land rather than farming. He also repealed the Whiskey Tax.

With the purchase of the Louisiana Territory in 1803, Thomas Jefferson gave frontier farmers free access to the Mississippi River system and the port of New Orleans for international trade, breaking the mercantile power base of the eastern seaports. The new lands also guaranteed an expansion of liberty for farmers. While Jefferson's actions provided land for yeoman farmers and planters, they displaced large numbers of Native Americans from their property and liberty and also created a greater demand for slaves and immigrant laborers. On the frontier, where Jefferson argued democracy flourished, class, racial, ethnic, and gender inequalities also populated the landscape.

As a result of Jefferson's agrarian policies, the frontier yeoman farm family became the predominant image of an expanding American democracy. The frontier economy and society, however, was considerably more complex. It was comprised of miners, loggers, and Yankee mercantilists as well as Native American, Mexican, European, and Asian immigrant groups, and Eastern farmers and laborers who produced the food and other local necessities for growing communities. The image of the yeoman family farmer denied recognition of not only class and racial struggles in American agriculture, but the transnational political and economic forces that produced them.

The myth of the self-reliant middle-class yeoman family farmer dominated the American identity because these production units reflected the dominant culture's religious values of hard work, flexible production strategies, labor sharing, mutual aid, thrift, kinship networks, and stable orderly communities. An important factor in the success of these strategies was the contributions of the daughters of farmers who became the iconic symbols of the virtues of rural life. Even when they worked off the farm, the industry and docility of farmers' daughters made them an easily exploited labor group. In the industrial sector in Eastern states, particularly in mills where farmers' daughters household skills as spinners and weavers were translated into wage labor, their wages were typically sent home to their fathers who used them to pay farm debts and keep the family farm afloat. While these jobs had relatively high status and were considered respectable for young farm women, Gilda Lerner argues, wage labor in the mills was "accompanied by a loss of status" for young women while at the same time adding to the status of their fathers (1969:11).

The class status of farm girl laborers was flexible, as they experienced mobility between work and farm, returning to the farm when needed or to marry and raise their own families (Lerner 1969:11). For these reasons, they were reluctant to enter into apprenticeships that would raise them above casual labor status in the least skilled and lowest paid jobs (11–12). Well into the twentieth century, fourteen-year-old daughters also worked in the fields during peak seasons, or left home to work as domestics or in factories, always bringing or sending their wages home to their fathers for household needs, land taxes, and mortgage debts. The daughters of farmers were also most likely to become the teachers in rural schools, and in fact, they are credited with filling a growing need to educate the children of frontier public schools (Lerner 1969:11). These salaries were also given to their fathers. The teaching profession did not contribute to the individual status of young women or their economic freedom as they did not earn enough to be self-supporting.

The daughters of the yeoman class were considered a class above the daughters of landless tenant farmers, however, who were more likely to be hired out and to work in the fields as their fathers did not own the livestock and the equipment for fully self-sufficient operations. Daughters of first-generation immigrant farm families were also considered a class below the daughters of yeoman farmers. Many immigrant daughters in the upper Midwest were farmers even though their fathers were not. They worked with their mothers to maintain subsistence farms while their fathers labored in logging camps (Jensen 2006). It was the work of these women that helped the family survive and provided food and necessary items for logging camps. This was particularly significant to the frontier economy because men who worked in logging frequently spent their earnings on recreation rather than return it to their families (Jensen 2006:49–50).

The daughters of immigrants were still more fortunate than the daughters of Native American farmers on the frontier, who typically lost their land to US government expansion. Many, however, retained enough land to sustain their subsistence farming and hunting economies. During the mid-nineteenth century, Native American farm daughters engaged in traditional community systems of agriculture, most of which were the province of women, while at the same time they learned to adopt white systems of individual homestead agriculture. They also learned to trade traditional craft items in local markets for additional household income or attended mission schools to learn white professions. They were placed at the bottom of the class hierarchy in all regions because of their traditional cultures. Despite the fact that their Native cultural traditions and identities persisted, their cultures were gradually transformed as many intermarried with other rural people of all ethnic groups, but largely in the working classes. Rarely did they experience upward class mobility even though they adopted many of the same economic strategies of their white neighbors. In most cases, they lost social status as tribal lands were increasingly taken from them and other economic opportunities were not available or offered to them.

Southern yeoman farmers were also considered a class below Northern yeoman farmers because of their less stable farm incomes. Steven Hahn (1983) argues that despite the focus on planters and slaves, most frontier Southerners were white yeoman farmers who also supplemented their farm incomes with seasonal industrial and logging wage labor while their wives and children sustained the household economies with their diversified production. As plantation agriculture expanded on the Southern frontier with increased production of cotton and the demand for still more slaves, the cult of white womanhood in the South preserved class distinctions for the daughters of planters, yeoman farmers, and slaves (Lerner 1969:12).

The yeoman farmer's daughter icon gained strength in the frontier period in American agriculture because it afforded young farm women opportunities for upward mobility as their fathers and future husbands acquired and developed cheap farm land. Each new immigrant group, however, from Europe, Asia, or Latin America was likely to be landless for at least a generation during which family members, including daughters, engaged in farm labor as the cheapest or lowest class of laborers (Street 2004:267). Margaret Ripley Wolfe argues that "except for the privileged few, rural women of all races have routinely worked in the fields, a practice that remained common into the twentieth century" (1995:59).

Out of economic necessity, many farmers' daughters left the farms during the nineteenth century to seek opportunities as domestic servants, wage laborers, or teachers in nearby towns or farther away in cities. They provided a large social web of contacts for economic opportunities for other family members who sought to avoid the all-too-present poverty and despair of farm life on the frontier. When daughters stayed, they are often credited with heroic deeds of survival, for themselves, their families, and other members of their communities (Jensen 2006). Frontier life was difficult for the daughters of farmers. They not only survived natural calamities, isolation, hostile environments, and the fragmentation of families due to early deaths but they provided the emotional strength, household skills, and family commitment that kept families and communities together. For these reasons, "their economic contribution was more highly valued, their opportunities were less restricted and their positive participation in community life was taken for granted" (Lerner 1969:12).

By age ten or twelve, frontier farmers' daughters engaged in field labor, farmyard chores, gardening, food processing, and household duties but were also expected to have freshly ironed tablecloths on rough-hewn tables and clean, starched curtains in the windows of sod homes. Farm daughters of the nineteenth century milked cows and assumed responsibilities for cooking, care of small animals, and butter making. These young women also attended school to learn to read and write when their families could afford it, thereby further expanding their labor opportunities. If they were poor, they had to stay home to care for younger children, older people, and the sick. If they were well-to-do, they could develop musical talents and engage in social activities in church and community that would enhance their social status and marriage options.

Despite the fact that poor and working-class women made up from 70 to 80 percent of frontier farm women (both mothers and daughters), they were expected to conform to notions of domesticity that generally applied to the middle class (Schlissel, Ruiz, and Monk 1988:43). They were expected to dress like middle-class ladies when they went to town or attended church, working late into the night washing and ironing "Sunday best" clothes for the entire family. Their sense of class consciousness was conflicted between the labor roles they enacted on the farm and the social roles they enacted in public. Neither gave them the agency to effectively change their class positions, although both enhanced the status positions of their fathers.

While they rarely sustained family farmers, American agricultural policies asserted the primacy and infallibility of the yeoman middle class. But
they seldom acknowledged the contributions of permanent farm laborer
families that rose out of the struggles of frontier farming who also contributed to the formation of the middle class. While government policies
like the Homestead Act promoted landownership for frontier farmers and
expanded the agricultural economy, there was little to offset the rising costs
of credit, market instability, higher land prices, weather disasters, crop failures, and soaring production costs that drove many of these frontier farmers into tenancy or laborer status, a status similar to that of the dependent
farmers of Iceland that Bolender discusses. Frontier farmers of the landed
and landless classes survived because of cultural traditions that respected
hard work and thrift for all members of the family and ethnic communities
that shared labor and engaged in mutual aid. Frontier farm families often
experienced a reduction in class distinctions as women in particular from all
racial, ethnic, and class groups worked together to survive natural calamities, isolation, hostile environments, and the fragmentation of families due
to early deaths.

The expansion of American agriculture allowed for upward class mobility for the daughters of native-born farmers who stayed in farming communities as long as unimproved cheap frontier lands were available and the
rural economy remained somewhat stable. Immigrants with large families
of exploitable laborers were able to realize the middle-class dream if they
restricted consumption in favor of land acquisition. Neither group, however, could count on government initiatives such as credit and tax policies
and global trade policies that expanded the agricultural economy to further
their dreams.

Social class analysis among frontier farm women is difficult because
of the fluidity and diversity of their experiences (Schlissel, Ruis, and Monk
1988:13). Many frontier women did indeed come from middle-class households in the East or the South. While their husbands and fathers saw the
frontier as an opportunity to sacrifice household comforts for greater access
to cheaper land, first-generation frontier farm women often experienced
great instability in economic and social status which transformed and threatened their class consciousness (Schlissel, Ruis, and Monk 1988:88). The lives
of the daughters of frontiersmen were affected most by the occupational
status of their fathers (Riley 1988:2). There were major differences between

women who farmed and those who ranched, and among ethnic groups. The labor of farmers' daughters and their subsistence production enabled cash grain farming to be highly productive in the labor-scarce Midwest (Flora and Stitz 1988:47). But daughters of all social classes could expect to improve their social and economic status within two or three years on the frontier (Riley 1988:23). This was due to their labor contributions, and to the expansion of the agricultural economy and the rise in land values, which benefited their fathers as landowners most of all.

On an individual level, the daughters of poor immigrant farmers on the frontier were much more aware of class inequality that intersected with ethnic or racial inequality when they became the victims of rape or forced abortions. Rural women's historian Joan M. Jensen found the story of Rosa Petrusky, a poor Slovakian Catholic immigrant farmer's daughter in northern Wisconsin. Rosa worked as the hired girl for a wealthy Protestant Anglo-American, where she became pregnant by one of the Pratts' sons. He forced her to have an illegal abortion, after which she died an agonizing death from septic infection. The Pratt family was accused by friends of Rosa's family of paying off the district attorney and the physician to avoid prosecution for the illegal abortion but were never brought to trial (Jensen 2006: 148–151). The Pratts did, however, pay for her coffin.

Era Bell Thompson (1946), the daughter of a black homesteader in North Dakota, had quite a different experience. Her autobiography revealed a hard frontier life but one free of racism, sexism, and classism in the multiethnic farming community in which she grew up. Neighbors of all ethnic groups valued each other greatly as they learned to depend on each other for survival. Era Bell's father came to rely on her to more than he could his sons to care for livestock, help with field work, and maintain the household after her mother died. While her class status as a farmer's daughter was limited by economic recession, her social or educational opportunities were not limited in the North Dakota farming frontier. She did not experience racism, sexism, or class prejudices until she struck out on her own in the city.

By the mid-nineteenth century, farm daughters of all races, classes, and ethnic groups gained greater control over their individual class interests in terms of property rights through inheritances, marriage choices, and labor opportunities. The farm family persisted, but individual interests within the family began to diverge. The family was no longer the fundamental economic unit of society (Carr and Van Leeuwen 1996:71).

THE CIVIL WAR ERA

Civil War casualties greatly reduced the number of American farmers, North and South, leaving many farm families in the hands of women and children. After the war, American farmers further experienced the negative effects of the expansion of the global market for agricultural products through greater communication controlled by middlemen and the high costs of railroad transportation. The American government offered them no protection in the world market where costs of production were cheaper elsewhere. This was worse in the South, where Northern industrialists took advantage of the devastated rural economy of poor farmers. Between 1860 and 1900, the average income of farmers in the South was only half of the national average.

Before the Civil War, the planter class defined the social relationships among poor white sharecroppers, white laborers, and immigrant laborers in the South within a "racialized regime" (Adams and Gorton 2006). After the war, the rich planters went into merchandising, banking, lumbering, and industry. They became the local business elites who advanced credit to small-scale sharecropper and tenant farmers who occupied their land (Adams and Gorton 2006). Independent yeoman farmers could no longer compete because they could not get labor or credit to grow anything but cotton. Through a false sense of class consciousness, most yeomen blamed the freed black slaves for their problems and worked to keep blacks from social, economic, and political equality to enhance their own status instead of forming alliances with them to address the power of the rich.

In Alabama, however, the Agricultural Wheel crossed racial lines as a highly class conscious organization. In Alabama, additional agrarian organizations that addressed class issues included the Grange, the Farmers' Alliance, and the People's Party (Rogers, Sr. 2001). These organizations understood the class consequences to farmers in the transition to an industrial and merchant economy after the Civil War that resulted in higher costs of farming and lower prices for their products throughout the nation. Between 1867 and 1869, Western farmers produced more bushels of wheat on more acres of land as prices dropped in half. Cotton prices dropped to a third between 1870 and 1898. In Georgia, the costs to produce cotton were greater than the prices farmers got for it. In Kansas, corn was selling so low in 1889 that farmers burned it for fuel.

While agricultural class experiences varied by regions in the United States depending on the availability of lands, local markets, transportation, labor, credit, technology, and racial and ethnic discrimination, it was clear that rural society was in danger after the Civil War. The nation's oldest national agricultural organization, the Grange, was founded to address this problem. In 1873, a financial panic brought greater class consciousness to farmers across the nation. The Grange opposed monopolies that limited equal economic opportunities for farmers. Operating at local levels across the nation, they sought to strengthen class consciousness and redistribute economic power.

The Grange's primary unit of organization, the family in the community, sought to unite farmers in the North and the South in a brotherhood founded on Christian values. It was the first national farm organization that attempted to organize African American farmers. The Grange admitted young men and women fourteen years of age and older as full members and was one of the first groups to admit women to membership in 1874. The Grange promoted appreciation for the abilities and contributions of women in agricultural life. It can be argued, then, that this organization, more than any other, recognized the class issues of farmers' daughters of all racial, ethnic, or regional circumstances throughout the nation.

In contrast to the Grange, the Farmer's Alliance, which was founded in central Texas in 1877 to address the power of land speculators and merchant middlemen, did not allow black farmers because the whites did not want them mixing with their wives and daughters at social gatherings (McMath 1975). Poor white farmers' daughters were also disadvantaged by the racist ideologies toward women that promoted the "cult of white femininity" as the ideal for Southern women. It was largely the plantation elitist notion of femininity. Yeoman, sharecropper, and tenant farmers' daughters could not expect to experience these ideals of sexual purity and domesticity. The "cult of white femininity" did not respect or protect the purity of poor women.

Class, race, and gender intersected in the South to define class for the daughters of farmers. In her examination of rape and rumors of rape in the South, Mary Francis Berry (1999) found that the law preserved a patriarchal white male class privilege regardless of the race of the accused or the accuser. This point is illustrated in the case of Annie Knuppel, a fifteen-year-old German immigrant daughter of a poor white pig farmer in Texas in 1886 (Berry 1999:207). According to Miss Knuppel's story, she was raped by "a colored man." A doctor's examination verified that she had been sexually assaulted. The man who was arrested seven weeks later and identified as the offender was tried and convicted by a local jury. An appeals court called for a new trial, after which the defendant was again found guilty. Texas appellate judges eventually reversed the convictions because at each trial, local "men of prominence" sided with the defendant's wealthy white patrons who argued that he was "their boy (208)." Berry found a similar case a year earlier in which a black man had been convicted of raping a poor Polish farmer's daughter and also released because of the testimony of his humble, respectful character by his white employer (208). Berry asserts that black women and poor white women in the rural South after the Civil War could not expect justice if they were raped by either black men or white men (212–213). Poor white women were devalued by the influence of wealthy white males (218).

THE POPULIST ERA

The 1880s brought an agricultural depression that politicians either would not or could not do anything about because they were aligned with the railroads and other big businesses. The depression was so severe that farmers mortgaged their land or borrowed money to pay taxes, living expenses, and production costs. By the end of the 1890s, a third of farms previously owned by farmers without debt were mortgaged and the number of tenant farms increased significantly, especially in the South (Hahn 1983). While farmers everywhere were unable to control the railroad costs of shipping their crops to market, the rates were two or three times higher in the South and West than in the North and East. Further, large shippers got rebates while small farmers did not. In addition, national banks were indifferent to the seasonal needs of farmers and foreclosed when farmers could not pay their loans on time.

By the 1890s, 80 to 90 percent of all cotton growers, black and white, owner and tenant, owed money to lien merchants who charged interest rates as high as 60 to 75 percent (McMath 1975). Merchants demanded payment at harvest when the market was most depressed. Merchants also demanded that farmers use all available land to plant cash crops rather than using some to plant gardens, forcing farmers to go deeper into debt to buy food from merchants. During this period, corporate giants challenged the producerism ideology that labor, not capital produced wealth with claims that capital was the primary driver of prosperity (Doukas and Durrenberger 2008:9).

In 1892, farmers formed a Populist Party to protect their interests and respond to the problems in the system: farmers paid the highest price for everything they bought and sold their crops at the lowest price. Populists wanted the government to store commodities and to treat their deposits as collateral until they could obtain more favorable prices. They also demanded government regulation of railroads and telegraphy companies and access to credit in national banks. Populism supported Jeffersonian ideals of independent yeomen farmer producers and recognized the class differences between those who produced and those who profited from producers. Populists worked to establish cooperatives that connected farmers to wholesalers and to get credit for these cooperatives through the federal government.

Plains Populists were attracted to the traditional ideas of social justice within local communities and the protection of their individual economic freedoms, which they saw threatened by commercialized agriculture (McMath 1975). The expansion of the global market for American agricultural products through commercialization meant a loss of local subsistence traditions and diminished family and community strategies for economic security. Populism also attracted white yeomen farmers in the South because they resisted powerful planter elites aligned with Northern capitalists. But Populists lost influence in the South because they were equated with attacks on the supremacy of whites and Southern views of womanhood for farm wives and daughters through their alliance with black farmers (McMath 1975). But two-thirds of the owner-operator small farms in the South belonged to blacks by 1900 (Adams and Gorton 2006:290), causing a deep rift in the movement.

Populists attempted unsuccessfully to unify industrial worker unions and racially and ethnically diverse farmers around common class issues everywhere in America. Labor organizers resented immigrant Chinese, Japanese, and Mexican farm laborers in California agriculture for working for lower wages, arguing that they were degrading farm labor and creating a new servant class (Hill 1973). Mexican and Japanese field hands formed their own union, but it was not recognized by the American Federation of Labor. Herbert Hill argues that the Chinese, Japanese, Mexican, and Negro farm labor force in California was marginalized and limited to low-paying, unskilled jobs through a system of "working-class racism" by refusing them membership to labor unions (1973:54).

Farm labor was seasonal in many areas of the country, particularly in the West and in the South. During picking seasons, migrant workers competed with resident laborers in the South (Adams and Gorton 2006:290). A new labor regime was created that placed black workers at the bottom and white elites at the top (Adams and Gorton 2006:290). In this system, neither blacks nor women were allowed to vote. Farm laborers, who were "undeniably a class systematically manipulated, kept down, and relegated to the fringe" (Street 2004:636), were just as important in the development of American agriculture as yeoman farmers. Entire agricultural sectors, such as the citrus industry, were developed by wealthy entrepreneurs who employed seasonal farm laborers, initially without labor agreements (Street 2004:498). These workers, including young girls whose wages went to their fathers, eventually formed labor unions in a class struggle against capitalist agriculture beginning in the early 1900s in California (Street 2004:454).

Underage farmers' daughters from the poor families had few choices in the negotiation for wages or labor conditions. They worked on farms or in industrial employment in cotton or woolen mills to help their families survive, often working about seventy hours a week for ten to twelve cents a day (Adams and Gorton 2006:290). The situation was so grim that a National Child Labor Committee began to address these problems only a few years before agricultural science developed in agricultural colleges to promote business principles in farm management. The Smith-Lever Act established agricultural extension services to rural communities before the first federal child labor law was passed and women were granted the right to vote. This clearly reveals the priorities of the federal government toward the rights of farm workers and the quality of farm family lives.

In the early twentieth century, it was clear that farm daughters had developed consciousness as a laboring class when the majority of farm households disappeared between 1900 and 1910 (Fink 1992:30). Mass media communication informed farm girls that they worked far harder than did urban girls and their lives were less enjoyable. At the beginning of the twentieth century, farmers' daughters were leaving the farm at a time when their labor was still very valuable to the farm family and the rural economy. The decisions of farmers' daughters to stay or to leave the farm family community were based on awareness of their opportunities as wage laborers off the farm and their potential for economic advancement through marriage to a nonfarmer wage laborer. And while staying on the farm seldom offered upward class mobility for farmers' daughters, marrying a farmer did still offer other valued rewards such as family continuity and the perpetuation of cultural values for future generations.

The Country Life movement led by Liberty Hyde Bailey addressed the problems of the agricultural laboring class and recognized the disproportionate burden farm wives and daughters bore to sustain the farm family (Bailey 1915:21). Bailey avoided a class analysis, however, in favor of a shallow moralistic diatribe. Bailey (1915) argued that the agricultural class was made up of men who owned their own land and labor, who should preserve a society free of class consciousness. His plan to improve the lots of women and keep farm daughters on the farm was more judgmental than helpful. Bailey and the Country Life Commission wrote that while rural poverty existed, it was the result of moral inadequacies in cleanliness, temperance, progressiveness, and thrift (1909:48). The data argue that it was more likely that farmers and their daughters lost control over the means of production, not their moral compass.

DEPRESSION/NEW DEAL ERA

While the Populist movement had largely failed to reform American agriculture, its sentiments lived on. In 1902, the National Farmer's Union was founded to address farm income and the stability of the farm economy. It formed the first marketing cooperative in 1903, which Bruce Field argues was the beginning of the Cold War (1998). In 1917, a Green Corn Rebellion was organized by poor farmers in Oklahoma with Socialist sentiments who opposed conscription to WWI, which they saw as a rich man's war (Burbank 1977). As a result of these activities, business interests saw a growing threat to American capitalism in the countryside and organized the Farm Bureau in 1919. It gained power through collaboration of railroad companies, the Chicago Board of Trade, banks, and chambers of commerce. The Farm Bureau posited alternative cooperatives that did not threaten capitalism by embracing their version with a doctrine of business (Durrenberger 1986:15).

The 1920s reflected relatively good years for urban families, but farm families earned only one-third as much as the average urban family (Durrenberger 1986:15). Despite efforts to professionalize farming, more and more farmers lost their land. Even in the Midwest, where farming had been relatively stable, many farmers feared they would become peasants (15). In 1921, nearly half the farms on the highly fertile soil of Black Hawk, Grundy, and Tama Counties in Iowa did not earn anything for the farmer's labor, did not make 5 percent interest on capital, and could not pay operation expenses according to the business model of calculating success (Munger 1921). In the South, immigrant farm laborers had little hope of ever becoming landowners (Adams and Gorton 2006:293).

While farm women earned the right to vote in 1920 along with their urban sisters, it did little to improve their farm labor circumstances and rural family lifestyles. Little immigrant girls age three and up were photographed in 1924 laboring in the fields during harvest time picking cranberries in New Jersey (Williams 1924: 71–73). Large-scale industrial agriculturalists that employed children along with their parents picking cranberries and other truck gardening operations were the target of health care professionals and children's rights activists, not farm organizations or federal agricultural policies. In many cases, children were taken into the fields and put to work because there was no place else for them to be minded or educated and because even their limited productivity was of some value to their families. This was largely because farm families had a tradition of exploiting the labor of every family member to survive in the global marketplace.[2] Had farmer alliances and organizations restricted the labor of farm children to improve the quality of rural life, they would have met with great opposition among family farmers who relied heavily on the labor of their children to make ends meet.

By the 1930s, social mobility was spiraling downward for most American farmers and their daughters. While New Deal programs helped to maintain a rural population and the farm family as caretakers of the land, these programs also were designed to expand production and rebuild the national economy. This accelerated economic inequality through technological and scientific developments (Danbom 2006:207, 209). Because the South received less of this assistance, Southern agriculture remained depressed. And while the Farm Credit Administration was established to address farm debts, lenders actually benefited as much as borrowers in avoiding bankruptcy auctions

(209). New Deal programs were often just an extension of the old deal in American politics. It was the farm economy that not only fed the nation but the national economy as well.

The business model promoted by the Farm Bureau promoted increased productivity, due to the fact that farmers provided the capital and the cheap labor. But this model did not provide a return on farmer's labor, that of his family, or their capital (Durrenberger 1986:16). The sharp decline in prices as a result of increased production prompted Roosevelt to establish the Agricultural Adjustment Administration, which paid farmers to not plant crops. The program did not distinguish between farmers and landowners, however. Landowners could benefit more from receiving payments to not plant crops than they could from renting to tenants. So they threw tenants and sharecroppers off the land, leaving them to compete with wage laborers for their livelihoods (Adams and Gorton 2006:297). Poor whites worked with black laborers in the fields and were barely able to survive. When FSA projects became available to poor families in the South in 1941, rural children were dying from malnutrition (Adams and Gorton 2006:299).

Throughout the 1930s, the class consciousness of American farmers was fully articulated in social movements that also involved industrial laborers (Denning 1966). Farmers across the nation had balanced agricultural and industrial labor opportunities to survive, learning that efforts to restrict union membership and progressive farm legislation were part of the same class war on working people to preserve elite power. When migrant farm wage laborers who were once small family farmers engaged in violent conflict with corporate agriculture, the American public began to understand these conflicts. John Steinbeck's *The Grapes of Wrath* articulated this rising class consciousness as a result of capitalism (Owens 1989:8). But while New Deal reforms addressed the symptoms and cured some of the ills, they did not alter the basic class inequities in American agriculture.

The daughters of farmers fared possibly worse during this time than any other time in American history as their typically flexible opportunities to engage in self-sufficient household production, wage labor, and stable marriages were all greatly diminished. Young farm women's experiences were further devalued by not only class realities but the enduring intersections of racism and sexism so apparent in popular culture images in America during the difficult years of the early twentieth century.

POST-WWII ERA

Class inequality among the farming sector in the 1950s grew more complex as a result of global trade and finance (Danbom 2006:251). At the same time, the rural landscape grew more homogeneous in terms of race and ethnicity. The changing nature of post-WWII farm technology, the once again expanding global market for agricultural products, and Cold War propaganda promoted an image of a stable rural middle-class. But these "middle-class" American farmers were increasingly divided into two classes of small-scale farmers and large industrial farmers as they grew more dependent upon global markets and government programs that manipulated their production systems. Their ability to manage the costs of production diminished as family farmers incurred greater debts to modernize. The high costs of capital lowered the value of farm family labor as profit margins narrowed.

By the 1960s, government programs played a central role in the rural economy throughout America in terms of subsidies, conservation and wildlife programs, and social security (Adams and Gorton 2006:300). As farm production increased, so did the size of farm operations. Small farms became less and less sustainable. The general trend in the 1960s was toward mechanization and away from farm labor, particularly the labor of the farmer's daughter. This varies by region and by modes of production, which were often culturally defined. Rachel Rosenfeld found that on modernized hog and dairy farms that demanded constant labor, daughters were still more likely to contribute to farm labor than on cash-grain farms (1985:30). She also found that daughters and sons over the age of ten were more likely than their mothers to contribute to labor on family farms in the 1964 census (31). While the labor roles of farmers' daughters are related to the structure of the family and the farm (Goss, Rodefield, and Buttel 1980:19), their value is a function of other labor values. The labor of farmers' daughters served as a reserve labor supply, the value of which increased as the costs of hired male farm labor increased (25).

Still, by the 1960s, the rise in farm technology diminished the need for hired male farm labor. Tenant farming also diminished at this time because of the high costs of production and limited credit. Class consciousness in the 1960s was complicated by the fact that while farm debts rose, incomes also rose. The modernization of rural life in general provided for a higher standard of living for most rural families. While credit was tight for farm operation expansion, landownership provided ready collateral for consumer credit. The reality is that many farm families went backwards while they were looking ahead to a better consumer lifestyle.

With the rise of women's freedoms and feminist consciousness in America during the second half of the twentieth century, young farm women increasingly desired greater freedom in the selection of marriage partners, individual self-fulfillment, and consumption of material goods available to them through expanding educational and career opportunities outside of farming communities. They also recognized that their participation as farm laborers was not as needed or valued as it had been in the past. Farms were increasingly specialized and mechanized so that livestock chores, gardening, and field work labor was much diminished. Also, farm families were smaller and household mechanization guaranteed that daughters were less necessary for family maintenance chores as well.

With their new awareness of wage labor and educational opportunities, many daughters of farmers increasingly did not want to contribute their labor to the family in return for risks and debts and little or no control over production decisions just for a chance to marry a farmer. Off-farm labor opportunities influenced all farm laborers' commitment to stay on the farm. Where there were no opportunities elsewhere, they stayed; when there were better opportunities, they left (Adams and Gorton 2006:301). The exit of farmers' daughters from the farm, despite their historical sacrifices for the family farm, makes it difficult to defend the myth of the propertied labor class and the middle-class yeoman family farmer in American agriculture much after the 1960s.

As farm commodity prices increased in the 1970s due to expanding global markets, farmers' daughters increasingly left the farms. There was little future for them on the farm or in the declining farm community. While many did farm chores while they were growing up on the farm, they also participated more fully in urban lifestyle activities that they saw as more attractive to farm life. As women gained educational opportunities and increasing equality in the work place, the farm girls were lured away from farms and small towns. The daughters of farmers did well away from the farm because of the survival skills that had been handed down through generations (Anderson 1996:241). They could reduce consumption and absorb stress due to the mental flexibility and resourcefulness they learned on the farm (Anderson 1996:241). Through hard work, education, and marriage choices, they could more easily experience upward class mobility off the farm than on the farm.

CONCLUSION

To understand class in American agriculture, we need to recognize farm laborers as individual fathers, mothers, sons, and daughters in specific regional and historical contexts engaged in processes of intersecting class dynamics. The labor roles and circumstances of young farm women reveal an ever-present class structure complicated by landownership, race, cultural norms, and gender. Despite early attempts to present a classless American agricultural society with the promotion of the stereotypical yeoman land-holding farm family, the farm labor in the American farm tradition is rooted in a class system of laborers without access to land or capital (Street 2004:635).

The American public largely ignored the structural factors that shaped obvious class differences that defined the economic and social value of farm labor in general and the labor of farmers' daughters in particular. Instead, popular culture representations of agriculture idealized one iconic image, the yeoman farmer's daughter, as the symbol of middle-class family and community stability, progressive entrepreneurship, and the quality of rural life. Agricultural scientists promoted the ideology that farmers represented the American ideal—the businessman (Durrenberger 1986:16). This class image served the interests of elites by devaluing or ignoring the labor con-tributions of various class, ethnic, religious, and racial groups throughout the United States. It denies the fact that young farm women in diverse pro-duction contexts contributed greatly to the survival of not only middle-class yeoman families but poor tenant and sharecropper families as well as to the protest of marginalized seasonal and migrant farm laborers. It obscures the widening class disparities that ensue from policies that promote the over-production of agricultural commodities for the global marketplace. Further, promotion of the homogeneous middle-class image has been damaging to yeoman family farmers by failing to recognize the increasing decline of this group.

Since the colonial period, the American agricultural system was always part of a global economic system as well as a gendered, class, and racial system. As agricultural production expanded, labor relations between the

daughters of farmers, their families, and local cultures were also transformed. The global political economy structured the class realities of
American farmers and their labor relations as government policies were
created to keep the economy expanding through increased production and
productivity (Durrenberger and Erem 2007: 207–209). Farm and trade policies that benefited farmers and their families were not directed primarily
for their well-being, but to expand profits for the elite institutions of the
nation that benefited from agriculture. This became more obvious when
national and international economic recessions and depressions destabi-
lized local economies and self-sufficient farm family household production. Government policies always responded to help the middleman and the
financial sectors first. Farmers were increasingly forced into relations with
capital that devalued their labor and increased their debt.

Still, many American farmers managed to resist identification with
class interests. The value of their farm labor was bound up in local cultural
and ethnic identities, demonstrating what Lipsitz argues, that there is "no
atomized class consciousness completely independent of ethnic identity"
in the United States (2001:39). Farmers further resisted class identities by
resisting the rise of industrial capitalism through economic independence as
a result of their landownership and the ownership of their own technology
(51). They thought of themselves first as patriarchs and community leaders,
then as businessmen, but not wage laborers. They did not look for a return
on their labor, but on their investments in land and technology.

Anthropologist Douglas Harper asserts that farming was a lifestyle
and one's status in the community and the accumulation of social capital
was more important than the accumulation of economic capital (2001:180).
Farmers maintained their political independence by controlling the local
rural community and their economic independence by controlling their
land, thereby avoiding the class struggles of those who worked for wages.
Solidarity for farmers was based on local community struggles for self-
sufficiency, survival of cultural traditions, and social order, not a broader
class identity. From the perspective of farmers, social capital minimized the
effects of class as well as the awareness of it (Walker 2006:96). Gaps between
rich and poor were minimized for the good of the larger community (98).
According to Walker, farmers in the South had a consciousness of rural
verses urban identities where rural people related to class in terms of local
political and economic power dynamics in which race and class shaped eco-

nomic inequality (100). These conceptions of class among American farmers have been fluid and flexible in response to changing power relations at several levels.

For the daughters of farmers, class consciousness and agency were experienced subjectively within specific cultural and historical contexts. Objectively, their relative class stratification in terms of wealth and power was the result of government policies that promoted monopoly capital (Schlissel, Ruiz, and Monk: 1988:78). Agricultural policy and agricultural structure clearly influenced the class realities of farm women (Flora and Stitz 1988). And while family structure defined inequality for young farm women, agricultural policy defined the class structure within which family systems of production emerged and were transformed. The changing labor roles of young farm women were highly class specific.

This brief comparison of diverse labor roles and class status for young farm women across time and space reveals culturally specific contexts. Thanks to feminist scholarship, gender relations within class, ethnic, racial, and cultural realms are now visible (Carr and Van Leeuwen 1996:38). The experiences of daughters of farmers in all classes reflected their father's social, political, and economic status as well as decision-making power within the family (Jones 1988:18). But despite their relative lack of power over decision making, daughters gained agency through meaning making (Osterud 1988:75). Osterud explains that while they may not have had a sense of class agency as farmers, they had a sense of agency over their lives in their identity with the family (77). This study argues that meaning making was translated to class agency when daughters decided to contribute their labor to the household economy or return wage labor to their fathers to support the family on the farm. Daughters understood that value was added to their labor through the meaning of belonging to the farm family and the farm community. When this was no longer the case, they left in pursuit of individualist strategies off the farm.

This study argues that agriculture in America was always maintained by working-class people. It is the structure of farm labor and not landownership that defines class in American agriculture. Small-scale operations survived because of the flexibility of the labor of the entire family and their underconsumption (Rosenfeld 1985:13). This was largely due to the roles of women, particularly those of the daughters. Large farms survived because of government programs (13). Daughters played a much smaller role in these operations. While the farmer's daughter is no longer the iconic image of self-reliant American agriculture that she was prior to the 1960s, and many farmers' daughters have left the farm, still others resist the ethnocide of the family farm by remaining on the farm and contributing their labor and educated skills to alternative farm family operations.

For the few remaining family farmers, the expanding global market for agricultural products is accompanied by a conscious effort to add value to their labor in locally sustainable markets. The challenge for this generation of daughters of farmers is to reach across class, racial, ethnic, and regional lines to build a coalition of young women who seek sustainable, stable, and just labor roles as well as social solidarity around family and community themes in American agriculture.

NOTES

1. See Heyman 2007 for a study of how Mexican immigrants perceive transnational capitalism and class relations.

2. For more discussion of the patterns and practices of the labor of farm children, see Riney-Kehrberg 2005.

REFERENCES CITED

Adams, Jane, and D. Gorton. 2006. "Confederate Lane: Class, Race and Ethnicity in the Mississippi Delta." *American Ethnologist* 33 (2): 288–309.

Anderson, Marvin L. 1996. "Reluctant Feminists, Rural Women and the Myth of the Farm Family." In *Religion, Feminism, and the Family*, edited by Anne Carr and Mary Steward Van Leeuwen, 223–245. Louisville, KY: Westminster John Knox Press.

Bailey, Liberty Hyde, Henry Wallace, Kenyon L. Butterfield, Walter H. Page, Gifford Pinchot, C. S. Barrett, and W. A. Beard. 1909. *Report of the Country Life Commissioner, Special Message from the President of the United States Transmitting the Report of the Country Life Commission*. Washington, DC: Government Printing Office.

Bailey, Liberty Hyde. 1915. *The Holy Earth*. New York: Charles Scribner's Sons.

Berry, Mary Frances. 1999. *The Pig Farmer's Daughter and Other Tales of American Justice, Episodes of Racism and Sexism in the Courts from 1865 to the Present*. New York: Alfred A. Knopf.

Burbank, Garin. 1977. *When Farmers Voted Red: The Gospel of Socialism in the Oklahoma Countryside, 1910–1924*. Westport, CT: Greenwood Press.

Carr, Anne, and Mary Steward Van Leeuwen, eds. 1996. *Religion, Feminism, and the Family.* Louisville, KY: Westminster John Knox Press.

Danbom, David B. 2006. *Born in the Country: A History of Rural America.* 2nd edition. Baltimore: Johns Hopkins University Press.

Denning, Michael. 1966. *The Cultural Front.* New York: Verso.

Doukas, Dimitra, and E. Paul Durrenberger. 2008. "Gospel of Wealth/Gospel of Work: Counterhegemony in the U.S. Working Class." *American Anthropologist* 110(2): 214–224.

Durrenberger, E. Paul. 1986. "Notes on the Cultural-Historical Background to the Middle Western Farm Crisis." *Culture and Agriculture.* 28: 15–17.

Durrenberger, E. Paul, and Suzan Erem. 1997. "The Way I See It: Perspectives on the Labor Movement from the People in It." *Anthropology and Humanism* 22(2): 159–169.

———. 2007. *Anthropology Unbound: A Field Guide to the Twenty-First Century.* Boulder, CO: Paradigm.

Farnham, Christie Anne. 1997. *Women of the American South: A Multicultural Reader.* New York: New York University Press.

Field, Bruce E. 1998. *Harvest of Dissent: The National Farmer's Union and the Early Cold War.* Lawrence: University Press of Kansas.

Fink, Deborah. 1992. *Agrarian Women, Wives and Mothers in Rural Nebraska, 1880–1940.* Studies in Rural Culture. Chapel Hill: University of North Carolina Press.

Flora, Cornelia Butler, and John Stitz. 1988. "Female Subsistence Production and Commercial Farm Survival among Settlement Kansas Wheat Farmers." *Human Organization* 47(1): 64–69.

Garkovich, Lorraine, and Janet Bokemeier. 1988. "Agricultural Mechanization and American Farm Women's Economic Roles." In *Women and Farming: Changing Roles, Changing Structures,* edited by Wava G. Haney and Jane B. Knowles, 211–228. Boulder, CO: Westview Press.

Goss, Kevin F., Richard D. Rodefeld, and Frederick H. Buttel. 1980. "The Political Economy of Class Structure in U.S. Agriculture." In *The Rural Sociology of Advanced Societies: Critical Perspectives,* edited by Frederick H. Buttel and Howard Newby, 83–132. Montclair, NJ: Allenheld.

Hahn, Steven. 1983. *The Roots of Southern Populism: Yeoman Farmers and the Transformation of the Georgia Upcountry, 1850–1890.* New York: Oxford University Press.

Harper, Douglas. 2001. *Changing Works: Visions of a Lost Agriculture.* Chicago: University of Chicago Press.

Heyman, Josiah. 2007. *Class Consciousness in a Complicated Setting: Race, Immigration Status, Nationality, and Class on the U.S.-Mexico Border.* Tucson: University of Arizona Press.

Hill, Herbert. 1973. "Anti-Oriental Agitation and the Rise of Working-Class Racism." *Society* 10(2): 43–54.

Jensen, Joan M. 2006. *Calling This Place Home: Women on the Wisconsin Frontier, 1850–1925*. St. Paul: Minnesota Historical Society Press.

Jones, Jacqueline. 1988. "'Tore Up and A-Movin': Perspectives on the Work of Black and Poor White Women in the Rural South, 1865–1940." In *Women and Farming: Changing Roles, Changing Structures*, edited by Wava G. Haney and Jane B. Knowles, 15–34. Boulder, CO: Westview Press.

Lerner, Gilda. 1969. "The Lady and the Mill Girl: Changes in the Status of Women in the Age of Jackson." *American Studies Journal* 10(1): 5–15.

Lipsitz, George. 2001. *American Studies in a Moment of Danger*. Minneapolis: University of Minnesota Press.

Little, Jo, and Patricia Austin. 1996. "Women and the Rural Idyll." *Journal of Rural Studies* 12(2): 101–111.

McMath, Robert C., Jr. 1975. *Populist Vanguard: The Rise of the Southern Farmer's Alliance*. Chapel Hill: University of North Carolina Press.

Munger, H. B. 1921. "Iowa Farm Management Surveys in Black Hawk, Grundy, and Tama Counties." Bulletin #198. Agricultural Experiment Station. Ames: Iowa State College of Agriculture and Mechanic Arts.

Osterud, Nancy Grey. 1988. "Land, Identity, and Agency in the Oral Autobiographies of Farm Women." In *Women and Farming: Changing Roles, Changing Structures*, edited by Wava G. Haney and Jane B. Knowles, 73–87. Boulder, CO: Westview Press.

Owens, Louis. 1989. *The Grapes of Wrath: Trouble in the Promised Land*. Boston: Twayne Publishers.

Riley, Glenda. 1988. *The Female Frontier: A Comparative View of Women on the Prairie and Plains*. Lawrence: University Press of Kansas.

Riney-Kehrberg, Pamela. 2005. *Childhood on the Farm: Work, Play, and Coming of Age in the Midwest*. Lawrence: University Press of Kansas.

Rogers, William Warren, Sr. 2001. *The One-Gallused Rebellion: Agrarianism in Alabama, 1865–1896*. Tuscaloosa: University of Alabama Press.

Rosenfeld, Rachel Ann. 1985. *Farm Women: Work, Farm, and the Family in the United States*. Chapel Hill: University of North Carolina Press.

Schlissel, Lillian, Vicki L. Ruis, and Janice Monk. 1988. *Western Women: Their Land, Their Lives*. Albuquerque: University of New Mexico Press.

Street, Richard Steven. 2004. *Beasts of the Field: A Narrative History of California Farmworkers, 1769–1913*. Stanford, CA: Stanford University Press.

Szatmary, David P. 1980. *Shay's Rebellion: The Making of an Agrarian Insurrection*. Amherst: University of Massachusetts Press.

Thompson, Era Bell. 1946. *American Daughter*. Chicago: University of Chicago Press.

Walker, Melissa A. 2006. *Southern Farmers and Their Stories*. Lexington: University Press of Kentucky.

Williams, Francis B. 1924. "Picking Our Greatest Crop Too Soon." *Hygeia: A Journal of Individual and Community Health*. American Medical Association, February 1924: 71–73.

Wolfe, Margaret Ripley. 1995. *Daughters of Canaan: A Saga of Southern Women*. Lexington: University Press of Kentucky.

Immigrant Heterogeneity and Class Consciousness in New Rural US Destinations

DAVID GRIFFITH

INTRODUCTION: IMMIGRATION AND SOCIAL CLASS

Immigrant groups tend to be associated with processes that fragment labor markets, work sites, communities, and other social spaces where class allegiances develop. Loyalties and affiliations are more likely to be based on local histories, ethnicity, national origin, enclaves, neighborhoods, important cultural places, or other dimensions of shared experience that may differ from time to time and place to place, such as church membership and political affiliation. Further, the growth and persistence of petty capitalist activity and multiple livelihoods among immigrants are corollaries to the fragmentation of production into enterprises that produce specific products, whether houses or hazardous toys, through subcontracting (Smart and Smart 2005; Griffith 2006).

These fragmenting processes became more common in organizing local economies and production during the last quarter of the twentieth century as corporations shopped in global labor markets for cheap labor and more recently as neoliberal economic policies swept large parts of the globe. What we once called the "new" international division of labor, in other words, is now over three decades old (Nash 1983; Sanderson 1985). The fragmentation of work breaks up realms of shared experience and frustrates class allegiances and class consciousness among direct producers, reinforcing the sustained political and cultural assaults on labor organizing that deepened after Ronald Reagan fired unionized air traffic controllers in the early 1980s (Griffith 1993; Hage and Klauda 1989; Newman 1988; Durrenberger and Erem 2005). Ironically, these divisive processes, while eroding most direct producers' power, at times create opportunities for direct producers to become petty capitalists and, usually by necessity, engage in multiple livelihoods to meet household demands for consumption and reproduction (Smart and Smart 2005; Zlolniski 2006). Janitors may become janitorial contractors, for example, by hiring their kinsmen and friends, or farm workers may work themselves into positions as farm managers or labor contractors, drawing on network and village ties to shape up their crews.

Given the proliferation and character of these disintegrative processes, examining immigrants' behaviors in concrete local settings may provide a window onto larger social and cultural trends sweeping across societies around the world. Not only have immigrants been linked, empirically, to fragmenting processes in local economies, their allegiance to class and their class consciousness can become further fragmented by attributes deriving from the immigrant experience. These include, most notably, as Heyman discusses in his chapter on the US-Mexican border, ties to home communities and transnational social fields, but also language differences, legal status issues, and differences of appearance, dress, food preferences and general consumption habits, and other distinguishing physical and cultural traits and practices. Immigrants develop social and economic ties to other more well-off immigrants and natives to form entourages that enable personal economic and political gain. This process draws allegiances away from social relations based on class and class consciousness and toward those based on common enterprise.

Here I use information from several years of ethnographic and survey work in four rural US communities and shorter periods of research in two regions in Honduras and one in Mexico[1] to explore the potential for immigrant class consciousness formation in relation to two social settings: criminal justice practices in central Iowa and consumption habits in southeastern and coastal North Carolina.

Referring to the rapid growth of immigrant populations since the 1986 Immigration Reform and Control Act (IRCA), social scientists have labeled these regions "new destinations" (Zuñiga and Hernandez-Leon 2005; Massey, in press). In both regions, early, primarily migrant populations of single males have developed into settled families of immigrants. Nevertheless, the two regions present slightly different conditions that facilitate or undermine class consciousness among immigrants.

Iowa's new immigrant population, for example, was drawn into the region initially to work in pork- and beef-packing plants, while North Carolina's early immigrants entered the state, by and large, as farm workers, only later transitioning into food processing (Fink 2003; Griffith 1993). Immigration into rural Iowa and the Midwest generally is taking place in a setting experiencing population loss of the locally born, particularly of young, working age locals. By contrast, immigration into the South accompanies population growth among US citizens, increasing the heterogeneity of its mix of ethnic groups, class backgrounds, and regional identities. At bottom, however, economic development has stimulated these migrations, altering the demographic complexions of the two regions beyond anything they had known in one to two generations prior to 1986 and allowing industry employers and managers in the two regions to construct working classes that have not yet achieved militance.

DRIVING WHILE BROWN:
CRIMINAL JUSTICE AND CLASS CONSCIOUSNESS

In the tiny crossroads town of Comstock, in central Iowa—a town with little more than a convenience store, a coffee shop, a grain elevator, a dairy, and a deputy sheriff—a local dairy farmer named Barry Connors, in 2000, hired sixteen Mexicans from Quarryville, a larger nearby town whose population had swelled by around 8,000 to 9,000 (20 to 25 percent of its population) after its meatpacking plant began recruiting Latino workers. Comstock could have been any one of dozens of communities in rural Iowa, Minnesota, Nebraska, or Kansas (Broadway 2007; Stull and Broadway 2001). In Iowa, meatpacking plants in Dennison, Marshalltown, Perry, Postville, Storm Lake, Sioux City, Waterloo, and several other towns have recruited Mexican and other Latino workers. Meatpacking plants known for recruiting immigrants and refugees are in Garden City, Kansas; Marshall, Worthington, and Faribault, Minnesota; Lincoln, Nebraska; and several other Midwestern locations. Meatpacking recruitment of immigrants has been so robust that border-crossing strategies have proliferated, leading to tragic consequences as occurred in October of 2002 in Dennison, Iowa, when the corpses of seven Mexican men and four Mexican women were found inside a grain car that originated in Matamoros, Mexico—a border-crossing tragedy that focused the nation's attention on the dangers facing the undocumented.

Barry hired the Mexicans from Quarryville because *quality* labor was scarce and Mexicans were seeking alternatives to meatpacking.[2] Since the mid-1990s, it had been hard for Barry to keep workers, and he couldn't expand production without secure labor. Barry's labor wasn't secure for several reasons. First, dairy work is difficult work that is poorly paid relative to the demands of the job, very much like meatpacking. Second, Comstock is within commuting distance of Des Moines, the state capital, and Ames, a large university town north of Des Moines, and alternative job opportunities were available to local native workers in these two cities. Third, Iowa has one of the highest emigration rates of young, able-bodied workers in the nation, leaving an available labor force with high proportions of the elderly and marginally employable (Marx's *lumpenproletariat*).

Although local labor was—in Barry's view—unreliable, in Quarryville, Latinos had been moving out of meatpacking into roofing, small manufacturing, casino work, restaurants, and other occupations, although the majority were still concentrated in meatpacking and most lived in neighborhoods adjacent to the meatpacking plant. Barry heard at the local coffee shop and at the Hy-Vee, the large supermarket (which also has a coffee shop) in Quarryville, that Latinos were good, hard workers and hoped that placing an ad in the local paper would get at least one to apply.

As a result of the ad Barry hired Felix Vargas from Michoacán and immediately asked if he had friends or relatives who might also want dairy work. Felix began bringing other Latinos from Quarryville to Comstock to work. They had come from Michoacán and Jalisco, the two Mexican states most represented among immigrants in Quarryville. Some of the Anglo workers at the Connor Dairy Farm complained of having to work alongside Mexicans, and soon all but six had quit.[3] Barry wasn't displeased; on the contrary, he was hoping the Anglos would quit. By that time Barry had a solid, reliable Latino crew: ten who were part of the original group Felix recruited and the other six what he called "floaters," who turn over from time to time, treating the work as seasonal even though it is, as Barry calls it, "24-7" work.[4] He replaces those who leave with new Latinos.

While working at the dairy, most of the Mexican workers continued living in Quarryville, about a half an hour's drive east of Comstock. Barry rented the only house he had for hired help to one Latino family, who asked if they could invite two other families to share the rent. Barry refused, saying that the people of Comstock would talk about him crowding Latinos into housing. Barry was sensitive to talk in the community because he was already something of a local rebel for hiring Latinos. News of the Anglos quitting had spread through the community, and the local deputy sheriff was suspicious of all the new faces on the roads to the Connor Dairy Farm. He routinely pulled them over, asking for licenses and registrations, engaging in a form of police harassment that has come to be known as stopping drivers for "driving while brown." After several weeks of this, and after several complaints from the Latinos working for him, Barry confronted the deputy. As a prominent local farmer and employer, as well as a voter, Barry's influence with the sheriff's department was substantial, and he forced the deputy to back off.

Barry's intervention between the local criminal justice system and his Latino work force was part of a general pattern of interactions between long-time residents and Latinos in Iowa, Minnesota, Nebraska, Kansas, and other new immigrant destinations. Aside from confronting the deputy, Barry offered the Latino dairy workers advice regarding regularizing their status, educating their children, handling their bank accounts, gender relations within their families, customary living arrangements, and a range of other subjects. By placing himself between the Latinos and local systems of culture, education, and criminal justice, Barry was setting himself up as both a spokesperson for the Latinos to the community and as a patron, friend, protector, and power broker for the Latino clients. This converted the employer-employee relationship to a multifaceted familial one.

His interaction with the deputy was significant to the Latinos because of the nature of the police and the criminal justice systems in Mexico and the United States. At bottom, many Mexicans accept, uncritically, Mexico's collective memory about the role the US courts played in the theft of Mexican privately held lands during the nineteenth century, combined with what they perceive as the US government's theft of half of Mexico's territory in the mid-nineteenth century. A recent Mexican text on the insertion of Mexican migrants into US labor markets opens with the observation, for example, "The migration to the United Status began more than one and a half centuries ago, when Mexico had to cede half of its territory to its more powerful neighbor."[5] Many Mexicans thus view the US system of criminal justice to be malleable and subject to manipulation by powerful class interests—a view that is ultimately more accurate than that of most US citizens, who are educated to believe in blind justice.

On the Mexican side of the border, the face of criminal justice complicates this collective memory with routine bribery—*mordidas* (literally, bites)—and corruption. The police chief in Quarryville, who had taken a trip to Mexico to learn more about the Mexican system of criminal justice, said that after he returned he took special pains to assure local Latinos that police in Quarryville did not take bribes, did not work for the INS (now ICE), and were not in the business of retribution or retaliation. Yet what the Comstock deputy was doing seemed more in line with Mexican police tactics than those of the police force in Quarryville, and when Barry intervened, he was negotiating with a local system of criminal justice that was clearly malleable.

In so doing, Barry redistributed power within Comstock in a way that increased his value to his workers and reinforced their obligations to him. In this context, the consciousness that the Mexicans achieved reflected their positions within the criminal justice system as mediated by their positions as workers on the Connor Dairy Farm. Whether it was *class* consciousness is an empirical question, but Felix and his relatives and friends from Michoacán were careful to point out to Barry something that reflected their identity: "They told me early on I was supposed to refer to them as Latinos, not Hispanics," Barry said. "*Hispanic* refers to a descendant of Spain, while *Latinos* are from Latin America." This simple distinction constitutes a critique of the prevailing appellation given to this new immigrant population (particularly by the US census), an appellation that tends to reinforce an imaginary homogeneity of the Latino population in Iowa, the Midwest, in other new destinations, and across the United States. Felix's rejection of this designation was a step toward actively distinguishing himself from his fellows, and perhaps a step toward active identification with his nation, his home state, and his natal community—each step further differentiating himself from other Mexicans and other Latinos. At some point in this branching of identity, Felix might achieve class consciousness, but only after exposure to events, literature, or information involving a formal or informal agent dedicated to speaking up on behalf of either new immigrants generally or some class of workers.

In and around Quarryville, the network of organizations providing services for the Latino population included the Catholic church (one of whose sisters operated a Hispanic ministry that addressed a wide variety of immigrants' spiritual and social needs), a nearby major state university, the hospital, the school system, the community college, the library, a local foundation established by descendants of one of the largest manufacturing companies in town, and a diversity committee that met periodically to discuss joint interests, problems, and initiatives, at times synthesizing the positions and issues of the other groups and catalyzing partnerships. Groups like these, either as part of their central missions or incidentally, generally educate immigrants about their rights and about where they can receive assistance for many of the problems that immigrants encounter.

At the same time, Quarryville was a heavily unionized town. Although some of the local unions were slow to recruit Latinos, by the time Felix and his fellow workers left the meatpacking plant, the union at the meatpacking plant—United Food and Commercial Workers Union (UFCW)—had brought in a Latino recruiter and had adapted its contract to include English as Second Language (ESL) classes for the Latino workers. The United Auto Workers (UAW) in Quarryville had only just begun recruiting Latinos, but stepped up its efforts after a strike in which many Latinos brought canned goods, clothing, and other supplies to the strikers. This show of solidarity and an expression of class consciousness struck a deep chord in the hearts of the strikers, most of whom were not immigrants but native Iowans.

CLUTTERED YARDS AND CLIPPED GOLF COURSES: CONSUMPTION AND CLASS CONSCIOUSNESS

We have Thorstein Veblen (1899) and Bill Roseberry (1996) to thank for drawing attention to the complex ways that consumption habits reflect class positions. Veblen wrote about conspicuous consumption and Roseberry about the subtler ways our coffee drinking tells about our class positions and class aspirations. Consumption habits of the rural South leave residues that some find aesthetically displeasing and others view as essential to their senses of self.

The horizontal outdoor storage of old wood, rubber, plastic, and scrap metal in various forms, from furniture to wiring to immobile cars, along with livestock and plants—resemble in some ways rural yards in migrant-sending communities of Mexico and Honduras. What appears to be junk can be used as spare parts or building supplies for various types of economic initiatives, such as penning livestock or repairing farm or food processing machinery. Many of the apparently idle or little-used goods, such as fish traps, baskets, or canoes, are awaiting seasonal activities such as shad runs or coffee harvests. These treasures provide safety from predators for fledgling poultry, encourages plant and insect growth that chickens and goats feed on, or camouflage enterprises such as growing marijuana that may be illegal or subject to theft. These collections of seemingly disparate material goods, piled up and clumped together in and around rural houses, barns, workshops, and yards, reflect rural livelihoods that contrast dramatically with those associated with the newly built environments of southeastern North Carolina.

New Hanover County, Wilmington, and coastal Brunswick County are among some of the fastest growing areas in the United States, adding new, high-dollar homes by the hundreds monthly (many over $1,000,000), hosting a modest yet enduring film industry and its occasional celebrities, and the site of several new, gated communities built up around marinas, golf courses, beaches, and other natural and enhanced landscapes that many find pleasing. Threatening this postcard image is the reputation of the region further inland for producing more animal waste than practically any area of similar size on earth, with several large poultry- and pork-processing plants and their associated confinement animal operations (Durrenberger and Thu 1995; Griffith 2006). More important to this discussion, however, is the change in the region's demographic composition. In addition to an influx of wealthy residents from the north, southeastern North Carolina has also attracted thousands of new immigrants, mostly from Florida, Latin America, and other localities to the south, originally to work in agriculture and poultry- and hog-processing plants. Increasingly, these new immigrants have moved into other sectors of the economy, clearing forests and draining swamps for golf courses and gated communities, building the high-priced houses inside the gated enclaves of the rich, and then cleaning and maintaining the golf courses, clubhouses, rental houses, hotel and motels.

8.1. TYPICAL RURAL YARD IN EASTERN NORTH CAROLINA

8.2. COURTYARD IN A RURAL VERACRUZ, MEXICO, HOME (PART OF A BAMBOO FURNITURE WORKSHOP)

Over 120 golf courses suffocate the coastal wetlands between Myrtle Beach and Wilmington, most associated with gated communities, marinas, and country clubs. Because golf courses need to be groomed for more than eight hours per day and would require paying overtime to a single crew, each golf course requires two crews of between twelve and eighteen workers. To avoid paying overtime, golf courses (or golf course management companies) swap crews. According to personnel managers who manage golf course crews, in 1989, only around 40 percent of the workers were Latino; by the mid-1990s, that percentage had risen to 75 to 80 percent. Today, nearly 100 percent of the applicants for golf course maintenance jobs are new immigrant Latinos.[6]

These Latino workers live in somewhat more modest accommodations than the elaborate homes they build around the golf courses and marinas they help to maintain. Some more recent immigrants, for example, live in rural labor camps of trailers without air conditioning or heat, yellow water, sheet rock flooring, and overpriced utilities. Working seventy to eighty hours a week, Latinos mow, weed, fertilize, and water the golf courses, performing a variety of tasks oriented toward keeping them trim, clean, lush, free of debris, and challenging. Although personnel managers consider them to be a unique, foreign-born component of a single working class, these Latinos neither all come from similar class backgrounds nor live in conditions reflecting similar circumstances.

At the least fortunate end of this continuum are men like Penín Simón,[7] a Chiapas-born emigrant with limited English or Spanish, two years of formal education in Mexico, and few skills marketable in a capitalist economy. Nevertheless, Penín's mere presence in North Carolina suggests that he had the resources to migrate—resources that range from access to loans or other financing to pay coyotes to the strength of character to risk crossing a militarized and dangerous border, as the gruesome discovery in the Dennison grain car showed. Once in North Carolina, Penín found work through an Anglo labor contractor named Duane Ash—a longtime local businessman who moved into labor contracting after marrying a Michoacán woman named Margaret Fernandez. Duane's businesses ranged from growing tobacco and other agricultural commodities to clearing land to fisheries and fish processing; after he moved into labor contracting, he added pornography and prostitution to his business services.

Duane and Margaret's relations with the local Latino population range from mildly paternal to highly exploitative, helping some with loans and job recommendations and milking others through housing at their labor camp, payroll kickback schemes, providing check-cashing services and high-interest loans, running lines,[8] and engaging in other practices common among labor contractors. Duane found work for Penín with a local golf course maintenance company—one of three that swap labor to avoid paying overtime—charging the company $12.00 per hour yet paying Penín only half that while charging him for rent, utilities, and for other goods and services. The company benefited by contracting with Duane because, as the immigrants' primary employer, Duane was responsible for assuring that they were legally authorized to work in the United States; this shielded the company from prosecution under current immigration law if, for instance, it should be discovered that Penín was not working legally.[9]

At the other end of this continuum is Margaret Fernandez, whose marriage to and business partnership with Duane Ash has enabled her rise into the local upper middle class of southeastern North Carolina. Margaret is part of a growing Latino middle class in new immigrant destinations across the United States. This consists principally of Latino entrepreneurs who have established businesses or entered into partnerships, through marriage or by other means, with locals who already own or control property, capital, or other resources. Many in this class cater primarily to other Latinos through country stores—*tiendas*—that provide wire transfer and transportation services; operate restaurants; sell food, spices, and other goods that Latinos prefer and desire; deal in a limited set of antibiotics and other pharmaceuticals (available without prescriptions);[10] and occasionally offer illegal entertainment such as selling controlled substances or sponsoring cockfights.[11]

Between Margaret and Penín are people like those from a family of working-class Latinos from a small community on the Guerrero-Michoacán border called Las Cuevas, some of whom were affiliated with Duane and Margaret, draining swamps, working in agriculture, and working the golf courses, and others who arrived later and took advantage of network ties and knowledge bases that earlier immigrants had developed to bypass labor contractors like Duane.

Over the past ten years, this extended family has colonized a small town called Vons, on the edge of Graffenried Swamp—a town that, little more than a crossroads on a map, is even smaller than Comstock. The oldest member of this family lives in Wilmington—a work-authorized, highly politically savvy, intelligent, skilled immigrant named Francisco Ortíz. Moderately well educated in Mexico (up to the ninth grade), after over two decades in the United States, Francisco spoke such fluent English that he at times had difficulty speaking Spanish; at one time in his life, he said that he felt as though he hadn't yet learned how to speak English well and had forgotten how to speak Spanish well. He has worked in jobs ranging from draining swamps for Duane (before Duane became a full-fledged labor contractor) to working in restaurants as a cook to running his own business building fences.

Francisco's early success in the United States, arriving prior to IRCA and becoming work authorized under its Special Agricultural Worker (SAW) provisions,[12] encouraged other family members to follow him, beginning with a cousin, Manuel Cortez. Drawing on Francisco's network connections, Manuel began working on Duane's tobacco farm, settling in Vons from April to September, during the tobacco season, and migrating to Florida to work in Florida agriculture during the winter—a seasonal itinerary he continues to the present day. He has been able to work himself into a position on Duane's tobacco farm that is common in rural North Carolina, acting as a foreman and supervisor of the seasonal tobacco workers, most of whom he recruits, and serving, with Duane's wife Margaret, as a liaison between the temporary farm workers and Duane.

Manuel has been in the United States nearly twenty years, but arrived too late to become work authorized under SAW provisions; for a brief period, he married a North Carolina woman with whom he had two children and through whom he acquired work authorization. After divorcing the *gringa*, he married a local Latino woman, but divorced her after a time and returned to Las Cuevas to bring back a much younger bride who has family in West Palm Beach near the farms where Manuel works during the winter. Over the next few years, several of Manuel's family joined him in Vons, some working with Duane but most finding work making cabinets in a small factory for the expanding market the coastal construction boom had created. They rented or bought houses and trailers in Vons, establishing the community as a kind of Las Cuevas annex. Currently, twenty interrelated families from Las Cuevas live in and around Vons.

After living in Vons now for several years, Manuel and the other Cortez families have settled into the consumer behaviors that characterize many Southern households and neighborhoods. Manuel's house has been built up from a mobile home, with a wraparound deck and new rooms added on in a way that now makes it anything but mobile.[13] Behind the main house are two trailers where Manuel houses temporary workers who work with him on Duane Ash's tobacco farm, as well as visiting relatives or those who have come to settle in Vons. Around the yard are small garden plots for growing vegetables, flowers, and herbs, pens for game cocks and hens, a storage shed, a greenhouse made primarily of plastic, and several other goods common in yards of this type: used tires, scrap sheet metal, car parts, recycled lumber, and so forth. Manuel's new wife, who speaks no English, works as a chambermaid at a motel along Highway 17, the road linking Wilmington and Myrtle Beach, and one of his sons works at a kiosk in a small mall built primarily for the golfing, retired, resident population. A second son builds cabinets with his uncles. Even the son who works with his uncles speaks little Spanish, like his brother who works at the mall, and Manuel frets that they have few ties to Las Cuevas, use English instead of Spanish, and prefer American to Mexican food. Manuel's lamenting about his sons' cultural preferences is interesting in light of his own hobby, which is following NASCAR and collecting racing team hats—a distinctly Southern rural cultural tradition. The hats are encased in plastic and, as if a milliner's wainscoting, line the walls where they meet the ceilings in two rooms of his house; models of NASCAR cars sit about on shelves as well.

Manuel's extended family is tied into the local economy and class system by many threads, generally in working-class positions, yet several factors frustrate their ability to achieve sustained class consciousness through their roles in the formal economy. Manuel and his wife, for example, leave Vons for half the year, migrating to Florida for work and family, and while in North Carolina, Manuel moves from his status as a farm worker to join Duane, the farm owner, in managing and housing the seasonal tobacco workers. He is also somewhat of an independent producer, using the resource of the yard surrounding his house to engage in repair work, gardening, raising livestock, recycling, and other informal economic pursuits.

Similarly, his brothers, cousins, and son—the cabinet makers—participate in the coastal construction industry in a remote way, manufacturing cabinets several miles from where they are installed in houses in gated communities and upscale neighborhoods of coastal New Hanover and Brunswick Counties. Throughout the construction industry—that part of Southern economies currently absorbing new immigrants at a rapid pace, often in the most hazardous tasks such as installing windows in high buildings and working with heavy stone—are fragmented and subcontracted. The plumbing and electrical contractors; framing, masonry, and finishing crews; the painting contractors and landscaping companies—all come to work sites by different paths and from different backgrounds, working on different jobs for different lengths of time.

In addition, construction in the South tends not to be unionized or based on systems of apprenticeship—two conditions that might foster class consciousness—but instead comprised of multiple companies ranging from independent contractors working more or less alone to large companies that specialize in skyscrapers, apartment complexes, prisons, and other large construction projects. These conditions frustrate the formation of relationships in work settings that could facilitate class consciousness.

Where Manuel and his family can achieve class consciousness is by comparing their levels and quality of consumption with the circumstances and living conditions of those who occupy the gated communities, lead lifestyles that seem excessively leisurely, and routinely benefit from the goods and services that Latinos and other working-class individuals provide. The material around one's house and yard, along with the house and yard themselves, reflect class positions and aspirations. The accumulations of what appear to some to be junk are actually sources of income and perhaps, eventually, wealth. Covenants, zoning laws, and other kinds of regulations designed to impose aesthetic standards on neighborhoods often meet vehement opposition by the working-class individuals, who often view them as conspiracies against their ways of life (Griffith 1999; Doukas 2003).

Another manifestation of this class consciousness can be seen in communities that provide migrants to US destinations like Las Cuevas, where the photographs that migrants send rarely depict the squalid conditions that many experience but highlight nice clothes, jewelry, *quinceañeras* ("coming out" parties celebrating girls' fifteenth birthdays), weddings, shiny automobiles and trucks, and other positive dimensions. These photos, often accompanying remittances, reinforce the belief among potential migrants that the migration experience usually results in material gain. Zamudio Grave (2005), writing about Veracruz, Mexico, and Isaula and her colleagues (2007), writing about Olancho, Honduras, both report that potential emigrants have highly distorted views and poor information about life in the United States.[14]

Immigrants' consumer behaviors in the United States often reflect middle-class aspirations. For example, Juan Jimenez, a Honduran construction worker, recently purchased a full-sized Dodge Ram pick-up truck for about $35,000. Such evidently excessive purchases are not rare: the priest at the Catholic church in Newton Grove, North Carolina, reported that one of his most significant and common interactions with new immigrant Latinos was blessing new trucks.

Married to a woman from Veracruz who sells tacos and enchiladas to Latino construction crews throughout the Durham-Raleigh-Chapel Hill triangle, the father of one US-born daughter, Juan has worked hard to learn English and has brought several of his relatives from Honduras to find them work in construction, renting them rooms in his house until they can afford their own housing. He and most of his relatives come from coffee-growing communities in Honduras, but his marriage to the Mexican woman, their raising a daughter in Durham, and his continuing success all point to an increasing attachment to North Carolina. When I asked him and one of his cousins whether they intended to return to Honduras to become coffee producers, they answered in a way that resonated with Roseberry's (1996) work on yuppie coffees: *No cafeteleros, pero café bebedores* ("Not coffee growers, but coffee drinkers").

DISCUSSION

I opened this chapter with a brief discussion of the ways work sites and production regimes have become fragmented, following with examples of immigrants confronting or participating in fragmenting processes and developing alternative allegiances and methods of making their lives more whole. A countervailing development occurring around many new immigrant populations is the several attempts to organize and enlighten immigrants in specific communities, bringing them together around community celebrations, in schools, in churches, and at other nonwork venues, and teaching them about resources available in local areas that assist immigrants with problems ranging from severe emotional or physical trauma to difficulties negotiating a supermarket.

Each member of the network of organizations, agencies, and individuals interested in immigrants' rights in Quarryville, Iowa, for example, provides immigrants information about one or more local resources, whether to address problems regarding health, language, education, housing, workers' rights, regularizing legal status, or others. Similar networks exist in all the communities experiencing new immigration that we studied across the rural United States, although they vary in terms of levels of organization, dedication, and power across communities. Immigrants who interact with these networks typically add to their knowledge about their rights in the communities where they reside (which may be greater, practically speaking, than their rights under federal statutes) and their human rights, including knowledge about sanctuaries from persecution, legal aid, and defense against discrimination and exploitation.

While these networks provide immigrants with the means to defend themselves against racism, police harassment, and other problems, they rarely stem the various processes that undermine class consciousness. Several developments in the international division of labor have made it possible for people to participate in production regimes without sustained social interaction with others in similar material conditions and similar economic opportunities, burdens, and risks—the circumstances that give rise to class affiliations and class consciousness (Durrenberger and Erem 2005). Two of the more important are subcontracting and the use of temporary workers (often called "contingent" workers), both hallmarks of flexible production systems as well as some industries that have historically drawn heavily on immigrant labor. Ironically, both practices encourage the continued strength of cultural heritage, cultural identity, and daily cultural practices, facilitating allegiance based on culture, yet discourage the social processes that facilitate allegiance based on class (Heyman, this volume).

The Mexican dairy workers in Comstock and the Mexican and Mexican-American cabinet makers in Vons are cases in point, deriving from different recent local and regional histories. Where meatpacking plants have provided a venue for unionization and its attendant class consciousness, the notoriously high turnover of labor combined with their dependence on immigrant labor, initially resulted in the military model of migration—single males colonizing an industry and living in barracks-like or dormitory conditions. Yet by the mid-1990s this had evolved into a Latino community in which families and co-ethnics not dependent on meatpacking have elaborated their cultural presence and multiplied their ties to local, native, and longstanding community members and institutions. Barriers between immigrant and native groups have been eroded and breached as a result, and more native industries and individuals have developed relations, including labor relations, with the immigrant population. As this has occurred, more and more immigrants have turned away from meatpacking and sought out other jobs in less-regimented industries, working in smaller groups where they have been able to develop closer ties, often of patronage, with their employers.

The two immigrant destinations profiled above have both attracted immigrants from similar regions in Mexico and Central America, and in both regions immigrants have been putting down roots, raising families, and becoming attached to the working class by various, more or less tenuous threads. The cabinet makers of Vons have not developed the same character of relations with their employers as the dairy workers in Comstock, but different structural conditions prevent them, too, from forming class allegiances.

The construction industry of southeastern North Carolina and the particular history of the Mexican colonization of Vons allow Manuel's cousins and son to participate in a monumental production project—one that has been altering entire coastal ecosystems—without traveling far from a small cluster of homes that, every day at noon, smells of tortillas toasting. Similarly, the dairy workers of Comstock may or may not have contributed to the UAW strike fund, but on the job their relations with Barry tend to be paternal rather than contractual or hostile. Some nascent attempts to foster class consciousness among immigrants do exist—such as farm worker unions and other collective organizations—but the fragmentation of relations of production have continued to result in driving immigrants and others of the working class into niches of identity based on cultural practices, paternal ties to employers, legal status, reactions to racist and nativist sentiments, multiple livelihoods and economic roles, and the semblance of upward mobility that comes from renting trailers to compatriots and supervising work crews.

Even when assuming management positions, these new (and now aging) immigrants remain in essentially working-class positions, hired by somewhat higher-class individuals to recruit and supervise co-ethnics whose labor continues to create value for those higher-class individuals. In each region, too, immigrant entrepreneurs have emerged, founding businesses ranging from country stores and restaurants to auto mechanic workshops and specialty construction services. Often these businesses revitalize ailing parts of the downtowns of rural communities, focusing immigrant activity and interaction in areas far from the outlying retail chains and shopping malls and enhancing local cultural landscapes for immigrants and natives alike. Yet more often than not these immigrant businesses depend on family labor and income from working-class occupations to survive, allowing their owners only limited separation from their working-class roots. As with US-born workers, who found taverns and restaurants with savings from fairly well-paid, unionized manufacturing jobs, these immigrants depend heavily on their former co-workers and contemporary co-ethnics to patronize their businesses, exposing themselves to more general economic trends (e.g., the health of the meatpacking industry). At the same time, they contribute to the illusion that they have freed themselves from the working class by leaping aboard the train of the American dream. Whether they are leaving behind or towing a grain car with eleven dead Mexicans remains to be seen.

NOTES

1. The bulk of research for this chapter was undertaken with Ed Kissam and Aguirre International (now the Aguirre Group of JBS International), for the US Department of Agriculture's Fund for Rural America initiative. This project involved analyses of six rural communities around the United States from 2001 to 2006 (two in the West, two in the Midwest, and two in the South). Additional funds were provided by the UNC Sea Grant College program to expand the study in rural North Carolina coastal regions. For the work in Mexico and Honduras, the research was funded by the National Institute of Occupational Safety and Health on the project, "El Puente (the bridge): Health Implications of Communication among Migrant Families" and the National Science Foundation on the project, "Migration and Knowledge." Many thanks to all these entities for their assistance; any errors or misrepresentations in the analysis are, of course, mine alone.

2. What constitutes *quality* labor is almost as variable from different class and ethnic positions as what constitutes quality food; employers want disciplined workers who show up on time, don't complain, and work at a productive pace (also subjectively defined), yet workers may consider a quality worker someone who questions prevailing methods of production because they endanger workers or because other methods of production could be more effective. Scholars of immigration commonly argue that immigrant workers become attractive not because of absolute shortages of workers, but because of shortages of workers who are willing to submit to conditions they believe are unfair or morally reprehensible (Hahamovich 1997; Griffith 2006).

3. It is unclear exactly why the local workers quit. However, this is not an uncommon local response to immigrant workers colonizing an industry or work force. Usually immigrants increase the pace of work or set higher productivity stan-

dards that employers then expect all workers to adhere to. When combined with racism and nativism, local workers have powerful material and cultural reasons to seek other work.

4. Mark Grey (2000) makes the point that many new immigrants in Iowa meat-packing treat their jobs as seasonal jobs, coming and going from them to attend to other responsibilities in other communities, states, and in Mexico, even though the jobs are stable, year-round jobs. Repetitive motion illness, a common complaint among meatpacking workers, encourages leaving meatpacking work periodically as well.

5. Author's translation of: "La migración a los Estados Unidos empezó hace más de un siglo y medio, cuando México tuvo que ceder la mitad de su territorio a su poderoso vecino" (Levine 2004:7).

6. The 1 to 3% or so who apply who aren't immigrant Latinos tend to be retir-ees looking for jobs as "rangers" (mostly older white men who perform a variety of odd jobs catering to golfers, primarily to golf for free).

7. This is a pseudonym, as are all the names of individuals, and some of the names of communities, in this paper, for reasons of confidentiality.

8. Running a "line" is similar to operating a country store, selling a variety of goods and services—from individual beers to sessions with prostitutes—to workers in labor camps whose costs are added to workers' bills and deducted from their pay each pay period. As with convenience stores in minority neighborhoods, the prices charged for these goods and services are often exorbitant.

9. Current immigration debates often ignore the fact that employers face severe sanctions for hiring immigrants under the Immigration Reform and Control Act's Employer Sanctions provisions. Although on the books for over 20 years, political will to enforce employer sanctions has yet to develop, leaving many critiques of the current status quo crying out for regulations that already exist.

10. According to some Latinos I've interviewed, some of the pharmaceuticals that are sold without prescriptions at these *tiendas* are expired and hence available in Mexico for little money; others report that they are simply purchased at Mexican *farmacias* and resold in the United States.

11. Occasionally, visiting these *tiendas*, there are many cars parked outside but inside the store only a clerk and perhaps one or two customers; this is because some of these stores have back rooms in which various illegal activities take place.

12. The SAW provisions allowed people to work legally in the United States if they could prove they had worked 90 days in agriculture over the previous three years. The program was a far bigger success than immigration reformers antici-pated, with over 2 million becoming work authorized under the provisions. This was what immigration reform advocates favoring punishing the undocumented today would call IRCA's amnesty provision and immigration reform advocates favoring documenting the undocumented would call something like "earned legalization."

13. Paul Durrenberger notes that this is also common in central Pennsylvania, where similar poverty and catch-all work encourage people to build onto double-wide trailers.

14. This contrasts slightly with Levitt's (2001) observations about the pools of information that migrants typically have prior to migration, and with the work of Grasmuck and Pessar (1991), among others who have written about transnational social fields.

REFERENCES CITED

Broadway, Michael. 2007. "Meatpacking and the Transformation of Rural Communities: A Comparison of Brooks, Alberta, and Garden City, Kansas." *Rural Sociology* 72(4): 560–582.

Doukas, Dimitra. 2003. *Worked Over: The Corporate Sabotage of an American Community*. Ithaca, NY: Cornell University Press.

Durrenberger, E. Paul, and Suzan Erem. 2005. *Class Acts: An Anthropology of Urban Service Workers and Their Union*. Boulder, CO: Paradigm Publishers.

Durrenberger, E. Paul, and Kendall Thu, eds. 1995. *Pigs, Profits, and Rural Communities*. Albany: State University of New York Press.

Fink, Leon. 2003. *The Maya of Morgantown: Work and Community in the Nuevo New South*. Chapel Hill: University of North Carolina Press.

Grasmuck, Sherri, and Patricia Pessar. 1991. *Between Two Islands: Dominican International Migration*. Berkeley: University of California Press.

Grey, Mark. 2000. "Immigrants, Migration, and Worker Turnover at the Hog Pride Pork Packing Plant." *Human Organization* 58: 16–27.

Griffith, David. 1993. *Jones's Minimal: Low-Wage Labor in the United States*. Albany: State University of New York Press.

———. 1999. *The Estuary's Gift: An Atlantic Coast Cultural Biography*. University Park: Penn State University Press.

———. 2006. *American Guestworkers: Jamaicans and Mexicans in the U.S. Labor Market*. University Park: Penn State University Press.

Hage, David, and Paul Klauda. 1989. *No Retreat, No Surrender: Labor's War at Hormell*. New York: William Morrow.

Hahamovich, Cynthia. 1997. *The Fruits of Their Labor*. Chapel Hill: University of North Carolina Press.

Isaula, Raquel. 2007. *Migracion y Remesas en Olancho, Honduras*. Tegucigalpa: Red de Desarrollo Sostenible.

Levine, Elaine. 2004. "Presentación." In *Inserción Laboral de Migrantes Mexicanos y Latinos en Estados Unidos*, edited by E. Levine. Mexico City: Centro de Investigaciones sobre América del Norte, Universidad Nacional Autónoma de México.

Levitt, Peggy. 2001. *The Transnational Villagers*. Berkeley: University of California Press.

Massey, Douglas. In press. *New Faces, New Places*. New York: Russell Sage Foundation.

Nash, June. 1983. "Introduction." In *Women, Men, and the New International Division of Labor*, edited by J. Nash and M. Fernandez-Kelley. Albany: State University of New York Press.

Newman, Katherine. 1988. *Falling from Grace: The Experience of Downward Mobility in the American Middle Class*. New York: Free Press.

Roseberry, William. 1996. "The Rise of Yuppie Coffees and the Reimagination of Class in the United States." *American Anthropologist* 98: 762–775.

Sanderson, Steve, ed. 1985. *The Americas in the New International Division of Labor*. New York: Holmes and Meier.

Smart, Alan, and Josephine Smart. 2005. "Introduction." In *Petty Capitalists and Globalization: Flexibility, Entrepreneurship, and Economic Development*, edited by A. Smart and J. Smart. Albany: State University of New York Press.

Stull, Don, and Michael Broadway. 2001. *Slaughterhouse Blues*. New York: Holt, Reinhart.

Veblen, Thorstein. 1899. *Theory of the Leisure Class*. New York: Modern Library.

Zamudio Grave, Patricia. 2004. "La Migración en el Estado de Veracruz: Una historia reciente." In *Los Grandes Temas de los Veracruzanos*. Veracruz: Xalapa Fundación Colosio Veracruz.

Zlolniski, Christian. 2006. *Janitors, Street Vendors, and Activists: The Lives of Mexican Immigrants in Silicon Valley*. Berkeley: University of California Press.

Zuñiga, Victor, and Rubén Hernandez-Leon. 2005. *New Destinations*. New York: Russell Sage Foundation.

NINE

Class Consciousness in a Complicated Setting

Race, Immigration Status, Nationality, and Class on the US-Mexico Border

JOSIAH HEYMAN

INTRODUCTION

The US-Mexico border is particularly interesting for examining the complications of class consciousness. Class relations and perceptions on the US side are deeply interwoven with race relations between Anglo Americans and Mexican Americans,[1] while racism and nationalism also affect understandings of Mexico in the United States and vice versa. The border inherently involves connections and comparisons across the international boundary, and the region is central to the current international division of labor in manufacturing. In turn, citizenship and immigration status strongly affect class and race in the United States, although none of these categories match up with the others in a simple way. Even a local, ethnographic study of consciousness thus demands consideration of regional, national, and transnational scales.

The goal in sorting out this complexity is not to privilege one set of relations, whether class, citizenship, race, or gender, and ignore the others or see them as disguises to be pulled away. Nor is it enough to say that inequalities intersect or combine (e.g., to use the label "class-race"). That is true, but by itself is not insightful, substituting a label for hard political and intellectual challenges. Rather, we need to examine the relationship between different orders of phenomena, the overall framework of capitalist relations, historically assembled regional frameworks (social-political orders and discourses), and lived experiences and understandings.

To untangle these complications, I begin by considering four levels of abstraction in the study of inequality. This helps us understand that the word *class* means several different things, helping us clarify the relationship between class and other social frameworks, such as citizenship or race. Next, I briefly review the history of the US-Mexico border, examining changes in the organization of inequality as we come to the present situation. The heart of the paper is a corpus of ethnographic material from the US side of the border (El Paso, Texas); although this is not a truly two-sided view of the borderlands, it does touch on consciousness of class in transnational connections. I conclude by suggesting that the border provides an illuminating case study of how to proceed in understanding other tangled cases of consciousness.

FOUR LEVELS OF ABSTRACTION IN THE ANALYSIS OF INEQUALITY

Here I offer four different levels of analysis of inequality, from more abstract to more specific. I draw substantially on Eric Wolf's discussion of power (1990), especially his distinctions among strategic power, tactical power, and immediate behavioral power.

1. The abstract class relationship between labor and capital: Marx's central concern, of course, and Wolf's core example of strategic power.

2. The organizing principles by which people are mobilized as "labor" or "capital," which fit with Wolf's tactical power. These may be race, nationality, and gender, as well as class itself (e.g., the factors that produce advantages and disadvantages in public schools).

3. The empirical distribution of material goods and social honor among individuals, households, and communities, much influenced by the mobilizing principles discussed in item 2.

4. Consciousness: the ways that people understand strategic, tactical, and empirical inequalities, using a variety of frameworks, class and otherwise.

Recently, and I think correctly, the idea of intersectionality (Collins 1998) has been used to summarize the simultaneity and interactions of class, race, gender, sexuality, and (more rarely recognized) citizenship and immigration status. The framework offered here aids our understanding of intersectionality by clarifying confusions derived from using the same words at different levels of abstraction, and by helping us analyze more deeply the specific character of intersections, such as the use of race or citizenship as means of recruitment into and lived experiences of strategic class relations.

FROM RACE TO CLASS ON THE US-MEXICO BORDER: A REGIONAL HISTORY IN TWO NATIONS

The US-Mexico borderlands deserve a lengthy stand-alone essay addressing the interactions over time and space of race, class, citizenship, and gender; all I can provide here are brief notes about how we arrived at the present situation (see Barrera 1979; Fernández-Kelly 1983; Ganster and Lorey 2008; Heyman 1991; Nevins 2002).

The current boundary was drawn by conquest and purchase in 1848 and 1853. After that, Anglo Americans used nationality, race, and culture (one cannot readily distinguish among them) as tactical principles of primitive accumulation to steal, by violence and law, resources from Native Americans and Mexicans. As industrial and agroindustrial capitalism grew from the 1870s onward, systematic racial discrimination (most often Anglo American versus Mexican American) pervaded workplaces, labor markets, and nonwork institutions such as schools. However, heroic labor, civil rights, and political struggles throughout the twentieth century broke the hold of formal racism, beginning in the 1940s and strongly taking hold from the 1970s onward.

Hence, the US borderlands have seen a shift of tactical and empirical inequalities from strict racism to a complicated mixture of race and class. It is precisely the point of interest in studying this case that class is no longer completely synonymous and hidden within race, but rather that both race and class frameworks are openly and widely available as raw materials for consciousness. However, as the militant civil rights struggles in the United States shattered the racist, unitary subordination of all Mexicans and Mexican-origin Americans, regardless of legal status and national location, this did not lead to the end of racism, but rather its reworking in terms of citizenship and immigration status.

Mexican labor migration to the United States, though it has a long history, grew dramatically after 1965, and the legal and social distinctions among citizen, legal immigrant (legal permanent resident), legal temporary worker, undocumented immigrant, and legal visitor became important to recruitment into unequal labor markets and educational pathways. To phrase this more abstractly, citizenship and immigration status are now important tactical grounds for the unequal mobilization and sorting of labor, class processes at their most strategic level (Heyman 2001). Mexican-origin people can and do belong to all of these legal categories, but often in US public discourse, the concept *Mexican* has substantially merged with *immigrant*, and *immigrant* has merged with *illegal alien*. Most borderlanders do a better job of making the relevant distinctions than interior residents, but the result is (again) an interesting complication of consciousness. Even in El Paso, among Mexican-origin people, there coexist discourses that objectify all Mexicans as subordinate or polluting outsiders, those that isolate current immigrants from Mexican Americans as citizens, and those that envision forms of class solidarity across boundaries of race, citizenship, and nation.

Racial inequality (indigenous/Hispanic Mexican) is important as a form of tactical power in many regions of Mexico, including some near the northern border, and there is widespread, if low-key, racism concerning skin color and culture. Nevertheless, the Mexican northern borderlands are explicitly organized by class at the tactical, empirical, and conscious levels, as well as in their strategic relationship to the world (mostly US) economy. As a result, the discourse of class is more often used on the Mexican side than the US side. Mexico's border region developed around a set of industrial farming and natural-resource extraction zones, together with transport and commerce with the United States, from the 1880s onward.

Beginning in 1965, and exploding after 1982, world-market-oriented export manufacturing plants, called *maquiladoras*, have located along Mexico's northern border cities. The million-plus workers are young women and men (note that abstract class roles are tactically organized in gendered and generational ways) and the capitalists major and minor US, Canadian, Asian, and European transnational corporations, and the resulting industrial mass rivals Engels's Manchester as exemplar of factory capitalism in a supposedly postmodern world. In addition to assembly-plant workers, however, Mexican northern border cities host burgeoning upper and professional-technical classes, and large numbers of formal and informal businesses and trades that often reach across the border; particularly visible in El Paso are cross-border commuting workers, including domestic workers, gardeners, and construction laborers.

El Paso itself also deserves brief contextualization. The largest owners of productive capital in this area—manufacturers, large-scale farmers, and housing and real estate developers—are Anglo American. However, large Mexican capitalists have substantial holdings and business dealings on the US side, and cross-border alliances abound among the elite. Bankers and the professions are disproportionately Anglo American but include a number of Mexican Americans and well-educated Mexican immigrants. In terms of external corporate capital, El Paso has sold itself for many decades on the basis of its large pool of low-wage and vulnerable workers.

From the 1950s to the 1990s there were large external and some local men's slacks manufacturers. Being a kind of transitional *"maquiladora"* zone within the United States, El Paso's low-wage manufacturing sector was devastated by the North American Free Trade Agreement (NAFTA) and Central American Free Trade Agreement (CAFTA), as blue jeans makers raced off to interior Mexico and Honduras. Indeed, this city that prides itself in its proximity to Mexico lost the most manufacturing jobs in the United States under NAFTA (Spener 2002). There has recently been an influx of external corporate call centers (El Paso offers a large bilingual labor force), but the garment and call center sectors mainly have different sets of workers. Finally, El Paso contains import-export businesses and receives cross-border wholesale and retail shopping from Mexico; owners include established Anglo families, niche ethnic groups (Lebanese, Koreans, etc.), and corporate chains, but many employees and some owners are Mexican American, able to speak Spanish to a Mexican clientele.

Perhaps the most dynamic employment sector in El Paso is, however, the US government, including extensive border control and intelligence agencies and, even more importantly, a vast and expanding Army base (Ft. Bliss). Government jobs vary a great deal in wages and working conditions, from enlisted private to FBI supervisor, but as a whole they offer relatively secure employment with federal benefits, allocated without regard to race; many African Americans and Mexican Americans as well as Anglo Americans work at all levels of this sector. Except for the military, which accepts legal residents, federal law enforcement jobs are reserved for US citizens. Leaving aside the challenging theoretical question of the relationship of state employment to strategic class relations in capitalism, this large set of jobs helps explain how class now cuts across the older labor market principle of strict racism: in the Department of Homeland Security, say, to be "Mexican" is no longer to be relegated to the lower sectors of the working class. At the same time, the importance of government employment strengthens consciousness of distinctions between US citizens and noncitizens (Heyman 2002).

In El Paso, to be a poorly educated, monolingual Spanish-speaking Mexican immigrant cleaning houses, gardening, or laying tile is precisely to be mobilized for highly exploitable class relations and for low income and no health insurance through the tactical principle of noncitizenship, although there are some naturalized and US-born citizens in this class segment.[2] Class, immigration status, and nationality thus align in daily experience. Likewise, being on the US versus Mexican side matters significantly to the surface characteristics of class—Mexico is a much poorer country than the United States, and has more starkly visible inequalities—even if analytically there are important transnational connections and commonalities. The interesting complexity of consciousness of US borderlanders is that they have some understanding of global class phenomena—undoubtedly more than most Americans—and yet their understanding is incomplete, being shaped by particular kinds of cross-border interactions and comparisons.

CLASS AND CONSCIOUSNESS: AN ETHNOGRAPHIC EXPLORATION

The Ethnographic Setting

Although my presentation is grounded in many years of formal ethnography and everyday life in the borderlands, in both Mexico and the United States, I draw here on a rather heterodox form of ethnography, electronic discussions from an online university course during spring 2007, recorded as written text. The course, US-Mexico Border Society and Culture, drew on students' own experiences in the borderlands (with two exceptions), mainly but not exclusively on the US side. Because online discussions and "classroom" materials may not be viewed as suited to ethnography, allow me to delineate the nature of this material.

In this course, students had a weekly discussion requirement that consisted of typed statements on a website that could be seen by the professor and other students. The week started off with a prompt from the professor, as well as assigned book and online readings (the latter, written by the professor, were the equivalent of a lecture).[3] The students replied to the prompt with a long statement (200 words or more), and then they were required to make at least two comments on other students' postings; they often made many more. In effect, a number of lines of conversation (threads) resulted from this structure. I rarely intervened in the discussions.

The prompt was as follows:

> National origin, immigration/citizenship status, and ethnicity are all obvious at the border. We easily refer to them in analyzing social interactions and culture. However, class also has an important role to play at the border, both in Mexico and in the United States, and in the many different kinds of interactions between the two. Discuss the role of class (class interactions and experiences within and across classes) in border society and culture.

Clearly, the prompt influenced students, but the flow of conversation broadly took its own path (as we will see); in my analysis, I have concentrated on the more personal, less reading- or professor-directed statements.[4] The typewritten corpus of conversations from this week was 72 single-spaced pages, while two years of the course yielded over 2,000 such pages. I analyzed the material from the focal week by identifying themes in all discussion contributions, tabulating the most common themes, and also identifying notable individual contributions. For this paper, I have also examined material from other weeks and the previous year's course in less-structured fashion. In addition, the fact that I obtained fifteen weeks of continual, often deep conversations by individual students, plus capsule self-descriptions provided for another course exercise, offers an ethnographically useful knowledge of the context of individual speakers.

It is worth briefly touching on the uses and limitations of an online discussion in the context of urban ethnography. Urban ethnography, with some exceptions, consists of one-dimensional encounters at single unifying settings of people living otherwise separated lives, unlike ethnographies in many small-scale societies and rural settings. On occasion we get to know some people and places more richly, but often we stitch together as ethnography bits and pieces of such partial encounters. An online course discussion board is one such partial, but internally rich and sustained, encounter of a substantial set of people. One can legitimately express concern that this material does not have the deep holism of immersion in a natural lived setting. But we can consider the discussion board to be a record of a deep, long conversation, something we value when we do naturalistic ethnography. In this regard, it should be emphasized that this conversation took place during the eleventh week of a fifteen-week course, when the students knew each other well and were relaxed and straightforward in their communicative styles. An obvious concern about online discussions is the idea that they are mediated by the computer and prone to falsification. Yet this was not a fantasy-role discussion board, and there is every reason to think that participants were sincere, just inflected by the normal presentation of self one finds in any public conversation among partially connected urban dwellers.

This course was taught at the University of Texas at El Paso (UTEP). UTEP is an urban commuter university with unselective admissions, and a strong sense of integration into the surrounding community. About 60 percent of students are the first in their family to go to college, a reasonable proxy measure for working-class origins. The university student body is 54 percent female, 72 percent US Latino (the vast majority of Mexican origin), and another 9 percent Mexican nationals/residents, who commute across the border. The 27 students in my specific course were 67 percent female. They included 25 US residents of entirely or partly Mexican origin, all of them residing in the El Paso area. No one dwelled in Mexico, though one student had changed residence from there recently and thus usually articulated a Mexican-side perspective. There were two Anglo Americans, both from nonborder regions of Texas, taking advantage of the online course. The US students of Mexican origin varied greatly among themselves, from dual nationals with close relationships to Mexico to very US-oriented Latinos and part-Latinos, and various cultural stances in between. The student body was thus reasonably representative of El Paso, except for their relative youth; however, the online format attracted more older students than a live course would have.[5]

Did Consciousness of Class Emerge in This Discussion?

The prompt about class as a distinctive phenomenon on the border was emicly comprehensible to almost all students. It did not receive the puzzled "Huh?" response characteristic of a locally incomprehensible ethno-graphic question. Admittedly, in a course setting with students aware that the professor would grade them, admitting that a question made no sense is unlikely, so I have examined their responses to see if they were relevant to the topic or manifested signs of assembling arbitrary and irrelevant state-ments to attempt to answer a poorly understood question. Of the 25 ini-tial responses, 23 (92%) showed comprehension of the question through a relevant reply. That is not to say that these were pure class analyses, nor perhaps should they have been, given the complexities of the borderlands. Indeed, what draws attention are the ways that class was comprehended in conjunction with other issues.

A few students provided systematic overviews of class in the border-lands (four strong postings and several other thinner ones). It is hard to tell whether this relatively small number is because of weak consciousness of class or poorly developed abilities to think about society and culture in sys-tematic terms at all. As anyone who teaches social science in the United States knows, students have potentials for such work that is rarely culti-vated. Hence, a less systematic, more personal contribution illustrates the latent awareness of class in the borderlands and how it was beginning to cut across the clearer framework of race division:

> When I was in elementary school (late 70's) I did not think there were any poor white people. When I finally met some I thought it was a tragedy. I thought it was worse to be a white poor person than a poor Mexican person. I'm not sure why I thought that. . . . One of my class-mates refers to herself as white trash because she does not have any money. She and her husband literally live paycheck to paycheck. She does not have extra money for things that come up. We recently had to buy a book for our class and if it weren't for a gift card she received she would not have been able to buy it. We have to look at each other as individuals with certain talents and needs.

It is worth contextualizing Maria Elena's (a pseudonym, as with all subse-quent names) surprising realization that class cut across ethnicity by consid-ering how strongly ethnicity aligned with class in her own, distinctly mar-ginalized Mexican-side and then US-immigrant background:

> Selling *aguas frescas* [freshly squeezed fruit juices] is certainly an honor-able job. My uncles helped feed their brothers and sisters by selling the

aguas. My grandfather abandoned his family and my grandmother was left to feed their 13 children. So my grandmother would make the *aguas* and my uncles would go out and sell them.

You are right [referring to another student] about (most) Mexicans teaching their children their "place" in society. I always knew my place. My parents always pointed out the fact that we did not have money and therefore we did not have certain rights. My parents never encouraged us to attend a University because only rich people could do that. I think this is why it is so important for me to finish my education even at the age of 39.

Maria Elena represents two strong tendencies in the conversation: students definitely did recognize class phenomena in their own lives and the lives of others they knew, but they also slid back and forth between class and other frameworks of understanding, such as race—note the ambiguous referent of her "place" (Mexican, not having money).

Two discussions involving eight individuals that emerged during the conversational period (after the initial postings were completed) indicate that class had a spontaneous presence in student consciousness, beyond responding to the professor's prompt.[6] One thread addressed the university's new policy of charging varying rates for different parking lots, using the symbolically loaded term "silver lots" for the closest and most expensive student parking. In markedly emotional postings, several students expressed personal affront at being differentiated by purchasing power. They also discussed the parking price increase in general, but that concern was expressed by fewer students and was more muted in tone. Nancy Fraser (1997) has argued that social justice involves both "recognition" and "redistribution"; in this case, students were more concerned with the symbolic recognition element than the material redistribution one. They did not, however, link this issue to the wider context of the border or the political economy of university funding.[7]

The other notable spontaneous discussion centered on a controversial redevelopment plan, involving eminent domain, multiple block razing, and corporate rebuilding for the southern edge of downtown El Paso. This issue is actually quite complex and contradictory from the point of view of class analysis of public policy.[8] The course discussion did not address those issues, but focused on a key aspect of class symbolism cutting across race in an interesting way. Claudia (a Mexican national living in El Paso and involved in US-side activism) noted:

An example of how important class is in the border is the plan to revitalize downtown, because the [investment] group Paso del Norte which
is proposing this project, targets specifically how to disappear an area
that reflects the environment of the working Mexican class. In the slide-
show that they are presenting to the enterprises and business, there is
an image of an old Mexican man, and they portrayed him as a lazy and
dirty; in the other slide in which they present the re-modeled version or
the group of people that this project will attract, they have pictures of
Penelope Cruz and Mathew McConaghey as their model of progress.

Then, Daniel (a dual national, living on the US side) affirmed her observation:

Indeed the current EP downtown revitalization plan that is proposed
is more about class perceptions than other aspects of classification
(ethnicity, for instance). I say this because in the Paso del Norte [group]
there are both Mexican and United Statesian members. And they are all
very rich and probably share many ambitions and a common outlook
on development. Their plan undermines other people (of various eth-
nicities) being affected with a different lifestyle, goals, ambitions, and
perspectives.

Claudia and Daniel's key point was that the plan was being promoted
through an image of improving the *class* appearance of the area in a way
that cut across Latino ethnicity (hence, the old man/Penelope Cruz contrast). Daniel also perceptively noted the cross-racial/national composition
of pro-redevelopment capital. They were not ignoring the relevance of the
racial composition of the stigmatized Mexican poor or Asian small store-
keepers, however. It is noteworthy that the two students who took the lead
in this conversation had backgrounds of Latin American critical political
consciousness.

In summary, a number of students offered critical class analyses, and
broadly understood the idea that class had become important as an explicit
feature of the social structure of the US borderlands. However, this does
not fully convey the overall tone, in which students often treated the emergence of class as potentially liberating. This came out spontaneously, early
in the weekly discussion, when there were several calls for and much admi-
ration of optimistic stories of upward class mobility.[9] The following self-
description by Laura came after a critical phase of the conversation that
addressed class unfairness as seen in lack of health insurance:

I understand where you're coming from especially needing that health insurance. I'm divorced, three kids and had to make a choice between finishing college to get a better paying job or continue working. I have to do without medical insurance but fortunately my kids have it. I was raised by lower class working parents and fortunately I have still had the opportunity to continue my education. . . . I am the 7th of 8 children and although we had to do without a lot while growing up coming from a low income household didn't impede our ambitions and desires for our future. We may not all be lawyers and doctors, but many of my brothers and sisters may be labeled as high-income families. I'm not trying to diminish the value of their stories, but just an example that even if you are from a low class society there is no need to be that all your life. Maybe we were just lucky, but my father was an illegal immigrant and both my parents were seasonal farm workers so I know there are opportunities here in the U.S. that allow for such progress.

And Martha added these heartfelt wishes:

It would be nice to read a novel about a "rags to riches" (or *colonias* to country club) experience [*colonias* are unplanned, informal settlements in the US borderlands, associated in most people's minds with poor immigrants, though the reality is more complex]. I personally have worked in the Texas A&M *Colonias* Program as a Parent/Child Trainer and would do home visits to the families in the program. I feel that many of the people I encountered had, in a way or another had their own success story, even if they were small accomplishments. Unfortunately these will never get published. The elementary school that I went to was in a "bad" neighborhood and yet this guy graduated valedictorian in high school, went to some great university, enrolled in the marines, married an ambassador's daughter, and is now some kind of overseas representative for the US. This is a great story, especially since his mother raised him and his sister on a factory worker's salary, and their father was out of the picture. Unfortunately, his sister was a *"chola"* [a tough street kid] in high school and had a very troublesome 20's. She was totally the opposite of what his story was. I also know this family of seven who came here as immigrants, the father and mother are hard workers; the children had to help them in the several family businesses that they had in order to make ends meet. The first four children have graduated from college and become a teacher, a financial consultant, an architect, and a broker for Merrill Lynch. There are many success stories within the Mexican immigrants but unfortunately these stories will never get the recognition they so much deserve which may help remove some of the stigmas that Mexicans have.

At least in the United States, many ethnographers have encountered this search for mobility and optimism in class consciousness, but a specific border theme emerges here, for example in the final remark on removing stigmas attached to Mexicans. Class ladders are seen as fairer in material and recognition terms than closed racial rules. As Aurolyn Luykx and I have written (Heyman and Luykx 2006), the University of Texas at El Paso and its students cocreate a populist vision of meritocracy for a "liberated" ethnic group, and thus help to mystify race and class sorting processes in education. But the appeal of this mobility vision must be understood through its contrast to past efforts to immobilize Mexican origin people as a servile labor force in the US Southwest.[10]

The Salience of the Poor Mexican Immigrant in Discussing Class

Strikingly, the topic of class brought strongly to the students' minds the figure of marginalized, poor, and unskilled laboring recent immigrants from Mexico. The two long quotes above concerning upward mobility from Laura and Martha, one a personal story and the other a distanced observation, are illustrative of this pattern. It is almost as if class is a code word for marginalized people, and that otherwise the students did not easily perceive their own class. To unravel this observation takes some analysis.

There is no unitary, bounded group of poor immigrant workers and households, but as we have seen, a set of marginalizing frameworks broadly overlap: insecure, highly "secondary" labor markets, noncitizen and sometimes undocumented immigrant status, Mexican origin and culture, Spanish-language predominance, residence near the border, in old urban *barrios* (Spanish for neighborhoods) or *colonias*, strong reliance on networks and household sharing to survive low incomes, and few to no public goods (pensions, health insurance, etc.).

A number of students grew up in and in some cases still live in these contexts. However, the larger number did not, and their experience of class extremes—whether the extremes of the market or extremes of stigma—is cushioned by a series of factors, including parental or their own civil service jobs or jobs in the private sector with (at least for the moment) security and an ascending career, health insurance and similar goods, legal security as citizens or legal residents, greater social honor, and generally less reliance on household and network resources and more reliance on dominant social institutions. This sort of contrast occurs, of course, throughout the United States and indeed the world, but its importance is heightened in El Paso, the poorest city over 500,000 in the country, in the poorest large region of the nation (the Texas-Mexico border), where contacts with and differentiation from the immigrant poor is quite salient to one's own perception of security, success, and status.

A main theme of the conversation was attacking biases against the immigrant poor, broadly a kind of class consciousness centered on the notion of honorable work. For example, the very first posting of the week was from Rick, a prosperous mixed Mexican and Anglo American, living in a neighborhood ranging from the well off to the marginal:

> I live in Palo Verde Acres where the existence of the social gap is very evident. I go and get my haircut down the street and in it I have seen both ends of the spectrum regarding class. Yes, there is a big evident physical difference in the two. I am part of the higher class but do not judge those of the lower any differently from anyone else. I have seen both classes sit away from each other on the benches when waiting for a haircut. I have seen a woman who was driving a Mercedes and dressed quite nicely with obviously expensive jewelry get up from the barber's chair because the stylist did not speak English. This woman was appalled at the establishment and made it very vocal. This stylist happens to be my preferred stylist and she told me that that sort of thing happens quite frequently and that she's getting used to it. It's a sad but true occurrence in our society. Every encounter I've had with anyone from the *colonia* area has been OK and never negative.

These simultaneous characterizations of the immigrant poor as distinctive and yet honorable do not just come from outside; Andres, an outstanding student, pointed out that he lived in a *colonia* and then told of his aunt, a domestic worker, to illustrate the importance but taken-for-grantedness of class:

> One seemingly obvious instance of social classes interacting goes back to the readings of last week and the undocumented maids. I shared a bit about my aunt and in her case, most of the people, if not all, that hire her are pretty wealthy as most of the houses she cleans are on the

west side of town, but the really nice west side of town up closer by the mountain. It's sort of odd in the sense that if anybody can afford to pay for anything, it would be people living in those 6 bedroom homes. My aunt gets treated fairly well and she has no real complaints. It becomes something that we just learn to accept, the social class division. Some people are meant to live in big houses, while others are meant to clean the pools, mow the lawns and make sure there is little dust for the people that live in big houses. [For more from Andres, see endnote 9.]

Both of these accounts are sympathetic, and while Rick's narrative could be seen as creating a favorable but still "othering" image of the hairdresser from the *colonia*, we would be hard put to say that Andres is othering himself and his formerly undocumented aunt (if anything, he others the rich people living on the mountain). What is noteworthy in this set of statements is that the archetypes of class are the very wealthy and the immigrant poor—rather than, say, the large civil service–based class fraction that hardly was mentioned despite its importance among the students.

Immigration status often reframed the conversation away from class (even as used by Rick and Andres). Key terms were *immigrants, undocumented*, or *Mexicans*, in the sense of recent entrants to the United States. Immigration status, though a relationship directly to the state, affects labor markets, work relations, and socially distributed goods in a number of ways (Heyman 1998, 2001; Zlolniski 1994, 2003). It is a tactical and empirical phenomenon that channels people into strategic relations of class, as well as a heavily policed fact of everyday life near the border. We thus should not be surprised that immigration and nationality sometimes becomes the conscious way of speaking about class.

At the same time, not all marginalized workers are immigrants, and especially not undocumented immigrants, and more importantly, immigration discourse can easily make class analysis disappear. For example, at one point in the online conversation, a Mexican American student had launched an attack on "illegal immigrants" taking health care resources deserved by her (US citizen) family. This sort of rhetoric about inclusion/exclusion from public goods is, of course, widespread in contemporary America, and has a substantial presence in El Paso (where there is, indeed, a modest but palpable maneuvering back and forth across the international boundary to utilize US services). However, while recurrent, immigrant-exclusion talk did not have a strong hold on the classroom conversation.

In this particular thread of conversation, a nonborderlander, Anglo American student who had had a serious set of illnesses, without insurance, and then worked in a hospital, insisted on discussing the realities of public health coverage and charitable care for uninsured citizens, legal residents, and undocumented immigrants alike (she was one of the students with a stronger sense of class awareness in the course, and considerable sympathy for immigrants). The overall point is immigration and nationality does play a role in class formation, especially near the border, and because of that— plus US political discourse—it tended to swallow up class analysis.

Comparisons to and Interactions with Mexico

Together with poor immigrants, the country of Mexico served as a predominant source of examples of class for the course discussion in two ways: encounters, mostly in service jobs, with visitors from Mexico; and observations and generalizations about class relations within Mexico. In the borderlands, there is a great deal of everyday shopping and leisure visiting from the other country, which means in El Paso that US students often serve middle-class to wealthy Mexicans in restaurants, stores, clinics, etc. There was thus a steady stream of complaining about rude, arrogant, and classist behavior of "Mexicans," not only in this course but also every course I have taught in El Paso. I cannot ascertain the validity and generality of these stories, not having provided services to prosperous Mexicans from a subordinate position (I teach commuting students from Mexico, but I am a professor). The basic narrative is plausible if overgeneralized, however, since Latin American codes of hierarchy often involve overt performance of domination/subordination, especially with service providers, as opposed to the egalitarian masking of inequality in North America. Be this as it may, many students held a strong notion that class is distinctly Mexican and the unmarked, contrastive notion that class is not American.

The nationalization of "class" came out in the frequent offering of examples of public class humiliation in Mexico. Martha contributed this typical example:

> Class is very important in Mexico compared to the US. This is especially true in the border area. Although it might spill over into the American side, it is of greater significance in the Mexican side. On the US side,

you can find people of totally different "classes" working in the same department, doing the same kind of job, going to the same schools, and sometimes living in the same neighborhoods. On the Mexican side it is not the case. The lines are very well defined and are meant to be abided by. This poses stress between the two classes: the ones who have money and the ones who don't. I have a cousin who worked in the night shift at the *maquiladora* near her home from the time she was in *"tercero de secundaria"* [9th grade], all thru *"preparatoria"* [college-preparatory high school] and up thru college till she received her Bachelors. She was able to obtain scholarships and was offered a full scholarship to get her MA in education. This was a real proud moment for my uncles, especially since she was offered a position as a professor at a "high" class *"preparatoria."* Nevertheless, she always stood out like a sore thumb at this high school. She commented on how the kids looked down upon her for not dressing right, not using the "correct" language, and thing as such that identify the difference in classes, what was worse is that she was their teacher!! They showed little respect for an older person of a lower class.

She followed this anecdote by explaining why class does not matter on the US side of the border: because class is all about occupation, and people from different occupations mix with each other in the United States.

If these sorts of stories emphasized the hierarchical stance of the rich and powerful in Mexico, that country was also represented in terms of its extremes of poverty. Students reported few direct reminiscences and observations of Mexican poverty, as opposed to the many personal discussions of US poverty (obviously, a US-side course selects for immediacy of US-side experiences more often then Mexican-side experiences, though there were exceptions). Generalized discussion of poverty in Mexico drew on either surface impressions or were taken from course readings that discussed street children, *maquiladora* workers, and marginal neighborhoods. The emphasis on Mexican material suffering, in turn, followed the "all poverty is Mexican" narrative delineated for El Paso by Pablo Vila (2000:110–111).

Vila shows with his analysis of Mexico-as-poverty narratives that class comes to be spoken in the language of international contrasts rather than as class formations found across nations. This was predominant, though not universal, among the students. What accounts for this central tendency? To begin with, students tended to see Mexico as distinctly class ridden and the United States as distinctly egalitarian. And it is true that Mexico has measurably higher wealth inequality than the United States. Such contrasts in empirical distributions, in turn, are readily apparent to US borderlanders, as are the cultural codes for performance of hierarchy discussed above. It is also often the case that Americans of Mexican origin grow up with stories of unfairness and suffering in Mexico as part of their familial migration narratives. Finally, the extremes of Mexican inequality are central to the mobilization of working people in ways that are evident to US borderlanders—if not usually deeply analyzed—such as the vast army of maids commuting daily to El Paso. Although partly reasonable, however, the conversion of class into nation stigmatizes Mexico, obscures class inequality in the United States, and bypasses the important interactions of two class societies at the border. And borderlands students do experience varied classes in both nations often enough that they periodically break out of the national narrative, as we shall see.

Consciousness of Transnational Class Relations

US borderlander students frequently verged on a global perspective. They spoke of it often in the narratives of immigrant lives and the language of differences between nations. Occasionally they brought up transnational capitalism or class relations across borders. One commentator (a US resident from an educated, professional Mexican background, and thus not typical of other students) noted that "if you place two wealthy people together, one Mexican and the other United Statesian, I think they will have more in common, (more shared life experiences, I say) than if you place each of them with a poor member of their own nationality." Indeed, transnational commonality is important to the upper circles of border society, for example the *maquiladoras* that typically combine US and Mexican managerial personnel. But no one in the course placed upper-class similarities and connections in the context of their role in the global economy. US borderlander students of working-class and middle-class origins rarely spontaneously envisioned the upper tier of transnational class processes, though they might have recognized such phenomena if they were pointed out.

There were also some mentions of the similarities between the poor of Ciudad Juárez and El Paso, though as one student noted, "poverty" was "arguably deeper and wider" in Mexico. Certainly, discussants understood the connections between poverty in Mexico and poor immigrants in the United States, as part of their own and others' experiences. What they did not do, however, was link workers across the international boundary. This gap is, of course, one of great questions of social science and frustrations of global labor and political activists.

Part of the answer, I think, requires us to understand that class involves various labor markets and ways that people are recruited into them. As pointed out, various arms of the US state employ a large workforce in El Paso, one that many students hope to be employed in. Those visions are essentially nationalist. Meanwhile, the vast *maquiladora* working class in Mexico is unquestionably global when thought of in terms of strategic relations, but on an everyday basis the *maquiladora* workers do not often move across borders, and if they do, it is in the tactical framework of immigration rather than as "workers of the world."

No student mentioned any personal or family experience in *maquiladora* work, and discussed it (if at all) in impersonal terms, from the course readings. Somewhat more surprisingly, no one mentioned work in one of the adjunct industries on the US side (plastics injection, stamping, warehousing). If they aspire to work for the *maquiladora* industry, with a college degree they likely aim to be part of management. The labor market segments where I saw mentions of experiences with transnational connections were service jobs where US residents sometimes worked with documented and undocumented immigrants, and informal economies that often span the border (such as selling Mexican foods in the US or second-hand US goods in Mexico). Informality and immigration do not erase class consciousness and solidarity, as Christian Zlolniski (2006) has shown, but they do make it more diverse and complex, and overlay class with cross-cutting tactical frameworks such as immigration status.

Globally mobile capital often sets locally rooted working classes against each other as jobs come and go. The disappearance of the El Paso blue jeans industry could easily have been understood in those terms. No student in the 2007 course mentioned the relocation to Mexico and Central America of men's slacks manufacturing, but students in a previous version of the course did discuss it. Interestingly, there was no sense of blaming Mexico or Mexican workers for the loss of jobs, and students did discuss how corporate economic interests cut across the two nations. The most criticism was reserved, however, for the US government for its limited and poor handling of retraining programs for displaced workers. A cluster of students had acquired that interpretation in their work with a militant organization of former garment plant workers and labor activists, Mujer Obrera (Working Woman).

Mujer Obrera accepts the globalization of garment manufacturing, and struggles to create an alternative community commercial, service, and small-manufacturing center (parallel to the Leipzig case discussed by Jancius 2006). Their tactics thus focus on pressuring the El Paso, Texas, and national governments to help this new vision, within a discourse that seeks to blend class and Mexican culture. Besides the political approach of Mujer Obrera, most of the garment plant workers were Mexican immigrants, many of them older women and men, and thus the ways that they had been mobilized for labor and then for unemployment did not favor blaming Mexico or Mexicans for their economic plight. It would have been tantamount to attacking themselves.

To understand consciousness of transnational capital processes and class relations, then, we need to keep in mind the precise setting of the issues. These include the power of state activities in people's lives, which make them more aware of national frames than transnational ones, patterns of cross-border personal interactions or absence of them, the fact that the two nations have related but not identical class distributions, the diverse interactions between different class members across the border, and the way that labor and political leaders and the mass media frame issues of polarization and solidarity (e.g., often in nationally bounded terms). Even at the border, then, the globalization of class is not necessarily empirically obvious, although it is strategically fundamental.

CONCLUSIONS

If the students at UTEP represent US borderlanders as a whole—and as I have said, there are good reasons to think they do—they are indeed conscious of class as an empirical distribution and organizing principle that cuts across other frameworks in the region, such as race and nationality. They certainly recognize the decline of strict racial inequality and the rise of a complex race-class pattern. At the same time, immigration status, national differences, and race/ethnicity often "recapture" awareness of class relations and processes. As well as the specific examples of discussion board postings presented above, the overall flow of conversation in that week began with class (the required agenda) and gradually evolved into race/ethnic culture, nation, or immigration status concerns, with class periodically resurfacing.

There are several possible causes of this incomplete appearance of class and tendency for it to be reabsorbed by other conceptualizations. One might posit a historical lag, that because race and nationality were so profound in the US borderlands' past, such understandings and phrasings are largely carried into the present (indeed, one of the signs of use of a direct class analysis is that it is "now" or "new"). Also, US public discourses (e.g., in the media) tend to racialize/ethnicize internal patterns of inequality and nationalize global patterns, while recently, immigration status has come to the fore. These frameworks do partly disguise class at the border, but the point is not that class is real, race (say) is not, and this is just all a simple and naïve mystification. Rather, such discursive frames interact with lived and experienced connections between strategic class and tactical nationality, immigration, race, gender, and class background, first as modes of recruitment and then as empirical markers in terms of resources and lifestyles.

It is thus helpful to recognize that the one word *class* covers four conceptually different phenomena: strategic relations of production, tactical forms of social mobilization to labor, empirical distributions, and patterns of identity and understanding. Let us take poor immigrants as a representation of "class," a major theme from my material: it is indeed important to understand how immigration status shapes segmented labor markets, as well as the way that people identify themselves and others in such class processes. At the same time, emphasizing this particular relation to the state highlights one side of these processes but reduces, at least in my course, the discussion of class consequences.

Consciousness in the US borderlands is, in some ways, heavily racialized (because of its history) and nationalized (because proximity to Mexico is ever present). At the same time, class is perhaps somewhat easier to conceptualize as a distinctive empirical and tactical phenomenon, by comparison to other regions of the United States that recently are becoming increasingly Latino and where racialization may be on the rise. First, by contrast with the situation discussed in David Griffith's paper, the Latino presence in the US borderlands is so long established and massive (over 80 percent in El Paso) that one cannot confuse Latinos as a whole with immigrants only. This, in turn, means that class among Latinos is not hidden by an overall classification as "newcomers"; among my entirely Mexican-origin students (minus the two nonborderlanders), Latinos were not understood as immigrants but rather immigrants understood as the honest poor among Latinos. Also, the fact that El Paso has so many Mexican Americans makes it easier to see the class differences among them, and thus that race is not all determining (recognizing, however, the disproportionality of Anglo Americans and Mexican nationals over Mexican Americans among regional capitalists and in the technical-managerial stratum). Finally, the proximity to Mexico, while making nation an ever-present theme, inevitably does raise awareness of transnational connections and also helps to understand that Mexico has complex class formations rather than viewing it as a simple icon of extreme wealth and poverty.

NOTES

1. There is no single widely accepted term for people in the United States of Mexican origin; I have chosen to use *Mexican Americans* here, which contrasts with the regionally used term *Anglo Americans* (or *Anglos*) for "whites." My (mostly Mexican American) students often used the local shorthand term *Mexicans*, which sometimes refers to people living in or visiting from Mexico and in other cases refers to people of Mexican origin—its referent can only be determined by context. There are, of course, smaller populations of Native Americans, African Americans, Asian Americans, and Asian Mexicans in the region.

2. I do not cover the tensions and solidarities (Vila 2000; Ochoa 2004) between US citizens of Mexican origin (Mexican Americans or Chicanos) and recent Mexican immigrants. However, the playing out of these differences and relations is strong evidence that the formerly unitary category of Mexican race has begun to pull apart. On one end of the would-be race group, the framework of citizenship permits mobilization of US "Hispanics" into various class roles, often in the secure working and middle class, while immigrant status and thus marked Mexicanness remains the crucial recruitment principle for the marginalized working class.

3. The week's readings, Richardson (1999:95–121) and Davidson (2000:3–79, 145–186) discussed *maquiladora* workers, Mexican street children, and forms of discrimination and exploitation in the borderlands. The previous week had covered *colonias*, farm workers, and undocumented maids. Clearly, these materials influenced the discussion to give something of an emphasis on poverty. On the other hand, students brought up this emphasis on class as poverty spontaneously during this week and in many others.

4. While one might idealize a disinterested research situation, agendas and relationships affect all ethnography, pure or applied. It seems willfully blind not to

be ethnographically observant while teaching, even as we recognize that pedagogy involves a particular kind of ethnographic relation, with some element of direction and authority on the part of the teacher. Students were informed that I would be using course materials for research on borderlands education and were given the opportunity to have their materials not used; all of them gave consent.

5. Confirmation of the representative character of my material is that it converges with the superior work of Pablo Vila (2000, 2005) on various narrative identities in El Paso, although our theoretical approaches are quite distinct.

6. A third spontaneous class analysis, more pronounced in the previous year's course than this one, concerned workplaces, in particular in mall and strip-development retailers and restaurants, which characteristically employ young people. Students offered an unflinching critique of US-side management/worker power relations interwoven with strictly nationalistic analysis of encounters between US service workers and prosperous Mexican customers.

7. Students rarely have the opportunity to learn about and discuss university funding and expenditures. Regrettably, I did not go over this topic in this particular course, though I always use it to illustrate economic anthropology in my introductory course.

8. Again, I would not have expected the students to know this, since it was not systematically covered in the course, and partisans on all sides oversimplified the issue. In a nutshell, the plan would enable an advanced capitalist real estate syndicate (involving both Latinos and non-Latinos but headed by a non-Latino) to displace very poor Latino apartment dwellers and small stores, many run by Asian immigrants, in favor of statusful franchise stores and higher-rent apartments. But it would also break a stranglehold of exploitative, regressive, mostly non-Latino landlords who own but do not invest in decaying buildings, in which typically the upper floors are abandoned while the street level is occupied—the dead hand of rent-capital in El Paso.

9. No students accepted this optimistic interpretation, however. Andres, for example, wrote: "It's not so much that I buy into fate thing and life being what it is. I myself am a first generation college student. For most of my life I have lived, and still live, in Eastside, which happens to be a *colonia* between [names two small outlying towns]. I am not implying that people should give up hope because there are those of us meant to be at the bottom of the food chain. What I meant is that the American Dream is just that, a dream that many people choose to follow. Some people will accomplish that dream and much, much more. We have read countless, too many to give examples, of people who have not reached that dream. Yes, indeed immigrants cannot and should not subject themselves to a mentality that no matter what they do they will only be victims of their own fate. I agree with you on that, as I agree with many of the other posts. Upward mobility and breaking out of poverty and social barriers is much harder than it seems. It's easy to tell people to

keep living the dream, but the reality of it is that some people just won't reach that dream, which isn't to say they shouldn't try, but rather that the number of illegal immigrants that have had it rough says it's not all hopes and dreams."

10. An apparently inverse, but I think related theme, was that Latinos who had risen in class and performed arrogant status displays were betraying their ethnic group. Class mobility is admirable when it is performed with a common touch.

REFERENCES CITED

Barrera, Mario. 1979. *Race and Class in the Southwest: A Theory of Racial Inequality.* South Bend, IN: Notre Dame University Press.

Collins, Patricia Hill. 1998. "It's All in the Family: Intersections of Gender, Race and Nation." *Hypatia* 13(3): 62–82.

Davidson, Miriam. 2000. *Lives on the Line: Dispatches from the U.S.-Mexico Border.* Tucson: University of Arizona Press.

Fernández-Kelly, María Patricia. 1983. *For We Are Sold, I and My People: Women and Industry in Mexico's Frontier.* Albany: SUNY Press.

Fraser, Nancy. 1997. "From Redistribution to Recognition: Dilemmas of Justice in a 'Post-Socialist' Age." In *Justice Interruptus: Critical Reflections on the "Post-Socialist" Condition,* 11–40. London: Routledge.

Ganster, Paul, and David E. Lorey. 2008. *The U.S.-Mexican Border into the Twenty First Century.* Lanham, MD: Rowman & Littlefield.

Heyman, Josiah McConnell. 1991. *Life and Labor on the Border: Working People of Northeastern Sonora, Mexico, 1886–1986.* Tucson: University of Arizona Press.

———. 1998. "State Effects on Labor Exploitation: The INS and Undocumented Immigrants at the Mexico-United States Border." *Critique of Anthropology* 18: 157–180.

———. 2001. "Class and Classification on the U.S.-Mexico Border." *Human Organization* 60: 128–140.

———. 2002. "U.S. Immigration Officers of Mexican Ancestry as Mexican Americans, Citizens, and Immigration Police." *Current Anthropology* 43: 479–507.

Heyman, Josiah McConnell, and Aurolyn Luykx. 2006. "Teaching about Structural Obstacles to Students Who Overcame Them." *Anthropology News* 47(8): 10–11.

Jancius, Angela C. 2006. "Unemployment, Deindustrialization, and 'Community Economy' in Eastern Germany." *Ethnos* 71: 213–232.

Nevins, Joseph. 2002. *Operation Gatekeeper: The Rise of the "Illegal Alien" and the Making of the U.S.-Mexico Boundary.* New York: Routledge.

Ochoa, Gilda L. 2004. *Becoming Neighbors in a Mexican American Community: Power, Conflict, and Solidarity.* Austin: University of Texas Press.

Richardson, Chad. 1999. *Batos, Bolillos, Pochos, and Pelados: Class and Culture on the South Texas Border.* Austin: University of Texas Press.

Spener, David. 2002. "The Unraveling Seam: NAFTA and the Decline of the Apparel Industry in El Paso, Texas." In *Free Trade and Uneven Development: The North American Apparel Industry after NAFTA*, edited by Gary Gereffi, David Spener, and Jennifer Bair, 139–160. Philadelphia: Temple University Press.

Vila, Pablo. 2000. *Crossing Borders, Reinforcing Borders: Social Categories, Metaphors, and Narrative Identities on the U.S.-Mexico Frontier.* Austin: University of Texas Press.

———. 2005. *Border Identifications: Narratives of Religion, Gender, and Class on the U.S.-Mexico Border.* Austin: University of Texas Press.

Wolf, Eric R. 1990. "Distinguished Lecture: Facing Power-Old Insights, New Questions." *American Anthropologist* 92: 586–596.

Zlolniski, Christian. 1994. "The Informal Economy in an Advanced Industrialized Society: Mexican Immigrant Labor in Silicon Valley." *Yale Law Journal* 103: 2305–2335.

———. 2003. "Labor Control and Resistance of Mexican Immigrant Janitors in Silicon Valley." *Human Organization* 62: 39–49.

———. 2006. *Janitors, Street Vendors and Activists: The Lives of Mexican Immigrants in Silicon Valley.* Berkeley: University of California Press.

Difference and Dispossession

Considerations on the Making and Unmaking of a Labor Elite at Saturn

SHARRYN   KASMIR

INTRODUCTION

The 1999 United Auto Workers (UAW) elections at General Motor's (GM) Saturn plant in Spring Hill, Tennessee, were hotly contested.[1] Flyers, newsletters, and palm cards flooded the shop floor, and representatives from rival union caucuses crowded factory doors, handing out campaign literature to workers who came in and out for their shifts. One palm card helped turn the election, break the monopoly on union power that the Vision Caucus had in the plant for over a decade, and dissolve Saturn's widely acclaimed labor-management partnership.

The card pictured a red SUV and carried the slogan, "The Vision Team is Leading the Way to 500K." On the front grille of the SUV were the words "Vision Team" and on the side panel "Vision 2002." The back of the card listed the Vision candidates for union office. At first glance, the message was simple: The Vision Team claimed that under its leadership, Spring Hill would finally get a much-needed new product and increase its annual production to 500,000 vehicles. The plant was seriously under capacity; sales of its long-stale subcompact never reached more than 278,000 units a year, and the plant never got a second product. Yet the palm card was not straightforward at all; rather, it called forth the complex history of GM's efforts to brand the Saturn Corporation as "A different kind of company," Saturn's inability to win investment from GM, and the trade-offs Saturn's union Local 1853 made to cooperate with management.

Someone close to the opposition caucus Members for a Democratic Union (MDU) learned that the red SUV was not a picture of a future Saturn but a photo of a Hyundai, downloaded from the internet. This discovery fueled leaflets, emails, and team-room discussions, and the plant ignited in controversy. One worker described the atmosphere:

> I saw a confrontation in General Assembly where the guy who supposedly created that thing was walking through a group of people, fifteen, twenty people, and some guy yelled out, "Hey Jim, nice job you did on that SUV. I heard Hyundai sales have gone up ten percent." And that guy had to feel small.

Despite the fact that the Vision Team did not intend to suggest that this was the new Saturn SUV—only that it could win such a model—workers felt deceived. Rather than assuring the plant's 7,200 workers that the Vision candidates could deliver a new product, this incident heightened workers' anxiety. In an overwhelming defeat, all of the Vision Team officers, many of whom had been in power since the plant opened, were unseated by MDU candidates.

MDU's victory was the culmination of a year-long campaign (1998–1999) carried out by union dissidents who were critical of Saturn's labor-management partnership and of their local union leaders. The Saturn Corporation made the ideological claim that its employees were "different" from other autoworkers because the labor-management partnership acceded them rights to participate in management. The corporation undertook to transform workers' self-concept in an attempt to produce this difference. Local 1853 collaborated in making this difference, and it distanced itself from the international UAW and repeatedly acted out of self-interest rather than solidarity with the international. In these ways, Saturn became an elite enclave within GM.

Saturn workers looked like what scholars have termed a "labor aristocracy," a privileged segment of the privileged North American working class. However, I argue in this chapter that the concept of the aristocracy of labor impedes our understanding of class processes, just as it hinders the ethnography of working classes. At the ethnographic level, insecurity was ever-present in the lives of Saturn workers, and I show how a "shadow of dispossession" was bound up with their privilege. Thus, I attempt a more dialectical consideration of class formation and consciousness to account for the ways that dispossession reproduces divisions and hierarchies within and between working classes, and privilege always rests on dispossession. Here, I tell the story of the making of Saturn's privilege, the insecurity and dispossession it supposed, and the organizing effort to unmake this difference.

DISPOSSESSION AND DIFFERENCE

I take my theoretical focus on dispossession from the recent work of geographer David Harvey (2003, 2005) who argues that dispossession has been the dominant form of capital accumulation in the post-1973, neoliberal epoch. Dispossession refers to the ways that capital seizes resources, denies access, or abrogates rights upon which institutions, social relationships, and expectations have been premised. There are myriad manifestations of dispossession worldwide: peasants and indigenous peoples lost communal lands; workers in advanced industrial regions lost pensions, welfare, national health care, and jobs; environmental and genetic materials were patented; water, communications, and other public utilities were privatized. When dispossession is unleashed on a global scale, its imprint is uneven; thus, capital accumulation creates difference and inequality (Harvey 2000). These insights would seem to invite an analysis of inequality that uncovers the connections between disparate working people and that takes the creation of difference as the subject of inquiry, yet Harvey unfortunately falls prey to typologies that naturalize rather than problematize difference (see Kasmir and Carbonella 2008).

Although the many forms of dispossession we see around the globe may have their origins in the dominance of finance capital that accompanied the ascendance of neoliberalism, Harvey attaches distinct logics to the struggles they engender. Despite the fact that he names capital flight as a signal feature of neoliberalism, he does not consider the struggles of workers in advanced industrial regions to maintain jobs, wages, and benefits to be a key dimension of the process of dispossession. Rather, he views them as misguided and backward looking. Instead, he sees more progressive political potential in the struggles against dispossession in the global South: "the long-drawn-out struggles against World Bank-backed dam construction projects in India and Latin America, peasant movements against biopiracy; struggles against genetically modified foods and for the authenticity of local production systems" (2003:166). Certainly these struggles have been crucial for local populations, as well as the developing global anticapitalist movement, yet by attributing distinct *logics* to these fights, Harvey makes the mistake of casting the divisions between and within working classes as *typologies* (see Kasmir and Carbonella 2008).

This error is readily apparent in Harvey's use of the problematic concept of "labor aristocracy." Harvey deploys this concept to charge that the labor movement in advanced industrial nations ignored the relationship of their own struggles to "preserve conditions and privileges gained within and around expanded reproduction and the welfare state" (2003:63) to the dislocations wrought by imperialism. As a result, he argues, "much of the labor movement in advanced capitalist countries fell into the trap of acting as an *aristocracy of labor, out to preserve its own privileges, by imperialism if necessary*" (2003:171, emphasis added). Here, Harvey effectively restates V. I. Lenin's concept of the aristocracy of labor, and he relies on a flawed intellectual tradition that categorizes rather than explains division and difference within and between working classes.

Lenin argued that imperialism divided the international working class into an upper stratum—unionized, stably employed workers and members of cooperatives—and a lower stratum—nonunionized and unemployed workers. According to this thesis, working classes in metropole regions generally support imperialism because it raises their standard of living (Lenin 1984:99–108). Yet, as Marxist scholar V. G. Kiernan has argued, Lenin missed the rapidly declining social position and prestige of the nineteenth-century labor aristocracy in the era of monopoly capitalism since he drew upon an economistic and *ahistorical* concept of imperialism that elided the very transformations of class it was meant to address (Kiernan 1974:54–59). Likewise, he credited capitalism with "too universal and omnipotent a direction of events" (Kiernan 1974:38).

A long line of historical and social-scientific scholarship uncritically accepted the labor aristocracy as an historical given. The thesis was revived by new-left scholars in the 1960s and 1970s who chronicled the ways that consumerism bought off the US working class, yet ignored the looming processes of dispossession that were already undermining its alleged solidity (e.g., Aronowitz 1991 [1973]; Ewen 1976; Goldthorpe et al. 1969). Consequently a historical moment of class stability, which turned out to be short lived, was transfigured into an evolutionary type. This typology does injustice to the actual processes and experiences of working-class formation and consciousness since it overlooks the many connections between privilege and dispossession.[2] The concept of labor aristocracy similarly misses what the ways that "political dispossession" of popular struggles—the erasure of the memory, social institutions, and political position won through collective struggle—is always part of the process of economic dispossession.[3] W. E. B. Du Bois's brilliant essay "On Work and Wealth" (1920) provides a template for overcoming both of theses shortcomings.

Du Bois wrote "On Work and Wealth" in the aftermath of the 1917 race riots in East St. Louis, when white workers set out violently against blacks. His sketch begins with the growth of industrial capital in the first years of the twentieth century. As East St. Louis experienced an industrial boom, dispossessed immigrants from eastern and southern Europe came to the city to look for work. Skilled tradesmen, in the main of northern European descent, held fast to their craft unions and their privilege, but the newly arriving workers struggled to build their own laborers' unions. Their standard of living rose during WWI, when immigration restrictions closed Ellis Island, the military commanded a share of the white work force, and they organized.

Just as labor gained power, however, northern capitalists looked south for workers, to "the greatest industrial miracles of modern days—slaves transforming themselves to freemen" (Du Bois 1920:88–89). Still, the migration of African Americans to East St. Louis did not immediately depress wages. African American workers joined the laborers union, and Du Bois suggests a moment of emergent solidarity in East St. Louis when African American, Italian, and Polish laborers together faced the skilled white workers and confronted capital.

Capital never acts alone, however, and the war-time government turned against labor. This collaboration between capital and the state opened the way for violence and racism, and it was then that the not-yet-white eastern and southern European laborers joined white workers to set upon blacks. Du Bois captured what moved the eastern and southern Europeans to violence:

It was not that their wages were lowered,—they went even higher. They received, not simply a living wage, but a wage that paid for some of the decencies . . . What they feared was not deprivation of the things they were used to and the shadow of poverty, but rather the definite death of their rising dreams . . . How far may men fight for the beginning of comfort?, out beyond the horrid shadow of poverty, at the cost of starving other and what the world calls lesser men? (Du Bois 1969 [1920]: 90–91)

We see in Du Bois's essay how dispossession washed unevenly over workers in one city, leaving behind aborted solidarity and new boundaries of identity and exclusion. We see also how insecurity—fear of the "definite death of their rising dreams" —shaped political reaction and led not-yet-white workers to seek racial privilege and what Du Bois would later call the "wages of whiteness" (cf. Roediger 1999. These processes are at work all over the globe, and they are the backdrop against which class consciousness, solidarity, and working-class power always struggle.

Sociologist Beverly Silver (2003) has attempted to assess the ways that working classes everywhere draw lines between themselves and other working-class factions in response to the vicissitudes of capital accumulation. At different times, different working classes identify and qualify themselves by race, nation, gender, and skill. These are not just wage or employment classifications, but "efforts to draw 'boundaries' delineating who will be 'cut in' and who will be 'left out'" (Silver 2003:21). They are sources of identity and alliance, and they create a spatial and social geography of solidarity and bias.

In an effort to capture the relationship of capital accumulation, class formation, and racialization, Karen Brodkin (2000) and Leith Mullings (2005) similarly direct our attention to division and exclusion within and between working classes. Eastern European Jewish immigrants in the United States were marked as nonwhite in the early twentieth century, Brodkin argues, when garment manufacturers introduced mass production and deskilled jobs. Jews sought work in the garment industry as unskilled laborers because American Federation of Labor craft unions kept them out of higher-paying jobs in the trades (241).

For Mullings, as well, the dialectic of accumulation and dispossession is at the heart of racialization; "all dispossession," she maintains, "is inextricably connected to accumulation and . . . structured disadvantage is the inevitable foundation of privilege" (2005:680). As these scholars make plain, capital is not an omnipotent force, rather the terms of who is cut in and who is cut out result from a negotiation between labor and capital, and workers "'actively construct identities that . . . exclude [other] workers from the community of rights'" (Silver 2003:21, quoting Rose). Silver uses the concept of "boundary-making" to describe this process.

Two processes operate simultaneously: On the one hand, capital accumulation requires and produces inequality; on the other, workers organize, access power, and form identities in the context of this global unevenness. In so doing, workers create alliances but also hierarchies and divisions. To capture these movements ethnographically, the notion of a historically situated, ongoing process of boundary making is much preferable to the static category of "labor aristocracy," as it encourages us to ask: How and when are boundaries made? What are their consequences? How can they be undone? These questions frame my ethnographic account of the dispossession and cleavages Saturn brought about when it created a privileged local within the UAW. These privileges were not premised on race, ethnicity, or gender—in fact, Saturn was racially and ethnically diverse and had more women workers than many GM plants—rather they were premised on a new, cooperative labor regime that set Saturn workers apart from other autoworkers.

"A FEDERATION OF LOCALS": DIVISION AND DIFFERENCE WITHIN THE UAW

The massive assault on labor that heralded neoliberalism hit auto cities hard. In the 1980s, GM downsized in Linden, New Jersey, (Milkman 1997) and shut its the Southgate, Fremont, and Van Nuys plants in California in an effort to cut a total of 80,000 jobs (Mann 1987:68). Flint, Michigan, lost 30,000 jobs from 1978–1992 (Dandaneau 1996: xxi.) Saturn workers came from these places and others like them; consequently, they lived through long layoffs, saw their home cities decline, and moved from plant to plant to secure work. Even those who had stable jobs were nervous. One worker described his home plant in St. Louis as "disposable." "GM made it almost seem like [we] were a disposable plant," he reflected. "They kept bringing in product, and eliminating product, and bringing in new product, and that worried me." Nearly 400 Van Nuys workers transferred to Saturn, but as one worker told me, they left behind "a few hundred, still in California, still collecting some benefits and unemployment."

This pervasive insecurity—made more acute by similar cuts in steel, coal, and other unionized industries—was an effective strategy for capital. Just as GM and other US automakers shut factories in the northern United States and created widespread anxiety, they offered some workers a new model of labor-management relations and a new self-concept to allay these fears. Automakers introduced just-in-time production, the team concept, worker participation, and other labor-management "jointness" programs to reorganize the shop floor and transform class relationships and identities. This new labor regime encouraged another round of boundary making.

Saturn origins were in this business, governmental, and cultural milieu of crisis and reform. In 1986, GM announced that it would spend $5 billion on the Saturn project—the largest single industrial investment in US history. The project was ultimately cut to $3.5 billion, still a vast sum (Sherman 1994:5). More than just an infusion of capital into a manufacturing facility, this was an investment in remaking the relations of power at work and at the negotiating table, and in redrawing the dividing lines within the US working class at the end of the twentieth century. Saturn was unusual in the mid-1980s for promising domestic capital investment and union jobs, and cities and towns across the country were desperate to win the plant. There was great fanfare surrounding Saturn.

Crushed by the decline of its steel factories, Youngstown, Ohio, bid for Saturn. Two hundred thousand school children and local residents wrote letters to then GM president Roger Smith touting the advantages of their city and imploring him to choose them. Youngstown realtors organized a 100-car caravan to GM headquarters to deliver the letters, and the city used public money to purchase billboard space and television time in Detroit to attract GM's attention (Russo 1986). In Loves Park, Illinois, former alderman Dick Kulpa, a comic artist by profession, drew "Race for Saturn," a comic that featured a superhero who promised "No Corporate Tax." A small record producer from Kentucky released the novelty song "Saturn" as a tribute to the frenzy. And after the 1985 National Governors' Conference, several governors appeared on the Phil Donahue show to sell their states to GM (Sherman 1994:98). Behind these stunts were staggering offers of tax exemptions, new highways, utility rate cuts, and free land. Tennessee finally won the bid after offering $80 million in incentives (Sherman 1994; Yanarella 1996:140).

There was competition at the negotiating table, as well. In 1982, under the new chairmanship of Roger Smith, GM demanded that the UAW reopen the national contract to negotiate a cut in the hourly wage. Union wage concessions had been granted during the Chrysler bailout in 1979–1980, and this set the stage for GM to demand givebacks from its workers. When the union refused, GM announced it would close four plants; within months GM shut Southgate in California, which had a largely African American workforce. The UAW soon reopened negotiations and agreed to $2.5 billion in wage and benefit cuts (Mann 1987).

Over the next years, GM changed tack. Instead of requiring concessions on the national level, as it had in 1982, it now required individual plants to compete with each other for new products. The winners accepted the team concept, quality-of-work-life, and other worker-participation programs, which were expected to reduce labor costs. While powerful UAW leaders, including Irving Bluestone and Don Elphin, pushed labor-management jointness, the Canadian wing left the International in 1985 over this issue (Yanarella and Green 1996:7). In the United States, Victor Reuther, brother of long-time union president Walter Reuter and critic of the cooperative strategy, founded the New Directions Movement, a dissident caucus of the UAW that condemned the concessionary stance of the UAW toward these pressures (Dandaneau 1996:7–33). New Directions saw cooperative practices as thinly disguised union-busting tactics, since just-in-time production brought a massive speed-up, and the team concept turned workers into petty managers of each others' efforts and robbed the union of control over job classifications and seniority rules, two sources of labor's power on the shop floor. The New Directions perspective was developed in the left labor journal *Labor Notes* (see Parker and Slaughter 1985, 1988, 1994).

Saturn was associated with these concessions. It was thus a controversial project, taking up considerable capital and fueling competition among union locals—a practice known as "whipsawing"—which came under increased pressure to concede on work rules in order to win new products. Victor Reuther feared that Saturn was turning the "UAW into a loose federation of locals competing among themselves" (quoted in Mann 1987:82). Whipsawing together with labor-management cooperation changed the social geography of identity and unity in the UAW. As August Carbonella (2005) has argued, localism has characterized the US labor movement since the 1935 Wagner Act banned solidarity strikes, mandated that local conditions amend national contracts, and in other ways helped to narrow the experience and aspirations of workers. In the 1980s, localism became all the more dramatic, as corporations used this moment of crisis to more fully utilize this tactic of power. Saturn's 1999 union elections and the fateful palm card had its origins in these processes of power and division.

"A TROJAN HORSE IN OUR MIDST"

As an opening salvo, when Saturn was still in the planning stages, Local 1853 scrapped the UAW national contract and negotiated a unique Memorandum of Agreement that eliminated the standard management rights clause and granted the union the right to participate in management. Union members were paired with managers at every level of the organization: they hired team members, organized workflows, consulted on advertising campaigns, and planned for the brand. Saturn's memorandum also eliminated job classifications and seniority rules so the team concept could be fully implemented, and it traded standard hourly wages for a formula that held a portion of salary "at risk" (12 percent at its highest) and paid rewards pegged to production and training targets. Advocates both inside and outside Saturn believed that Local 1853 and its leaders were pioneering a new model of unionism (Bluestone and Bluestone 1992; Rubinstein 1996; Rubinstein and Kochan 2001). Indeed, Local 1853's leadership named itself the "Vision Team" to signal what it considered its visionary role in redefining unionism.

When 1853 accepted the labor-management partnership in the mid-1980s, other UAW locals fought bitterly to defeat the team concept and this new unionism. The president of a local in Warren, Michigan, charged, "Saturn had become a Trojan horse in our midst. Armed with the threat of plant closing, the company is now playing local against local to see who will meet or exceed Saturn's give-backs" (quoted in Mann 1987:82). An international UAW official I interviewed believed that "Saturn was a drain on every plant in the system." Similarly, the head of Central Tennessee's Service Employees International Union told me that 1853 was estranged from the regional labor movement; he thought that Saturn was "good internally for their people, but not good externally." While give-backs meant concessionary contracts for locals throughout the country and a weaker international union, Saturn workers were anointed the new elite among autoworkers.

Though their average base pay was $4,000 less than that of their GM counterparts, bonuses reaching $10,000 in the mid-1990s more than made up for this shortfall, but the differences extended well beyond pay. UAW vice-president Don Elphin, a leading architect of Saturn, emphasized that "the keynote of . . . worker participation programs is to change the *self-concept*" of workers (quoted in Mann 1987:87, emphasis added). Saturn set out to make this new self-concept. The public relations campaign that launched the brand portrayed Saturn employees as a new breed of workers who were neither alienated from the product of their labor nor from the consumers (Aaker 1994; Kasmir 2001; Rogers 1999). Saturn was saturated with technology, language, and images (including Saturn commercials broadcast on an in-house television station) that encouraged workers to see themselves as distinct from and superior to other autoworkers (see Kasmir 2001, 2005).

Saturn's method for disciplining workers is exemplary of this initiative. Errant workers were sent to "coach and counsel" where they were asked to improve themselves. These sessions were presided over by a union-side "module leader" (one of the managerial positions union members occupied) together with his/her management counterpart.

I sat in on one session while I trailed Betty, a union-side module leader, during a week of night shifts. Cindy, a middle-aged white woman, who looked decidedly tired and worn out, sat at a long table in a meeting room where she was asked to explain why she had stalled the cockpits team's work and stopped the line.

Cindy did not have the parts she needed to do her job, and she told her module leaders that though she had ordered them (something she is responsible for under the team concept), the person working delivery had not come through. Betty had done some investigating before the session, and she learned from someone whom she trusted that the request for parts had come too late to keep the line moving.

Betty and her management-side partner told Cindy they saw a developing pattern: She made mistakes on the line, and she was a drain on her team's performance. The module leaders instructed her to think about how she could improve herself, and they issued her a warning. This was one of many techniques that Saturn used to try to summon workers to be self-improving and self-disciplining. More than this, it was one of many occasions when union members were asked to discipline their fellow workers.

Teams were another technique of this self-concept. Teams took on managerial tasks, such as controlling inventory, producing within budget, assigning jobs, and allocating labor hours. This shared responsibility meant that team members were in a position to oversee each other's work (and

Cyndi's teammates had complained about her to their module leaders). It also blurred the line between labor and management.

Workers went to team and plant-wide meetings, traveled to visit suppliers, and, in order to receive reward payments, completed 92 hours of training per year. These responsibilities took them off the assembly line, and made their jobs seem "white-collar," as one worker told me. Moreover, all employees were given a Franklin Planner in which to schedule these meetings, trips, and classes. This planner was more than a calendar; it was a system for improving the self. In addition to entering appointments, workers who used their planner properly spent time each day thinking about their goals. Weeks, months, and years had larger areas for writing mission statements and plans to realize one's potential. Workers could choose classes, credited to their 92-hour load, to learn to use the planner and to aspire to the self-actualization it preached.

While some classes taught technical skills, many, like the Franklin Planner class, were more ideological (see Yanarella 1996). I attended "Team Saturn," a ten-hour session that was mandatory for all employees. The class was held at a training center in a local strip mall, where I gathered with thirty or so workers and supervisors early in the morning.

We began the day with introductions, and participants were asked to introduce themselves by recounting the story of how they came to Saturn. As each person spoke, a trainer marked their year of entry on a timeline that represented important dates in company history; this represented an effort to tie each person's own life story with Saturn's, and it asserted a link between the individual and the company (see Kasmir 2001, 2005).

Next, we were instructed in corporate history through a montage of Saturn commercials that sounded the brand theme, "A different kind of company." A series of videotaped interviews with Saturn presidents replayed this message. Later, we had a lesson in brand image, and we listened to audio tapes of customer phone calls. We were told not to try to solve the problem the customer presented but to think about how the employee might improve his/her handling of the call. One call was from a woman who was having problems with her sedan. Some of the workers in the room remembered a problem on the line that resulted in just such a defect in the model the customer purchased, and they were energetic in suggesting what the customer could do to repair the car. The trainer repeatedly reminded them to restrict their comments to ways the operator could better handle the complaint, but they nonetheless continued to talk about the defective car.

Workers' inability to stay on point during the customer phone calls suggests that the company's attempts to rally them to better themselves and to summon their capacities to continuously improve the company were not wholly successful. Durrenberger and Doukas (2008) document a similar pattern in New York and Pennsylvania, where corporate efforts at remaking workers according to Andrew Carnegie's "Gospel of Wealth" have also failed (see also Doukas 2003). In fact, aside from this one outburst of energy, Saturn workers were, in the main, bored and tuned-out during the first half of the day.

They came to life, however, during the financial presentation, when they were shown charts about the troubled US small-car market, Saturn's steep losses, and the competitive advantage Toyota and Ford had over them. The session was intended to rally them to cause of profitability, but instead it signaled to them that their jobs were insecure and their unique labor agreement and legacy of difference had left them particularly vulnerable. The trainers were unable to control the room, as workers shouted questions about the promised SUV and budget details that the trainers were unable to answer. This small rebellion at "Team Saturn" was reflective of the larger rebellion that pushed the Vision Team from union office.

INSECURITY AND VULNERABILITY AT SATURN

After a strong year in 1996, sales fell 10 percent in 1997, and another 20 percent by March 1998 (*Newsday*, August 23, 1998:F8). Meanwhile, GM gave Spring Hill's much-awaited new product, a midsized sedan, to Wilmington, Delaware. This was the first Saturn model to be produced outside of Spring Hill. Workers had seen the brand as theirs, and they felt betrayed. Meanwhile, declining sales of the subcompact led to loss of overtime, a slow down in production, and a cut in their reward pay. In 1997 bonuses plummeted to an average of $2,000, and Saturn workers were earning less than their counterparts in GM. At the same time, many had taken on considerable consumer debt, including mortgages, car and truck payments, and boat loans.

Greg is a Euro-American man in his late forties who transferred to Saturn in 1988. He was divorced, and his ex-wife and daughter stayed in St.

Louis. In Tennessee, he bought a small suburban home, which he furnished nicely. He had a new GM truck and a Saturn in his two-car garage, and a recently purchased bass boat docked in the lake where he went fishing with his girlfriend.

His girlfriend was not a Saturn transplant but from the Spring Hill area. To her, Greg was "rich." Greg laughed as he told me this; he was proud that she saw him this way, but he was also nervous, since his lifestyle depended upon paychecks padded with overtime and bonuses. Greg made a lot of money; as a skilled tradesman, his hourly rate was high, and like many at Saturn, he supplemented this with overtime.

Saturn had a unique work schedule, another thing that differentiated it from the rest of the UAW. Each crew (there were three in all) worked four ten-hour days, then had two days off. Days off did not necessarily fall on weekends, as the plant operated on Saturdays but not Sundays. Following the two-day break, there was a shift change, and those who had been on days worked nights. After four days on nights, they got five days off. Workers often used this five-day stretch to work overtime, and in this way, they were able to boost their pay considerably. In combination with the loss of thousands of dollars in bonuses, the drying up of overtime was a serious blow to household budgets. Greg told me that some workers were already filing for bankruptcy. He was concerned that he would fall behind in his truck and boat payments.

Workers also feared for their jobs. When Saturn representatives went to GM plants around the country to recruit workers, they promised a new and better work regime and job security. They billed Saturn as a "hundred-year car company," suggesting long-term job security for workers and their children. Workers weighed relocating their families, selling their homes (and in places like Flint and Detroit, housing prices were severely depressed) and sometimes forfeiting a spouse's employment, against a careful assessment of their futures.[4] Bill is an African-American man in his fifties who made this calculation:

> I got laid off in '88. And I had gotten an application [for Saturn] back in '88. I was working as a security supervisor, and it was pretty much a desk job. It was a paper-pushing kind of thing. I had filled the application out, and I carried that application in my briefcase for a year and a half. Finally, in early '90, I decided that I needed to retire. And I did not want to start over again. And so I sent the application off, finally. It was a very difficult

decision to do that. Finally, I came to the conclusion that we needed to retire.

John, a Euro-American in his forties, worked in a GM plant in Syracuse, New York, since he was nineteen. He came to Saturn in 1992 after long considering his future at GM:

> People had come up to our plant in '90, recruiting people to come down. I went to listen. I was interested. At that time, my plant was doing good. We were working overtime, but I started seeing things change at our plant. I noticed the way management was acting . . . The biggest thing was we purchased new machinery that was four to five years old. Management locked out ten machines. We were told "Don't take parts off those machines." In my mind they put "sold" signs on those machines. I would take out the [Saturn] application and fill it out a bit at a time, take it out from time to time when things looked bad, but then they would look better again, and I would put it away.

Even while his job in Syracuse was secure, John monitored his plant for signs of layoffs. He read investment patterns in the machines and scrutinized management for evidence of capital flight. John made a union wage and worked in what he was told was a stable plant, but he was on the look out for dispossession, and he filled out his Saturn application as he saw indications of capital flight. He was now watching again at Saturn.

Insecurity has historically been a persistent condition in auto production; cars are highly subject to downturns, and autoworkers have long waited through periods without work. But the specter of layoffs had a distinct meaning at Saturn. Saturn's labor agreement forfeited transfer rights and other layoff protections (such as, sub-benefits and guaranteed income stream) in favor of language that promised no layoffs except in case of a "catastrophic event" or "severe economic conditions."

Workers now worried how this language would be interpreted (Slaughter 1998). Workers already faced extended down time and plant closures in the 1980s back home; not a few worked in two or three other plants, and they had already uprooted their families when they transferred again to Saturn. In Tennessee, they had to find new houses, schools, and churches. Together with the long hours, nontraditional shifts, and the intensity and insularity of Saturn's work culture, this took a toll on families and marriages. A representative from the international UAW believed that "Saturn very insidiously isolated people from the larger social fabric":

> The family comes in and the boy wants to play in little league, Boy
> Scouts, but the father can't do any of those things with him [because of
> irregular shifts]. Same for what the girl wants to do. [Since spouses who
> both work in the plant can't be on the same crew] parents can't belong
> to a bowling league together. Can't belong to any type of social thing
> together. There were 8 x 11 placards on people's refrigerators. All 365
> days of year blocked out in color-coded blocks for the crews. The rota-
> tion for each spouse is different. They are not even off together.

Not surprisingly, there was reportedly a very high divorce rate in the plant.

This job had come at a high price for many, and the prospect of losing it was fearsome. Some responded to this insecurity by wanting to move
back home (if their plants were still open,) but they gave up GM seniority
when they hired on at Saturn, and they now had low priority for transfer.
Others wanted desperately to stay in Spring Hill and save their jobs. In this
"shadow of dispossession," many workers were ceaseless in their attention
to production numbers and products. Stories circulated about late-night
transfers of hundreds of cars from the plant parking lot to an off-site location, where evidence of slow sales could be hidden. One worker worried
that "Saturn now has over a hundred day supply."[5] This meant a disastrous
breakdown of just-in-time management and suggested not only that sales
were off but that managers were failing in their jobs. Workers I interviewed
second-guessed GM, arguing that they saw the need for a minivan or SUV
years ago, and they worried that even if they got one now, it might be too
late. In this atmosphere of insecurity, the palm card with the red Hyundai
SUV inflamed emotions.

UNMAKING BOUNDARIES

Amidst growing anxiety in the plant, a small group of dissident union members calling themselves Concerned Brothers and Sisters met in the winter
of 1998 to discuss their dissatisfaction with the corporation and with their
union leaders. Over the next several weeks, they gained support on the shop
floor, and they organized a meeting of 600–700 workers in the Spring Hill
High School gym, which they rented when their union officers would not
grant them use of the union hall. At this meeting, they agreed that Local
1853 should return to the national UAW contract, thus gaining the layoff
protections, seniority rights, and hourly wages that they had given up. Their

proposal for a referendum on the national contract was ratified at the next union meeting by a vote of 87 percent.

Concerned Brothers and Sisters then enlisted workers to send letters and emails to the international UAW, detailing their criticisms of the Saturn contract and of Local 1853 leadership. They asked for support from the International. "Please, brothers and sisters of the International," wrote one worker, "don't forget us down in 1853 for our local leadership has lost the way." The International helped to orchestrate dissent from its offices in Michigan. The campaign centered on job security, pay, and transfer rights but also expressed the conviction that to return to the national contract was an act of solidarity. The referendum to adopt the national contract was defeated by a vote of 2:1. Despite their loss, however, dissidents were emboldened by their growing ties to the International and by their success, for the first time in Saturn's history, in orchestrating dissent. For its part, the Vision Team interpreted the vote as a mandate for its partnership-style unionism.

Concerned Brothers and Sisters rallied the plant again in July 1998, during a strike that began at GM's Flint Metal Center parts plant over the outsourcing of work to nonunion plants. A second Flint parts facility struck in short order, and strikes spread throughout GM, some plants walking out over local issues, others forced to close for lack of parts.[6] There was widespread concern that GM planned to spin off the Delphi parts division and leave some 53,000 parts workers outside of the GM system—a fear that was, in fact, realized later that summer. Thus, the combined action of the locals had the distinct appearance of a solidarity strike in support of Delphi workers fighting for their jobs. A total of 186,000 workers were out, and twenty-seven of twenty-nine assembly plants and scores of parts facilities were shut down in the biggest labor stoppage in GM since the 1970s. Local 1853 members, however, were still at work.

This situation recalled Saturn's isolation during a 1992 strike at GM Lordstown, when Local 1853 president Mike Bennett complained to the press that the International should allow Lordstown workers making *Saturn* parts to cross the picket line (Parker and Slaughter 1997). In effect, Bennett suggested that rather than expecting Saturn to show solidarity with another local, the striking Lordstown workers should respect Saturn's difference and support its maverick experiment. It looked as if Saturn employees would once again stand apart from their fellow autoworkers in 1998. "In the name of preserving the nation's best-known experiment in cooperation between labor and management," reported the *New York Times*, "they have set aside union solidarity by assembling cars using parts from Japan and at least one nonunion American company, instead of parts from Flint" (July 22, 1998:A1).

Workers were deeply troubled by the fact that they were still working while most of GM was on strike. As one activist, a Mexican American man from Van Nuys, told me:

> Before the shutdown, a lot of the people went on their five [five days off after night shift] up to Michigan. And they had relatives, and they were being harassed.
>
> A lot of them told me, "I have a brother-in-law just gave me a hard time. I couldn't even drink a beer with him, because he says, 'How can you justify my being on strike and you guys are out there working, it's not right. What kind of a union are you guys?'" And a lot of them, I think that had a lot to do with it, when they went home, some of their own family members, their dads, brother-in-laws, asking them, "What kind of a union do you guys belong to?"

Concerned Brothers and Sisters began to organize the membership to urge their local leadership to support the strike. A member of the group explained:

> [W]e kept the membership informed of what was going on. We'd get our news off the internet, and we'd put it out on the floor and keep them informed. And also we started a write-a-letter campaign . . . And then addresses of the UAW, Solidarity House, AFL/CIO, the UAW website. And we encouraged the workers to write letters in opposition to what was going on in Saturn, the outsourcing of the parts.

This shop-floor militancy, combined with increasing pressure from the International, led Local 1853 to hold a strike authorization vote. It was the first time Saturn workers had taken such a vote, and it was an exciting and emotional time. A worker in General Assembly recalled:

> That was the greatest thing that ever happened to this place. There were tears in my eyes. I mean the roads were jammed. People coming on a Sunday, an off day, to vote. I couldn't believe that people came together. It was really amazing. I've never seen anything like that. I wish you had interviewed me when it happened, I was jumping I was so excited.

> The strike vote got the International behind us again. I think that it showed the International that we were union and that we would help the International. I think it helped our relationship with the International.

The strikes were a month-and-a-half old when the Saturn vote was taken, nevertheless, Saturn's decision to join them was momentous. Dozens of national and international newspapers covered the story, carrying headlines such as, "Elite car workers ready to strike" (*Independent*, July 21, 1998:13). Saturn's union leadership agreed to talk to management for thirty days before they called a walkout, and Mike Bennett used the threat of a strike to get Spring Hill a promise of an SUV. The strikes were settled before Saturn ever walked out, but the vote strengthened workers' solidarity with the UAW, unleashed their dissatisfaction with the Saturn difference, and won them a commitment from GM for investment in a new model.

Feeling confident after Mike Bennett secured a promise from GM for the SUV, the Vision Team called union elections early, in February 1999. Concerned Brothers and Sisters rallied once again to support candidates from the opposition MDU Caucus. This caucus ran on a platform of reform and vowed to change the Memorandum of Agreement to bring Saturn closer to the national contract.

These were the events that lent the palm card so much power. When the membership learned that the photo of the promised Saturn SUV was actually a Hyundai, it spoke to the inability of Vision Team to secure their jobs, and it suggested that the boundaries they had made, which had been so painfully and publicly displayed during the strike, had finally won them little. The union elections became, in effect, a referendum on the Vision Team and on Saturn's difference from the rest of the UAW. All thirteen Vision Team candidates were defeated. Some months later, the new officers negotiated a change in the Memorandum of Agreement to bring Saturn closer to GM wages. In 2004, Local 1853 scrapped the labor-management partnership altogether and adopted the national agreement.

The seniority, transfer, and call-back rights provided by the national contract have proven crucial to Saturn workers who ultimately won the SUV (after they agreed to a speed up) only to find that their jobs are permanently under threat. In 2005, GM announced a massive corporate restructuring: it would shut twelve plants and lay off 30,000 North American workers by 2008. GM did not initially identity the plants it would close; instead it instigated another round of whipsawing and concessions to determine which plants would be rewarded. Saturn learned it would lose one production line and 1,500 jobs. No new product was promised; thus workers transferred, retired, and took buy-outs, and the workforce was quickly reduced to 4,200. The Saturn brand subsequently underwent a much-heralded revival, but none of the new vehicles were made in Spring Hill. In March of 2007, Spring Hill manufactured the last of its subcompacts and the last of its much-fought-for SUVs. It was not until months later that workers found out that they would get a new Chevrolet. Twenty-five hundred workers were laid off for twelve to eighteen months while the plant was retooled for the new model; they were relying on their recently regained layoff protections, guaranteed in the national contract, to keep them afloat.[7]

CONCLUSIONS

In this chapter, I have argued that the concept of the "aristocracy of labor," long used by scholars to characterize a structurally privileged segment of the US working class, inhibits rather than advances our understanding of class processes. I have suggested, instead, that we gain greater analytical rigor and theoretical insight if we attend to the dialectic of privilege and dispossession that contributes to the making of working classes and the boundaries among and between them.

In the late 1970s–1980s, GM and other manufacturers deployed a manifold strategy to manage the crisis of profitability and to discipline the US working class: They shuttered factories and cut tens of thousands of jobs in advanced industrial regions, thereby creating mass insecurity among union and nonunion workers alike. At the same time, GM put labor-management cooperation on the table as the sine qua non for winning capital investment, and it required UAW locals to compete with each other for products. The new cooperative work regime brought with it a corporate ideology that sought to transform workers' self-concept and to promote identification with the company rather than the international union. Meanwhile, competition among union locals limited the reach of labor solidarity and encouraged narrow localism.

Dispossession and privilege are corporate strategies for producing insecurity, unevenness, and difference, but as the case of Saturn shows, workers and their unions are also active agents in this process. Saturn's Local 1853 helped craft a labor accord and devise a management regime that stood for over a decade as the model of labor-management cooperation in the United States, and the local and its leaders were credited with pioneering a new form of unionism. This new unionism was premised on the dispossession of other UAW locals and on the creation of an elite enclave in Spring Hill. Though many scholars would see a labor aristocracy at Saturn, I argue against such a typology. My purpose in rejecting this concept is not to ignore or erase or privilege but to document its making, detail its consequences, and signal its instability. My intention is to turn an analytical lens on difference among and between working classes and to make it a starting point of anthropological investigation.

Dispossession shadowed Saturn workers, even as they were better off than other autoworkers. They came to Saturn from cities that suffered profoundly from the effects of capital flight, and many had moved from plant to plant to secure their futures at GM; despite years of affluence and difference at Saturn, insecurity was pervasive. When the small-car market slumped in the late 1990s, and their bonuses, overtime, and jobs were threatened, workers did not, however, turn inward toward the company and the labor-management partnership; rather, they looked outward to the international union. This wave of dispossession thus led them to new alliances, as their strike authorization vote in the summer of 1998 attested. They expressed this new geography of struggle when they elected union leaders who vowed to reform Saturn's labor-management partnership and when, later, they scrapped their labor accord and returned to the national UAW contract.

It might be argued that the Saturn case merely documents a realignment within the privileged North American working class, which (*pace* Harvey) is simply out to defend its own privileges. Indeed, Local 1853's new relationship to the International is a very small political moment, yet the significance of this case resides in the fact of Local 1853's move from isolation to alliance, and what that development suggests about the possibility of wider, even international, connections and more radical transformations. The case of Saturn indicates that we don't know a priori the effect of dispossession—toward exclusion and violence or toward solidarity—rather, this is an ethnographic question that requires we understand particular histories of working-class formation and experience. In our haste to categorize popular struggles and organizations across the globe, we must not overlook these instances of solidarity if we are to build an anthropology of labor that recognizes dispossession and difference but can also imagine new connections, alliances, and consciousness.

NOTES

1. This chapter is based on fieldwork conducted at the Saturn factory from 1998–1999. I carried out this research while a fellow at Vanderbilt University's Robert Penn Warren Center for the Humanities. I thank my colleagues in the seminar for their valuable contributions to my work. I owe a great debt to Sherry Willis who expertly transcribed my interview tapes. Additional research was funded by a grant from the National Endowment for the Humanities. This chapter owes a great debt to August Carbonella, with whom I have worked through much of the theoretical argument of this paper. An earlier version of this paper was presented at a panel entitled "Possession/Dispossession" at the American Anthropological Association meetings in 2007. I thank the participants and discussants for a lively panel. My sincere thanks to August Carbonella, Paul Durrenberger, Chris Matthews, Kirk Dombrowksi, and Cheryl Mwaria for their criticisms of and suggestions on earlier drafts of this paper.

2. George Baca (2004) critiques Harvey's characterization of Keynesianism/ Fordism as too widespread and unitary. Baca reminds us that many peoples and regions, even within the US, never won the social gains afforded by Fordism. For those people and places, Baca argues, Fordism's demise into a regime of accumulation by dispossession does not represent the radical break that Harvey's theory supposes.

3. Manning Marable (2006) sees the silencing of the radical history of the African American struggle—specifically, the legacy of Malcom X and the erasure of Du Bois's pan-Africanism, anticolonialism, and socialism—as political dispossession, akin to the capital accumulation by dispossession Harvey describes. Kasmir and Carbonella (2008) likewise use the notion of "political dispossession" to describe how neoliberalism undid the position and power of the US working class. See also Jerry Lembke (1991–1992).

4. The job market in Spring Hill and surrounding towns was tough for Saturn spouses. Employment opportunities were limited in the area, and since Tennessee is a right-to-work state and has low union density, wages were low.

5. Letter from Saturn worker to Richard Schoemaker, UAW vice president, GM Department, February 6, 1998.

6. Like Harvey, Silver understands capital flight as a singular "spatial fix," and she sees that waves of dispossession spur working-class boundary making, but beyond this time-space fix, Silver stresses the import of political, product cycle, and technological/organization fixes, as well. Silver argues that just-in-time produc-

tion (an example of a technological/organizational fix) will backfire on management, since job action in one location can now stall a whole corporation. She sees this dynamic in the 1998 GM strike, where a walkout in Flint stopped production across North America in short order. While I appreciate Silver's attention to the technological/organizational fix, she fails to account for the impact of management practices and ideologies that go hand-in-hand with just-in-time production, and she misses the ways in which workers are, at the same time, politically dispossessed by labor-management cooperation. As the case of Saturn shows, worker participation and labor-management cooperation draw lines between union locals, encourage whipsawing, and damage solidarity. This work regime disempowered workers by inspiring narrow localism. The GM strike points not to a new microgeography of production, but to the need to overcome localism if this fix is to have genuine political potential for workers.

7. Pete Richardson's (2010) research on Ford workers offered buyouts suggests an infinite fractioning of the workforce, as workers make their decisions based on individual calculations. Richardson shows that Ford workers are now encouraged to see their jobs as their personal property, transferable into a buyout package. In this way, their sense of collective rights and union power has been dealt a decisive blow.

REFERENCES CITED

Aaker, David. 1994. "Building a Brand: The Saturn Story." *California Management Review* 36(2): 114–133.

Aronowitz, Stanley. 1991 [1973]. *False Promises: The Shaping of American Working Class Consciousness.* Durham, NC: Duke University Press.

Baca, George. 2004. "Legends of Fordism: Between Myth, History, and Foregone Conclusions." *Social Analysis* 48(3): 169–178.

Bluestone, Barry, and Irving Bluestone. 1992. *Negotiating the Future: A Labor Perspective on American Business.* New York: Basic Books.

Brodkin, Karen. 2000. "Global Capitalism: What's Race Got to Do with It?" *American Ethnologist* 27(2): 237–256.

Carbonella, August. 2005. "Beyond the Limits of the Visible World: Remapping Historical Anthropology." In *Critical Junctions: Anthropology and History Beyond the Critical Turn*, edited by Don Kalb and Herman Tak, 88–108. New York: Berghahn Books.

Dandaneau, Steven P. 1996 *A Town Abandoned: Flint, Michigan, Confronts Deindustrialization.* Albany: State University of New York Press.

Doukas, Dimitra. 2003. *Worked Over: The Corporate Sabotage of an American Community.* Ithaca, NY: Cornell University Press.

Durrenberger, E. Paul, and Dimitra Doukas. 2008. "Gospel of Wealth, Gospel of Work: Hegemony in the U.S. Working Class." *American Anthropologist* 110(2): 1548–1433.

Du Bois, W.E.B. 1969 [1920]. "Of Work and Wealth." In *Darkwater: Voices from Within the Veil.* New York: Schocken Books.

Ewen, Stuart. 1976. *Captains of Consciousness: Advertising and the Social Roots of the Consumer Culture.* New York: McGraw-Hill.

Goldthorpe, John H., David Lockwood, Frank Bechhofer, and Jennifer Platt. 1969. *The Affluent Worker in the Class Structure.* New York: Cambridge University Press.

Harvey, David. 2000. *Spaces of Hope.* Berkeley: University of California Press.

———. 2003. *The New Imperialism.* New York: Oxford University Press.

———. 2005. *A Brief History of Neo-Liberalism.* New York: Oxford University Press.

Kasmir, Sharryn. 2001. "Corporation, Self, and Enterprise at the Saturn Automobile Plant." *Anthropology of Work Review* 22(4): 8–12.

———. 2005. "Activism and Class Identity at the Saturn Automobile Factory." In *Social Movements: A Reader,* edited by June Nash, 78–95. Malden/Oxford: Blackwell Publishers.

Kasmir, Sharryn, and August Carbonella. 2008. "Dispossession and the Anthropology of Labor." *Critique of Anthropology* 28(1): 5–25.

Kiernan, V. G. 1974. *Marxism and Imperialism.* London: Edward Arnold Publishers.

Lembcke, Jerry. 1991–1992. "Why 50 Years? Working-Class Formation and Long Economic Cycles." *Science & Society* 55(4): 417–446.

Lenin, V. I. 1984. *Imperialism: The Highest Stage of Capitalism.* New York: International Publishers.

Mann, Eric. 1987. *Taking on General Motors: A Case Study of the UAW Campaign to Keep Van Nuys Open.* Los Angeles: Institute of Industrial Relations Publications, University of California.

Marable, Manning. 2006. "Resurrecting the Radical Du Bois." In *Living Black History: How Reimagining the African-American Past Can Remake America's Racial Future,* 67–120. New York: Basic Books.

Milkman, Ruth. 1997. *Farewell to the Factory. Autoworkers in the Late Twentieth Century.* Berkeley: University of California Press.

Mullings, Leith. 2005. "Interrogating Racism: Toward and Antiracist Anthropology." *Annual Review of Anthropology* 34: 667–693.

Parker, Mike, and Jane Slaughter. 1985. *Inside the Circle: A Union Guide to QWL.* Detroit: Labor Notes.

———. 1988. *Choosing Sides: Unions and the Team Concept.* Detroit: Labor Notes.

———. 1994. *Working Smart: A Union Guide to Participation Programs and Reengineering.* Detroit: Labor Notes.

————. 1997. "Advancing Unionism on the New Terrain." In *Unions and Workplace Reorganization*, edited by Bruce Nissen, 208–227. Detroit: Wayne State University Press.

Richardson, Pete. 2010. "Buying Out the Union: Jobs as Property and the UAW." In *The Anthropology of Labor Unions*, edited by Paul Durrenberger and Karaleah Reichart, 79–102. Boulder: University Press of Colorado.

Roediger, David. 1999. *The Wages of Whiteness: Race and the Making of the American Working Class*. New York: Verso.

Rogers, Brishen. 1999. "The New Myth of the Happy Worker." *Baffler* 12: 41–50.

Rubinstein, Saul. 1996. "Saturn, The GM/UAW Partnership: Impact of Co-Management and Joint Governance on Firm and Local Union Performance." PhD dissertation, Sloan School of Management, Massachusetts Institute of Technology.

Rubinstein, Saul, and Thomas Kochan. 2001. "Learning from Saturn: A Look at the Boldest Experiment in Corporate Governance and Employee Relations." Ithaca, NY: Cornell University Press.

Russo, John. 1986. "Saturn's Rings: What GM's Saturn Project Is Really About." *Labor Research Review* 9: 67–77.

Sherman, Joe. 1994. *In the Rings of Saturn*. New York: Oxford University Press.

Silver, Beverly. 2003. *Forces of Labour: Workers' Movements and Globalization since 1870*. New York: Cambridge University Press.

Slaughter, Jane. 1998. "Union Votes to Keep Separate Contract—As Sales Slip, Saturn Workers Worry about Job Security Under 'Cooperation' Regime." *Labor Notes* April (229): 16.

Yanarella, Ernest J. 1996. "Worker Training at Toyota and Saturn: Hegemony Begins in the Training Center Classroom." In *North American Auto Unions in Crisis: Lean Production as Contested Terrain*, edited by Ernest J. Yanarella and William C. Green, 125–157. Albany: State University of New York Press.

Yanarella, Ernest J., and William C. Green, eds. 1996. *North American Auto Unions in Crisis: Lean Production as Contested Terrain*. Albany: State University of New York Press.

ELEVEN

Do Hair and Class Gel?

KATE GOLTERMANN

INTRODUCTION

Americans spent over $50 billion on cosmetics and toiletries in 2006 (Singer 2007). That is more than the US government spent in the same year on elementary, secondary, and vocational education combined, according to the US Office of Management and Budget report. As sales in luxury items continue to grow, an upscale hair salon offers a space to consider the expression of class and status by working-class hairdressers and the leisure-privileged middle-and upper-middle-class patrons.

This work is based on fieldwork over a three-month period in the summer and fall of 2003. I spent about ten hours a week hanging out and conducting informal and formal interviews in the Mike Miller Salon and Spa, an up-scale Aveda salon in a mid-sized city in Florida.[1] Before I started fieldwork in the salon, Mike said to me, "There's only one thing . . . It's your outfit . . . Well, we all dress in a certain *way*." I knew immediately what he meant and wore only black and white clothing to the salon for the next three months, just like the salon workers.

The goal of my analysis is to explore the constraints of class by examining the material culture (see Miller 1995:148) of an Aveda hair salon that publicizes a policy of profits with principles. It is structured in three parts. In the first, I show how Aveda's corporate ideology shapes its marketing campaign and the material culture of the salon and how that in turn shapes the subjectivity of the female customers. In the second, I explore how Mike frames beauty work as an expression of concern for the upkeep of his customers' individualism and specialness, which results in a uniquely modern and American feeling of doing good. In the third, I examine how the store's policies on customer service are an attempt to make the salon appear to be a site of one-class society—that of the privileged upper class. I found that the salon is *not just* a place that people visit because it is a relaxing pastime but a site where lofty ideals are put on display, where the hierarchy of class and status seem to collapse, and where beauty work is the symptom of and antidote to women's anxiety about aging.

Because this fieldwork took place in 2003, about eight years before the publication of this book, I am positive many things have changed in the salon. Changes occurred the minute I stepped out of the salon for the last time, and changes have been occurring ever since. In fact, I last heard that Mike was having personal issues related to his marriage and financial trouble with his business; many of the original hairdressers that I knew left the salon to work other jobs. And, my own analysis has changed based on exposure to new literature and viewpoints. Thus, this study looks at a specific location where particular cultural and social interactions took place within a specific time frame and is written from the standpoint of a researcher with her own theoretical background, personal opinions, and agenda.

This paper should be understood as the exploration of one slice of the complexities of the Aveda Corporation and its dealings. Mike's salon demonstrated a culture of work and class interactions that are at the center of this particular piece of writing, but the salon exists amid a multitude of other relations. There are varying degrees of interactions among local, national, and international actors such as, for example, other franchise owners, Aveda salon "affiliates," Aveda corporate workers, Estée Lauder parent company employees, United States–based NGO partners, media associates, contract workers, international governments, international NGOs, and indigenous cooperatives and communities. If the Aveda Corporation is at the center of this web, these actors provide gossamer threads of connections to the center that sometimes tangle and overlap with each other. Because of the diverse interests of these people (i.e., salon owners in New Jersey or Ohio are probably more concerned with the daily operations of their salon than with the land rights of indigenous people), there are often contradictions and divergent perspectives. Despite this, all are loosely tied by delicate strands. And from these strands, people's thoughts, perceptions, and outlooks emerge, often without offering perfect, neat answers to the questions I posed. But, there is a narrative worthy of being told precisely because of this messiness and very nature of incongruous views—they are part of what make us human. While this paper cannot discuss all of the components that make Aveda such a dynamic company or convey the versatility and intricacies of the workers and clients who graciously shared their lives with me, I do think that there is value in trying to cut through some of the layers that made the salon such a multifaceted site.

AN INTRODUCTION TO THE AVEDA IDEOLOGY

Daniel Miller observes that the study of material culture, once the purview of archaeology, has returned as the "vanguard precisely because of its ability to focus on the commodity and its social significance" (Miller 1995:148). Material culture is crucial to understanding how Aveda tries to shape the social relations between staff and client and between company and customer. The products are the entry point to understanding the production of "the Aveda image." Part of Aveda's appeal is its recycling policy. To advertise its Uruku makeup line, Aveda focuses not only on the quality of the cosmetics, but on the packaging. In one promotion pamphlet I found in the salon, there is an image of a lipstick tube that looks like a pillar of molded wood chips standing upright next to another lipstick tube that rests inside a case that looks like pulpy, egg-carton material. Below this image the caption reads:

> Uruku is packaged with the Earth in mind: in a new environmentally-responsible lip color system—a reusable case that can be refilled with your favorite Aveda Lip Pigment. Its base is *up to 65% post-consumer recycled aluminum*; its geometric cap is *30% natural flax fibers*. And the lip pigment tube itself is *90% post-consumer recycled resin*. All housed in an innovative *100% recycled newsprint* shell using up to 70% less energy and creating 73% less air pollution than packaging with virgin fiber. *(Sources: U.S.

Forest Service, Environmental Protection Agency) Refillable color—easy
on the Earth (emphasis and U.S. Forest Service citation in original).

The success of all-natural makeup and natural packaging marks a shift
in the marketing of beauty products to the middle and upper-middle class.
Companies like Aveda now ask their customers to imagine their beauty routine as something responsible yet luxurious, expensive yet basic. In order
to harmonize these seemingly contradictory demands, Aveda utilizes the
popularity of the green movement.

The endorsement of green principles in the US economy is visible
in the promotion of organic produce and energy-efficient light bulbs, the
endorsement of free-trade and organic products such as coffee; the charm
of hybrid cars; and corporate-sponsored carbon-cutting programs. Whether
these green agendas will improve the environment is still to be seen, but
Crane argues that there is no such thing as truly ethical products, only "ethical attributes" and "ethical augmentation" (Crane 2001).

The question, then, is why are women so eager to spend so much
money on Aveda products that most likely work just the same as something
from a drugstore? (see Wolf 1991; Etcoff 1999; Foulke 1992). The answer lies
not only in the appeal of environmental responsibility, but also in the appeal
of a culturally and socially responsible policy.

In the early 1990s, Aveda partnered with the Yawanawá, an indigenous
group in Acre, Brazil. The Yawanawá grow and harvest urucum, a plant
that produces a red pigment, which Aveda uses in its Uruku makeup line.
The relationship between Aveda and the Yawanawá is complex; it is not a
Manichean battle between a domineering corporation and a naive local
community (see Posey and Dutfield 1995; Morsello 2004, 2005; Marinova
and Raven 2006; Mayers 2000).

One aspect of the contract between this company and community is
Aveda's commitment to invest in social projects that promote the well-being
of the Yawanawá. With company support, the Yawanawá designed wells
for drinking water and toilets, built a health clinic, installed solar panels in
the main village, updated their communication tools, and secured 93,000
additional hectares of land and boats to patrol the borders. Of securing the
land, the chief of the Yawanawá, Tashka Yawanawá, said, "After years of
struggling together, it is extremely special to us to regain this important
land. We thank Aveda so much for always supporting our efforts" (http://

Aveda.Aveda.com/about/press/pdf/NR-YawanawaDemarcation–8–07.pdf).
The Yawanawá have gained cultural and political benefits, while Aveda has
gained brand trust and soaring profits.[2]

In 2003, Aveda contractually agreed to pay the Yawanawá in exchange
for the use of their images in advertising. For example, Aveda's website
pictures Yawanawá people dressed in colorful headdresses and face paint.
These images imbue them with authenticity as environmental stewards.
The ads potentially bestow customers with feelings of connectedness to a
global cause rooted in images of the Amazon. When Aveda's customers buy
its products and support its recycling program, they declare their superiority
as responsible consumers (Marchard and Walker 2008; Kelley 2004). And,
their conspicuous consumption of expensive pampering products is justified by their conviction that they are helping.

Aveda's products are expensive because customers are willing to pay
for positive feelings associated with products that are environmentally low-
impact and culturally sensitive, while catering to their desire to be sexy and
hip at the same time. Aveda products, wrapped in ethics, transfer these values to the people who purchase them.

These notions of efficacy and worth are tied to use and exchange value
(Marx [1867] 1978). *Use value* represents the function of the commodity
(i.e., shampoo cleans the scalp), while *exchange value* represents the amount
of money people are willing to pay for products based on their social as
opposed to economic worth. Orser calls this placement of value on objects
"esteem" or "aesthetic" value (Orser 1996: 192). These values show that
commodities are socially endowed with characteristics that may have nothing to do with their composition or uses.

The Aveda corporation must foster the esteem value of its products if
its salon clients are to pay between $10 and $70 for conditioner, depending
on the size of the bottle. They did this by overlaying the commercial transaction with meaningful social interaction. As long as customers see a social
value in getting their hair cut and buying expensive makeup, they need the
services of the working-class hairdressers. "The mystical character of commodities does not originate, therefore, in their use value . . . The product
must be not only useful, but useful for others" ([1867] 1978:320–322).

Customers can buy shampoo at any local grocery mart and wash their
hair themselves, but they don't. They come to Mike's to buy their shampoo and have him wash their hair because he offers special, personalized

indulgences. The salon offers physical pleasures, such as the immediate offering of coffee and tea when a customer walks in the door, and mental comforts, such as confirmation that a certain product is "perfect" for a certain customer, asking about the state of people's jobs, and inquiring about children by name; this makes customers feel good about themselves and helps maintain their loyalty to the salon. Aveda's products, narratives, and images offer the women a script in which indulging in expensive products helps indigenous people and reduces waste.

Despite the critiques and hazards of capitalizing on these "essentializing" images (Brosius 1999; Conklin 1997), lumping indigenous people into a singular group (Agrawal 1995), and Americans' obsession with "everything eastern" (Lau 2000), the Yawanawá's objectives might be best realized by presenting a united, fixed, and romanticized representation of their shared identity. For example, the Aveda corporation realized that the Yawanawá's images were more important than the actual production of urucum, so agreed to contractual payments beginning in 2003 (Michi 2007:100–101). This illustrates how communities can use resources that are important to companies as a basis for bargaining power (Vermeulen and Mayers 2007:134).

ARE THEY JUST WALKING HEADS WITH WALLETS?

> Sexy is . . . when a woman can transform herself into something new. Still as beautiful, she allows her versatility to control her style, giving her freedom to express herself and her love for creation. These styles aren't about making yourself over completely, they're about taking what you have and seeing the potential that's already there—unmasking something fresh and invigorating. (Salon Select 2003)

I was next to Mike's haircutting chair when he said to me, "*Again*, it goes back to this is a person [the customer]. This is not a walking head. We want to make people feel *good* . . . The way lifestyles are now, people need to feel nurtured. If there's a problem and we can help, why shouldn't we?" This exemplifies one of the salon's paradoxes. On one hand Mike is saying that how women look naturally is a "problem," but on the other hand he tells them that they're more than "just a walking head." Mike, by way of his specialized knowledge, is able to talk about his clients like an architect might talk about remodeling a kitchen. He talked about the necessity of his work, the aesthetic value of his work, and the altruistic nature of his work.

Mike went on to say, "Everyone sitting here [the hairdressers] likes to help and make people feel good and help their self-esteem." In this instance, Mike appeals to the hairdressers' "inherent" desire to help people. With wallets full of cash and access to powerful social networks, the customers are temporarily at the mercy of the hairdressers for their self-esteem. By deeming the hairdressers "amateur psychologists," Mike pumps up the self-esteem of the hairdressers and blurs the class divide between the hairdressers and their customers. This salon-speak is double edged. It convinces Mike's costumers that his services fulfill an a priori need that justifies his services.

Mike's entire business thrives on selling people fantasies to go along with their cuts and styles. Mike's attitude meshes with Aveda's philosophy that people must pay more money to receive a sustainable, high-quality product.[3]

A month into my fieldwork, Marcy, one of the stylists, introduced me to Hannah, a concierge at a five-star hotel who said:

> It's like *Steel Magnolias*. It's like family. You look forward to coming. I just love the service . . . You know what? It's *the ritual*. Bella [the receptionist] needs to answer the phone . . . There's always a little change; you look forward to the change. They're so up on the products and forward education. It's service you don't find in your average day spa. And I would guess that's why people come here.
>
> I love that they offer water, tea. It's those little things . . . You don't know you miss them 'til you don't have them. I don't even look at rates anywhere else.

I asked her if she colored her hair and she replied laughing, "I swore I would never color my hair, but then I got older."

Standing behind her cutting chair, Marcy interjected, "Aging gracefully."

Hannah smiled, "Yes, aging gracefully."

Hannah embodies the complexities of the beauty myth. On the one hand, she goes to the salon to relax; on the other hand, the whole experience confirms that there is something ungraceful about aging, something shameful and undesirable.

I met Lacy, a woman in her mid-thirties, the day after I spoke with Hannah. Lacy whole-heartedly embraced the ethos of the salon and basked in the attention that Mike gave her. She told me that she had heard about Mike Miller from friends and had come with one of them to get her hair cut.

"Twenty of my friends come here now . . . At least!" she told me.

When she first went to the salon, Lacy needed her hair cut shorter to legitimate her position in the corporate world. She told me she was wearing business suits for work and could only wear her hair up or back, and she wanted "more flexibility." The implication was that she had to alter her appearance to be more masculine to fit in with the work and justify her earning power, and the salon did this without appearing at all to be enforcing this male-dominated view of how a woman should look in the office workplace.

Various authors have claimed that the process of beautification through hair and makeup is an expression and affirmation of class and status (Wax 1957; Goffman 1959; Gimlin 2002; Ewen 1979; Etcoff 1999), a desire to create a new self (Perutz 1970; Synnott 1989), a sign of the beauty standards (Banner 1983; Wolf 1991), and a sign of the pressures of a male-dominated society (Ewen 1979; Dellinger and Williams 1997). Aveda's literature glorifies makeup and hair products as goods that enhance one's life.

The first time Lacy came to the salon she got "hi-lites" and said of the experience, "The first time I came in I was a little nervous about it, but I told Mike, 'I'll trust you.' I don't use anything that's not Aveda—shampoo, conditioner."

Hannah and Lacy both suggest the services of the salon's workers make women feel individually special and different from customers who go to cheaper or more generic hair salons. The salon's customers must at the same time be collectivized as a "consumer base" to secure brand loyalty to Aveda *and* individualized within "aspirational clusters" (Hebdige 1994) to provide the customers with maps of what they could like to be. The salon offers "temporary relief from worries and insecurity by providing something to believe in, or at least follow, and by releasing the person from concern with his own ego" (Perutz 1970:51).

A beauty ideal created by living and working in a male-dominated society and the insecurity of being part of the "petty bourgeoisie" contributes to women's insecurities. Yet, the panacea for the insecurity seems to lie in a leisure activity that the women themselves perpetuate—getting their hair done. But in *this* space it is synonymous with the ability to buy an image that simultaneously confirms one's social standing to oneself and those in proximity (Veblen [1899] 1994). Beauty rituals can be a relaxing way to spend time, but paradoxically, beauty work heightens people's insecurities while appearing to alleviate them.

Salon employees and clients complicitly agree not to mention that their relationships are based on the staff's ability to make a profit by selling customers as many products as they can. The workers made the customers feel that their personalities and some kind of "intrinsic worth" were the reasons that they received special pampering, and the customers seemed willing to ignore that their money had anything to do with gaining the esteem of the salon owner and workers. The staff offer services as a business, and customers bask in the emotional fulfillment of individual attention. While customers were aware of Aveda's influence in the salon, including the staff's drive to sell products, they made it clear that they felt the Mike Miller salon was different from others in ways that validated the extra cost of the services and products.

Mike needs to give constant emotional attention in order to maintain customer loyalty. During my first interview with him in early August, I asked, "People come in here and spend a lot of money for the services, so what do you think brings them in here?"

Mike responded, "We give value-added service. We focus on the client. Make them feel special. I try to get the staff to recognize the guest as an individual."

Etcoff claims that one message promoted by beauty companies and perpetuated by customers is one of the "democratic spirit" or "hard work and money" (Etcoff 1999:46). Mike realized that as a business, his salon had to sell more than just products in order to keep his clients happy. He had to sell the idea that his customers deserved to be pampered "The Aveda Way." This particular "way" reinforces that environmentally conscious spending on expensive products is not just pampering, but "helpful pampering" and affirms that the women are justified in spending their money being indulged because they deserve it.

The act of going to the salon created a sort of "checklist" (Wobst 1977: 327) by which women can compare themselves to other consumers and the larger world outside the salon. By surrounding themselves with Aveda's material culture and adopting the messages behind the products, they are saying, "'I am an individual who belongs to social group x' . . . [and] . . . in conformity with the other behavioral norms and the ideology behind those norms . . . It allows individuals to summarize and broadcast the uniqueness of their rank or status within a matrix of ranks or statuses, or to express their social and economic group affiliation toward outsiders" (Wobst 1977: 328). The uniqueness of Aveda products, if only in packaging and image, reflects back at the women who are trying to gain a certain uniqueness within their own ranks. If a woman can pare out an identity that is uniquely valued in this culture—the beautiful/responsible consumer (what could be better!)—she takes on the image of the commodity, becomes the commodity, and participates in a shared discourse around images of ethical beauty, including herself.

Customers embraced changing their bodies, as well as their attitudes. Perhaps the change was only temporary while they were in the salon, but through their words they expressed how completely they embraced the remedies to their insecurities. The salon and the workers in it offered a quick fix to anxieties like growing older, being ugly, spending irresponsibly, and fitting into a man's world. The customers became walking, talking advertisements for the commoditization of themselves. Women went to the salon specifically to be molded and displayed as finished products analogous to commodities on a production line. But unlike stamped packages, the women are told that they are treated with individual care and that their service is extraordinary because they deserve it. But, as on the production line, someone must do the work. And that relationship is difficult to disguise.

THE EXPERTS STRUGGLE TO BE MORE THAN JUST SERVICE-SECTOR EMPLOYEES

They're famous, and let's face it; they all look fantastic at 40 and beyond. But don't hate them because they're beautiful. Read between the lines (or in this case, the lack thereof), and you might just spot a secret to their enduring splendor. Sure, we can chalk it up to charisma and killer genes, but there's also some technique for the taking behind their Hollywood hair and makeup. So, we've asked the experts to spill the beans behind these ladies' lasting looks. (Berke 2003:68)

The identities of Mike's salon staff are just as managed as those of his customers. Mike's stylized behavior as an educated professional emits the message that he is worthy of a social and economic position that is close to that of his customers. He is a hairstylist, and not just a guy who cuts hair.

Invisible from the cutting room, signs posted just inside the back room state various policies and mottos. There were four main printouts made by Mike and his wife. The first dealt with service:

3 Steps of Service[4]

1. Warm Welcome
   Escort to Destination

2. Anticipate the Guests Needs
   Assist Before Asking

3. Fond Farewell
   Escort to Front Desk
   Complement

The second printout explained the necessity of teamwork:

Mike Miller Salon Definition of Teamwork

- Two or more people setting goals and working towards them Deriving from that Success
- Trusting each individual of the group to hold their own
- Respecting individual feelings
- Accepting and Seeking Responsibility
- Respect all Ideas
- Give the group credit not an individual
- Winning Attitudes
- Learning from your teammates
- A Passion for Excellence
- HAVING FUN

The third printout stated the salon's motto:

Mike Miller Salon and Spa Motto:

We are ladies and gentlemen serving other ladies and gentlemen
—RITZ CARLTON

We are what we repeatedly do. Excellence, then, is not an act, but a habit.

—ARISTOTLE

Finally, there was a list of twenty steps to follow within the salon:

Mike Miller Salon and Spa 20 Basics

1. All must energize the credo

2. We are Ladies and Gentlemen serving Ladies and Gentlemen
   Who you are and how you should behave
   Mutual respect for one another and ourselves

3. The 3 steps of service will be used in each interaction with our guests
   and co-workers

4. The Employees Promise is the foundation of our guest service and
   will be honored by all employees

5. All employees will successfully complete training certification and be
   involved in customer service reinforcement

6. Company objectives are communicated to all employees and it is
   everyone's responsibility to support it.

7. To create pride and joy in the workplace, all employees have the right
   to be involved in planning

8. It is every employee's responsibility to identify defects within Mike
   Miller Salon
   If there is a problem take it to the source

9. Teamwork is the responsibility of every employee

10. Basic housekeeping is the responsibility of every employee

11. Each employee is responsible for anticipating guest needs
    Mr. Miller likes his coffee with cream

12. Each employee is responsible for instant guest pacification no matter
    whose guest

13. Always smile make eye-contact and have positive ATTITUDE
    towards guests and CO-Workers

14. Always speak positively about your salon in and outside of work

15. Escort your guest to their destination

16. Use proper phone etiquette
    Thank You for choosing Mike Miller Salon and Spa this is Marcy
    How May I Help You?
    May I please put you on hold?

17. Take pride in your appearance

18. GO THE EXTRA MILE!!!!!!!!

19. Respect all assets of the Mike Miller Salon including yourself and other coworkers

20. Have a passion for what you do!

In the previous section, I claimed that the customers were receptive to being molded into idealized representations of themselves because they felt they were given individualized, tailored attention. From the guidelines of service above, it would seem that the treatment of all customers is standard, but constantly needs to be maintained and monitored, so Mike leaves the principles up every day. Indeed, Mike talked a lot about standards in the salon, saying that the staff needed to change their voices on the phone and in person, "to be more enthusiastic so that clients know you're on top of it." Mike also suggested the idea of giving a shampoo bottle with a picture of a baby to each expectant mother. "We should acknowledge anything in a person's life. A loss, a move . . . I think that's good business."

Mike has positioned himself as what Hochschild identifies as "the upper class . . . the tycoons . . . the imperial decision makers" (Hochschild 1983:155). "Their notions of what is funny, what to be aware of, how grateful to feel, and how hostile one should be to outsiders will become an official culture for their top employees" (1983:155). But Mike is only posturing as a member of the upper class. Undeniably, he dressed well and drove a Mercedes, but these are more markers of his status, as Weber defines it. Maybe Mike did make as much money as his clients (I never knew his salary).[5]

During the run-through for something called "Feel Good Friday," Mike's wife, Susan, asked me, "When you first came here, was it what you thought it'd be?"

I tried to think of a good answer, and with my mouth full of cheese and crackers I said, "Well, yes and no." Apparently I did not understand what she was driving at.

She quickly added, "Because we work so hard to create an . . . " She did not finish her thought, snacking on her chicken salad contemplatively. "I mean, we're all so looked down upon."

"You mean the salon?" I asked without really thinking.

"Hairdressers in general," she said.

She told me that they try to combat that image with the aesthetics of the salon that "are Aveda and the Mike Miller salon." Later in the conversation, to impress the point that her husband's salon is more than just a place to get one's hair cut, she told me that they "do a lot of pretty famous people's hair." Debra Gimlin pointedly notes, "Hairstylists reinforce the importance of commercially managed beauty as part of their own efforts to nullify status differences between themselves and their customers" (Gimlin 2002: 47). By telling me that the salon does famous peoples' hair, Susan was elevating hairdressing to a more professional standing, something trend-setting. At the same time, if famous people and hairdressers both find it important to manage their beauty (as Gimlin would say), then symbolically this links the two worlds together and legitimates its necessity. The statement conveys that hairdressing is more than just manual labor. It is something famous people *need* from the experts, like the expertise only a doctor can give to a sick person.

This "social leveling" (see Furman 1997) is a technique that the staff used to close the status gap between themselves and their clients, but it also showed how high the stakes were for the stylists. For example, their black-and-white attire not only looked sharp—it was a status symbol. It blurred the line between "stereotypical hairdresser" and professional business person. Gimlin explains, "Beauticians, by way of their low status and unsuccessful claims to professional identity, are more vulnerable than their clients to the pressures of the beauty myth. While their middle-class customers may very well resist the demands of beauty ideology in favor of the demands of the workplace, stylists' work simply serves to reinforce—at least among the stylists themselves—the importance of attaining some notion of beauty ideal" (Gimlin 2002:47).

Beauty work is not all rouge and hair dye. It is hard work, even "deep work." (Geertz [1972] 1991). But, the hairdressers in Mike's salon are not only vulnerable to the middle-class standards of beauty notions, nor can they merely gain entrée into the middle class by looking like their clients. Working for the Aveda company, the hairdressers consciously associate themselves with the morals of social and environmental justice that are also the values of the clients and a marker of the middle class.

In addition to stressing their expert knowledge or fashion sense, the workers were acutely aware of the higher social and class standing that they gained by working for Aveda, which holds liberal principles. One day I asked Bella, the receptionist, "How does the salon reflect the idea of 'Aveda'?" She quickly said, "Even us! No perfumes. We even try as far as recycling our empties [meaning empty boxes] . . . our boxes.

"Me personally, when you go somewhere else you're not likely to buy synthetic stuff. We're likely to buy Aveda. I can even walk by the Dillard's perfume stuff!

"I mean, everything in the salon—even the furniture is old, natural—ties into the Aveda concept. Window treatments. Things like that. What we have is all-natural. From paint to knick-knacks to furniture. We tend to keep everything neat, in place. I don't want to say . . . " Bella paused for a second and changing her mind said, "Yeah! *The Aveda Way*. In other Aveda salons it's like that, too. In order, in place. Each one of these guys in here is genuine. We fit in with Aveda. With what Aveda thinks [laughing]."

Aveda's ideology shapes the class consciousness of its employees, including the franchise owners like Mike and the lower-level employees like Bella. And, this indoctrination into the "Aveda Way" is purposeful and calculated. Aveda's senior vice president of global marketing and design, Chris Hacker, captures the dynamic in the salon saying, "Typically, our customer is someone who has had an experience of the brand that was transforming. Most often, that experience began in a hair salon. We help stylists to become evangelists for environmental behavior. It can be a very powerful catalyst for a trusted stylist to ask a simple question like, 'Do you recycle?' " (http://www.enlightenedbrand.com/pages/ebj_2004-4.php).

Aveda's official rhetoric is that it offers its employees *more than* typical vocational training and working-class employment as hairdressers. Both Mike, the owner, and Marcy, a hairdresser, stressed to me the comparative costs and class hours of college and cosmetology school. Although the staff did take about one college-year's length of cosmetology classes, paid about $11,000 in tuition, and drove nice cars (including a BMW, Mustang, and Lexus), the average income of hairdressers is much lower than that of the clientele at Mike's salon.[6] The stylists tried to take on a status position close to that of their clients (who were mostly middle-and upper-class white women) by confidently expressing their expertise and stressing the aesthetic and social worth of Aveda's products, but it was at the cost of continual emotional work.

CLASS AND STATUS: REFLECTIONS

"Though Beauty May be Truth, there is nothing true about beauty"
(Perutz 1970)

Aveda's products play an active role in the constitution of the social relations in the salon, and they are also instruments for the enactment of commitment to specific morals. The products' design, packaging, and narratives help the wealthy, white customers imagine an ideal world in which
social distinctions are collapsed into an ideal, multicultural world. However,
the work of the working-class hairdressers in the salon reflects the reality
of class relations outside the salon in which only the wealthy are afforded
the luxury of spending daytime hours paying for expensive services and
products.

The material culture of the salon differentiates its female clientele from
the larger world by uniting them as ethical, elite consumers who can afford
to pay a premium for environmentally correct products. Images of the
Yawanawá evoke an exotic preindustrial secret to eternal youthfulness that
connect customers with something pristine and untouched by vulgar consumerism, which they try to avoid by buying Aveda's products and patron-
izing Mike's salon. By buying Aveda's products, consumers support the con-
tinuation of what they perceive as an authentic, unspoiled wild way of life
that they can know only vicariously.

I argue that the customers did not simply make an appointment with
the salon to get a haircut or hairstyle. The true transformative value does
not lie in the realm of aesthetics or technique (i.e., shorter hair, longer layers, highlights, etc.), although certainly some women did feel confident
about the way they looked, but in the fact that they do not have to recycle,
be environmentally conscious, care about or know about people with dark
skin—because the products do these things for them. The customers were
trying to attain something else, something they did not have. One could
look at them as parvenus, but this would obscure another important point.
The point is to look at how the commodities facilitated and produced a
desire for the upward mobility that was such a prevalent ideal in the salon.

So, how did the commodities produce this desire? One must look at a
layer deeper to see how the commodities facilitated the relationships that
made these desires possible. To judge the participants' adherence to their
beauty "rituals" as just the success of patriarchal control would be deeply

misleading. Just looking at the salon in this way would miss the meaning that I found in the cracks and imperfections of the interpersonal relations of the salon. Within the constraints of Aveda's convincing ad campaign that capitalizes on notions of natural beauty ideals, the customers and hairdressers actively participated in and created the power relations that constituted the relationships within the salon. The relationships are founded on Aveda's ability to "dye" traditional marketing by tapping into social and class issues such as globalism, health, well-being, humanitarianism, and prestige. The company tied these lofty, abstract ideas to rouge, lipstick, eye shadow, hair gel, shampoo, conditioner, aromatherapy, books, retreats, and much more.

And, this site allowed me to see how people, who were sometimes acutely aware of their positions in society, dealt with the insecurities of their class and status, which are firmly rooted in historically based issues. So, the consumption of commodities is also the consumption of an entire value system. Consuming, then, becomes an act of believing in a set of signals.

The commodities signaled something exterior (the fantasy of the self-less, eternally young, environmentally conscious consumer) and interior (the relationships that perpetuated these exterior ethoi). Although the standards for youth, beauty, and power are impossible to meet, the women espoused them in their loyalty to Mike's salon and workers (as people often do until something goes awry) and returned to the salon appointment after appointment to get their hair cut. The customers are not blind participants in beauty rituals but complicated social actors limited by and participating in the class and prestige narrative of the salon. Actualizing beauty standards is not so much the point of going to Mike's salon, as is the *doing* of beauty principles (i.e., aging appropriately, using products that help the environment, and buying products that support indigenous groups) in a meaningful way, although they will never be fully realized (thus, people return time and time again to salons).

Mike realized that a certain manner and appearance were needed to maintain the prestigious image of his Aveda salon and marketed himself, his staff, and products so that customers were not only willing but eager to exchange a lot of money for his services and products. Mike used the stylish image of Aveda to reinforce the elitism of the working-class hairdressers and his own self image. The division of labor in the salon had to be continually reinforced within the broader context of the upper-class arena of the salon through image control (rules, mottos, dress). The seemingly mundane everyday space of the salon was *not* a preexisting space for the expression of identity, but a space that was continually remade for the renegotiation of consumer subjectivities within the constraints of class and gender.

The "power" of the products allowed women to use Aveda's environmentally conscious products, believe in the ideology behind them, and then jump into their very expensive SUVs at the end of their appointments. The stylized talk from Mike made the customers feel special. Combining this feeling of specialness with ones of environmental responsibility led to a showy liberalism. Being eco-friendly gives way to fuzzy feelings, and this gesturing comes from well-orchestrated advertisement, salon-speak, and a charismatic leader (Mike).

In the everyday rhythms of a hair salon, workers, customers and I were constantly reformulating what we were telling ourselves about ourselves and about each other. These formulations were emergent from activity, not *reifications of* what people *already were*. The salon was a site of things *happening*—of workers working, workers trying to sell an image that their customers would want to buy, customers trying to recapture their youth, and consumers trying to reformulate their persona with different haircuts. The entire salon offers a space for the power dynamics between the working-class hairdressers and conspicuous consumers of the upper and middle class to express their status and wealth at the appropriate time, in the appropriate place.

NOTES

1. All workers' names and the name of the salon have been changed.

2. For discussions of the potential benefits to company-community partnerships see, for example, Marinova and Raven 2006; Mayers 2000; Morsello 2004, 2005; Posey and Dutfield 1995; Ros-Tonen et al. 2008; Vidal and Donini 2007; and World Bank 2006.

3. However, in 1997 Aveda's moral conviction was in question when Amnesty International found out that Aveda was taking palm oil out of Malaysia, where authorities were imprisoning protesting indigenous people and deforesting their lands to make way for companies interested in harvesting the oil. Aveda did rectify the situation by striking a deal with a Brazilian women's cooperative to supply babassu oil, a palm oil substitute (LaFranchi 1997). And, in February 2007 Robby Romero, an Apache who proved that Aveda had withheld compensation for its use of native plants in its "Indigenous" line, won a lawsuit against Aveda in the New

York Supreme Court. Romero told the UN Permanent Forum on Indigenous Issues in May 2007, "Unfortunately, there are corporations . . . that have been enriched from the use of indigenous peoples' natural resources, culture, philosophy, creativity, resources, intellectual property, traditional knowledge, images, names, and likeness. And often, those corporations manage to circumvent indigenous peoples' rights to free, prior, and informed consent and to benefit sharing."

4. All statements in bold, capitals, and exclamations are emphasized as seen in the original copies. The grammar has been reprinted as it appeared in the originals.

5. My sense was that Mike made more money than his staff, but as of 2006 his business and marriage were struggling, and most of the original staff had left the salon.

6. The mean annual income for hairdressers in the state of Florida in 2006 was $24,740, according to the US Department of Labor Bureau of Labor Statistics.

REFERENCES CITED

Agrawal, Arun. 1995. "Dismantling the Divide between Indigenous and Scientific Knowledge." *Development and Change* 26: 413–439.

Aveda. 2003/2004. "Coalition for Environmentally Responsible Economies." http://Aveda.Aveda.com/protect/we/ceresreport2003_2004.pdf, accessed June 14, 2006.

———. 2003. "One World, Many Voices." http://216.74.173.138/enter/style/fp_02/oneworld.html, accessed December 1 and 2, 2003.

———. 2004. "Mission, Vision, Beliefs." http://Aveda.com/about/beliefs_vision/default.asp, accessed February 23, 2004.

———. 2007. "Celebration of Color: The Story of Brazilian Urukum." http://Aveda.Aveda.com/protect/we/uruku.asp, accessed May 3, 2007.

———. 2007. "Mission Statement." http://Aveda.com/customerservice/ourmission.tmpl, accessed May 3, 2007.

———. 2007. "Aveda Celebrates the Success of the Yawanawá Tribe in Securing the Rights to 93,000 Hectares of Sacred Land." Press release. http://Aveda.Aveda.com/about/press/pdf/NR-YawanawaDemarcation-8-07.pdf, accessed January 5, 2007.

Banner, Lois W. 1983. *American Beauty*. New York: Knopf.

Berke, Amanda. 2003. "Over 40 and Fabulous." *101 Hairstyles* 11:68.

Brosius, Peter J. 1999. "Green Dots, Pink Hearts: Displacing Politics from the Malaysian Rain Forest." *American Anthropologist* 101(1): 36–57.

Celebrity Style 101 Hairstyles. 2003. http://www.mmimags.com/101Hairstyles.html.

Conklin, Beth. 1997. "Body Paint, Feathers, and VCRs: Aesthetics and Authenticity in Amazonian Activism." *American Ethnologist* 24(4): 711–737.

Crane, Andrew. 2001. "Unpacking the Ethical Product." *Journal of Business Ethics* 30: 361–373.

Cultural Survival. 2007. "Indigenous Rock Star Wins Lawsuit against Aveda." July: 31(2).

Dellinger, Kirsten, and Christine Williams. 1997. "Makeup at Work: Negotiating Appearance Rules in the Workplace." *Gender and Society* 11(2): 151–177.

Enlightened Brand Journal. 2004. "The Natural Beauty of Aveda: A Discussion with Chris Hacker." Autumn. http://www.enlightenedbrand.com/pages/ebj_2004 -4.php, accessed November 27, 2007.

Environmental Working Group. 2005. "FDA Warns Industry to Follow Law on Untested Ingredients." http://www.ewg.org/issues/cosmetics/FDA_Warning/index.php, accessed June 27, 2006.

Etcoff, Nancy. 1999. *Survival of the Prettiest: the Science of Beauty.* New York: Random House, Inc.

Ewen, Phyllis. 1979. "The Beauty Ritual." In *Images of Information: Still Photography in Social Sciences,* edited by Jon Wagner, 43–57. Beverly Hills, CA: Sage.

Foulke, Judith E. 1992. "Cosmetic Industry: Understanding the Puffery." *FDA Consumer.* http://www.fda.gov/fdac/reprints/puffery.html, accessed June 24, 2006.

Furman, Frida Kerner. 1997. *Facing the Mirror: Older Women and Beauty Shop Culture.* New York: Routledge.

Geertz, Clifford. [1972] 1991. "Deep Play: Notes on the Balinese Cockfight." In *Rethinking Popular Culture: Contemporary Perspectives in Cultural Studies,* edited by Chandra Mukerji and Michael Schudson, 239–277. Berkeley: University of California Press.

Gimlin, Debra L. 2002. "The Hair Salon: Social Class, Power, and Ideal Beauty." In *Body Work: Beauty and Self Image in American Culture.* Berkeley: University of California Press.

Goffman, Erving. 1959. *The Presentation of Self in Everyday Life.* New York: Doubleday.

Hebdige, Dick. 1994. "After the Masses." In *Culture/Power/History: A Reader in Contemporary Social Theory,* edited by Nicholas B. Dirks, Geoff Ely, and Sherry B. Ortner, 222–236. Princeton, NJ: Princeton University Press.

Hochschild, Arlie R. 1983. *The Managed Heart: Commercialization of Human Feeling.* Berkeley: University of California Press.

Kelley, Annie. 2004. "The Rise of the Ethical Woman." *New Statesman* 133: 26.

LaFranchi, Howard. 1997. "For U.S. Company, Tribe Partnership is Bottom Line." *Christian Science Monitor International,* November 20. http://www.csmonitor.com/1997/1120/112097.intl.intl.1.html, accessed February 16, 2004.

Lau, Kimberly. 2000. *New Age Capitalism: Making Money East of Eden.* Philadelphia: University of Pennsylvania Press.

Marchard, Anne, and Stuart Walker. 2008. "Product Development and Responsible Consumption: Designing Alternatives for Sustainable Lifestyles." *Journal of Cleaner Production* 16: 1163–1169.

Marinova, Dora, and Margaret Raven. 2006. "Indigenous Knowledge and Intellectual Property: A Sustainable Agenda." *Journal of Economic Surveys* 20(4): 587–605.

Marx, Karl. [1867] 1978. "Capital, Volume One." In *The Marx Engels Reader*, edited by Robert C. Tuckers, 294–442. New York: W. W. Norton.

Mayers, James. 2000. "Company-Community Forestry Partnerships: A Growing Phenomenon." *Unasylva* 51(201): 33–41.

Michi, Leny. 2007. "O papel do Estado nas Parcerias Comercias entre Povos Indígenas Amazônicas e Empresas na Comercialização de Produtos Florestais Não Madeiras." MA dissertation, Programa de Pós-Graduação em Ciéncia Ambiental, University of São Paulo.

Miller, Daniel. 1995. *Acknowledging Consumption*. New York: Routledge.

Moore, Karl. 2006. "Environmentalism Rising." *Marketing Magazine* 111(33): 14.

Morsello, Carla. 2004. "Trade Deals between Corporations and Amazonian Forest Communities under Common Property Regimes: Opportunities, Problems, and Challenges." In The Tenth Biennial Conference of the International Association of the Study of Common Property, *The Common Goals of an Age of Global Transition: Challenges, Risks, and Opportunities*. Oaxaca: Universidad Nacional Autónoma de México.

———. 2005 "Company-Community Non-Timber Forest Product Deals in the Brazilian Amazon: A Review of Opportunities and Problems." *Forest Policy and Economics* 8(4): 483–494.

Orser, Charles E., Jr. 1996. "Beneath the Material Surface of Things: Commodities, Artifacts, and Slave Plantations." In *Contemporary Archaeology in Theory*, edited by Robert W. Preucel and Ian Hodder, 189–201. Boston: Blackwell.

Perutz, Kathryn. 1970. *Beyond the Looking Glass*. New York: William Morrow.

Posey, Darrell, and Graham Dutfield. 1995. *Beyond Intellectual Property: Toward Traditional Resource Rights for Indigenous Peoples and Local Communities*. Ottawa: International Development Research Center.

Ros-Tonen, M. A. F., Tinde van Andel, Carla Morsello, Kei Otsuki, Sergio Rosendo, and Imme Scholz. 2008. "Forest Related Partnerships in Brazilian Amazonia: There Is More to Sustainable Forest Management Than Reduced Impact Logging." *Forest Ecology and Management* 256(7): 1482–1497.

Salon Select. 2003. *Hairstyling Trends*. Winter.

Singer, Natasha. 2007. "Skin Deep: Should You Trust Your Makeup?" *New York Times*. February 15. http://query.nytimes.com/gst/fullpage.html?res=9A02E0DF173 EF936A25751C0A9619C8B63, accessed November 27, 2007.

Synnott. 1989. "Truth and Goodness, Mirrors and Masks—Part I: A Sociology of Beauty and the Face." *The British Journal of Sociology* 40(4): 607–636.

Veblen, Thorstein. [1899] 1994. *The Theory of the Leisure Class*. New York: Dover.

Vermeulen, Sonja, and James Mayers. 2007. "Partnerships between Forestry Companies and Local Communities: Mechanism for Efficiency, Equity, Resilience and Accountability." In *Partnerships in Sustainable Forest Resource Management: Learning from Latin America*, edited by Mirjam Ros-Tonen, Helen van der Hombergh, and Annelies Zoomers, 127–145. Leiden: Brill.

Vidal, Natalia, and Gabriela Donini. 2007. "Promising Business Models for Community Company Collaboration in Brazil and Mexico." *Forest Trends* 1–29.

Wax, Murray. 1957. "Themes in Cosmetics and Grooming." *American Journal of Sociology* 62(6): 589–593.

Weber, Max. 1999. "Class, Status, Party." In *Social Theory: The Multicultural and Classic Readings*, edited by Charles Lemert, 115–125. Boulder, CO: Westview.

Wobst, Martin H. 1977. "Stylistic Behavior and Information Exchange." In *From the Director: Research Essays in Honor of James B. Griffin*, 317–342. Anthropological Papers, No. 61, Museum of Anthropology. Ann Arbor: University of Michigan Press.

Wolf, Naomi. 1991. *The Beauty Myth.* New York: Doubleday.

World Bank. 2006. "Beyond Corporate Responsibility: The Scope for Corporate Investment in Community-Driven Development." Social Development Department and Sustainable Development Network. Report no. 37379-GLB.

TWELVE

Dreams, Illusions, and Realities

Conclusions

E. PAUL DURRENBERGER

Michael is using interest from his trust fund to pay for this trip. I am grateful, but also angry at the inequalities in our realities. No matter what I say or do, he can't understand what it's like to scrabble for the money for rent and heat and food. Worse, he thinks he does understand.

I worked an entire summer once to pay my own way on an Outward Bound trip, he says.

I roll my eyes.

Big whoop, I say. Working a whole summer for a want, not a need, is not the same. There's no desperation there. No life or death. No crisis should you fail. If I miss a payment I'll be chattering in the dark, or worse, asking my family for help.

Don't be so melodramatic, he says. Your family would help.

I look at him like he's from the moon . . .

I was raised to be self-sufficient. It is a virtue in our family. A virtue born of necessity, perhaps, but a proudly held virtue just the same.

You wouldn't understand, I say (Latus 2007:79–80).

I quote from a memoir of an abused woman, not an anthropological work. But I quote it because it's a familiar situation to anyone from a working-class background trying to make herself understood to someone from the managerial middle class. In 1994, Rubin wrote:

> Two decades ago [1973] Richard Sennett and Jonathan Cobb wrote
> that one of the most destructive of "the hidden injuries of class" is the
> stigmatization of working-class status, the disrespect for the men and
> women who work with their hands, and the belief that it's nothing more
> than their own inadequacies that keep them from climbing the class lad-
> der. An analysis that's as true now as it was then. (40)

And it continues to be even more true today as the class divides become more exaggerated. Or, as Michael Zweig (2000:11) puts it, "Class is about the power some people have over the lives of others, and the powerlessness most people experience as a result."

The managerial middle class are the people at least temporarily in positions of command or authority. "Their job is to conceptualize . . . what others must do. The job of the worker, blue or pink collar, is to get it done" (Ehrenreich 1990:133). Ehrenreich continues: "The fact that this is a relationship of domination—and grudging submission—is usually invisible to the middle class but painfully apparent to the working class."

Recent anthropological works ostensibly about issues of class in the United States (Newman 2000, 2008 ; Newman and Chen 2007; Newman et al. 2004; Ortner 2005) do remarkably little to clarify fundamental theoretical, empirical, or methodological issues about class; in fact, they do more to obscure issues than enlighten them because they stay within the terms of reference of US culture that deny and obfuscate the existence of class. Anthropologists who do ethnography like June Nash (2007) and thus see the world from the ground up rather than from the middle down develop a different picture, one that is both ethnographic and global, one that sees each locale in its global political-economic context.

Criticism from the formerly colonized and women so decentralized Euro-American white male definitions of the objective world that the promoters of postmodernism reduced all reality to a semiotic world of signs and symbols and dismissed understandings of gender and ethnicity in terms of processes of neoliberal globalization as vulgar determinism (Nash 2007:23). While the champions of postmodernism disparage ethnography,

June Nash argues that the experience of activist collaboration with those we study overcomes the postmodernists' tendency to question the reality of social problems, provides new insights, and reflects the concerns of people who "are transforming the structures of domination both at home and abroad" (2007:3).

Like ground-penetrating radar, the broad comparative and holistic vision of anthropology helps us to see beyond the confusions of the surface to the realities under it. Fried's (1967) concept of differential access to resources defines widespread human practices that we can see underlying many cultural forms through time and space.

A nuanced and complex concept of evolving systems of relationships to define access to resources in China and Mongolia provides a way for archaeologist William Honeychurch to understand the connections among extensively scattered sites as they change through time. Douglas Bolender uses the same notion in the narrower confines of settlement Iceland to understand the changes in forms and placement of house structures that archaeologists have located and mapped in time and space in their survey of a northern fjord.

Keeping track of who has access to what resources allows Ann Hill to understand the complexities of the Nuosu system of stratification in which slaves may collect rent from aristocrats and lets us see the continuities as Nuosu relationships with China change from being "frontier barbarians" of the imperial Chinese to being an "autonomous" region in a Communist system and then in the contemporary Chinese system.

One salient conclusion of these last two studies is that Fried overstated the extreme fragility of stratified systems that did not develop states. It is clearly possible to enforce asymmetric access to resources by means other than states, though those means may themselves introduce instability as feud did in both Iceland and among Nuosu; they do not necessarily mean that those with privileged access to resources will make common cause and become the ruling class of a state. The systems may become appendages of other states as both Iceland and Nuosu did.

When we project asymmetrical access to resources from the local to the global system, we can see a global system as yet ungoverned by a global state mechanism. And as Fried suggested that such asymmetry required enforcement, Trawick indicates the role of the Global North and the United States in particular in enforcing that asymmetry and describes the response from the South. He finds hope for these social movements in the ethnographic and archeological observation that people can and do equitably manage resources such as water, fishing rights, and common lands.

The last six studies focus on dimensions of class in the United States and accept the challenge of culturalists such as Ortner (1998, 2005) to understand the cultural products of the US system of class, especially since it seems to be ever-so-much more complex than the Marxian dichotomizing objectivist discourse would suggest. Ortner writes:

> A good deal of the post-Marx debate has concerned what to do with the middle class, who are neither "owners," broadly speaking, nor workers. Yet the middle class has been the most dynamic part of the structure of capitalism, growing in size, wealth, and political importance over the course of the past century. (1998:2)

It may be true as John Kenneth Galbraith (1998) observes, that the people of the class that most pride themselves in their hard work never work, but, as Newman (1988) observes, they most certainly think they do and even make that fantasy the center of their sustaining ideology. But when ethnography is capable of going beyond the cultural dreamwork to see the structures behind it, we can see the basis of different contemporary North American views of Ragnarök, the end of the world, in different class positions as Dimitra Doukas shows us. Gender is one of the poles of identity that anthropologists may dance around like strippers in a bar to distract the denizens from the grimy realities of their lives, but Barbara Dilly is able to use the lens of ethnography to show how daughters' positions in the rural economies of production and their cultural treatments changed over time.

David Griffith reminds us of the importance of mobility both for immigrants and for maintaining the myth of classlessness. He shows how one can move from the disassembly line of an Iowa meatpacking plant to work on a dairy farm and how an immigrant can hope to become involved in a business enterprise. If the archaeologists rely on the evidence of houses occupied in the past, Griffith shows us the conceptual difference in houses between the occupants of the houses of gated communities and the people who build them. The one is for display and investment while the other is a place for storing things of use and of potential use. The one is a market commodity; the other is the center of a household economy. The one is for enjoyment and transforms the use values of the other into eyesores and nuisances.

The border of the United States and Mexico is fraught with as many contradictions as the borders of China to the north where Honeychurch explored Mongols or the southwest where Hill discussed the fate of a "tribal" group. Josiah Heyman dissects the complexities of place of birth, documentation standing, residence, and job to vividly illustrate how people on the border construct their identities of the materials of their lives, how they think about and experience them, and how these cultural artifacts are related to the underlying realities of the political economy of the border and the more brutal facts of national control of resources that define the relationships among nations and how those trickle down into the lives of the people of the place.

Unions are one means for working-class people, who undeniably must work, to organize to pursue their common interests against the owners of capital. Because of a more than three-decade-long battle against unions in the United States, their place in the cognitive maps of North Americans is almost as obscured as that of class itself. But one of the survivors going into the twenty-first century was the United Auto Workers, UAW.

General Motors established new relationships with the UAW when they established their new Saturn plant. Sharryn Kasmir shows how those relationships divided the Saturn members from the rest of the UAW and how management used the allocation of privilege to divide the members against themselves. GM proved the old Inuit saying, familiar to anthropologists, that gifts make slaves just as whips make dogs. But what GM could give with one hand, they could take away with the other, and if they could establish a new factory, they could close others and keep the threat alive from year to year. Kasmir shows how the ruling class can erode the solidarity of the working class by using their cultural constructs and potentials against them. She reminds us that the fundamental reality is that of class and that there are no aristocrats among workers.

Kate Goltermann takes us from the factory floor to the beauty parlor where working women do the body work for other working women who are pleased to think of themselves as sufficiently meritorious that they deserve to be pampered. But they want to be unsullied in their exercise of privilege. They want their consumption of products and work to benefit the planet and its people. Goltermann shows us how a corporation has managed to leverage this penchant into a product line and a salon practice that feeds and develops these cultural constructs to make the illusion deeper and more realistic. So in Goltermann's exploration of the shadow world of the dreamwork of class, we see the corporate underpinnings in a global political economy that connects the working women of the salon, both those in the chairs and those behind the chairs, to Native Americans in South America who serve as symbols of the natural.

All but the last of these works are based on long-term engagement of anthropologists with the fine-grained empirical materials of archaeological or ethnographic observation. The one exception is that of the newcomer to our field, Kate Goltermann, who continues to explore the world she mapped in her contribution to this volume.

These works lend weight to Ehrenreich's (1989) observation that the people content to imagine themselves rightfully middle class are structurally no different from those who know by brutal experience that they are working class. The ruling class has given these sycophants the privileges of living in fancy houses, driving big cars, sending their children to good schools to raise them to the same managerial skills and cultural conceits. But Ehrenreich correctly diagnoses the nervousness of the middle class as fear of falling because they know, because they do it on behalf of the ruling class as GM managers did at Saturn, that gifts of privilege can be withdrawn on a whim.

When management responds to union organizing drives by offering workers new health and dental plans, maybe some raises, places on continuous quality councils and the like, organizers warn workers that such gifts are not contractual. And the ruling class has no contract with the middle class, as Katherine Newman (1988) found. But as those along the edges of the middle class begin to fall into the ranks of service employees, flipping burgers and changing sheets for the sick, the rest draw up their cultural drawbridges and steadfastly cling to their dreamwork, and may even find an anthropologist like Ortner to ratify it for them.

The anthropologists whose work is collected here responded to the organizing theme that we would explore class via Fried's insight that privileged access to resources defines classes. Access to resources was key for Fried. When access to resources is equal, there may be egalitarian social relationships, as he defines them, as many positions of prestige as there are persons capable of filling them.

But there may not be. Some people may live in different kinds of houses, have different clothing, be addressed by different titles than others. There may be fewer positions of prestige than people capable of filling them, what he calls *rank societies*. But in these, the people still have equal access to resources. The archaeological signature of rank societies may be different in differential mortuary practices and different house types, but as long as people have equal access to resources, there are no classes. If the redistributive economic system that Fried suggested accompanies such social organizations failed to satisfy the needs of the people, they could repudiate and change it.

Edmund Leach (1954) and Thomas Kirsch (1973) described the dynamics of such a system and how the people in it can change it from one state to another. The theoretical debate was about the relative weight of internal cultural factors and external ecological factors, but never about whether anthropologists should accept as their own the cultural concepts of the people in the system. Anthropologists took such Kachin words as *gumsa* and *gumlao* and Leach went to great lengths to describe how people thought about these categories. But Leach's understanding of how the system worked was rooted in concepts of ecology, politics, and economics, not local cultural terms.

Nor should anthropologists accept the cultural dreamwork of North Americans as the basis for theoretical or empirical understandings of class, even if it is the dreamwork of their own people. Dreamwork is nonetheless dreamwork no matter whose dream it is. And as long we as remain inside it, we cannot transcend the dream to see the realities behind it. We remain like Dorothy in the Wizard of Oz, dazzled and fascinated by the images in the fog without daring to look behind the curtain at the man working the illusion machine. As Marvin Harris famously put it:

> Ignorance, fear, and conflict are the basic elements of everyday consciousness. From these elements, art and politics fashion that collective dreamwork whose functions it is to prevent people from understanding what their social life is all about. Everyday consciousness, therefore, cannot explain itself. It owes its very existence to a developed capacity to deny the facts that explain its existence. (1974:6)

The works collected in this book continue the tradition of anthropology tearing away the curtain of illusion and asking questions about the realities beneath them. Like Fried, Leach, Kirsch, and Nash, we use the methods of historical materialism, cultural ecology, and political ecology to understand the realities of class and how they evolve.

REFERENCES CITED

Ehrenreich, Barbara. 1990. *Fear of Falling: The Inner Life of the Middle Class*. New York: Pantheon.

Fried, Morton. 1967. *The Evolution of Political Society: An Essay in Political Anthropology*. New York: Random House.

Galbraith, John Kenneth. 1998. *The Culture of Contentment*. New York: Penguin.

Harris, Marvin. 1974. *Cows, Pigs, Wars, and Witches: The Riddles of Culture*. New York: Vintage.

Kirsch, A. Thomas. 1973. *Feasting and Social Oscillation: A Working Paper on Religion and Society in Upland Southeast Asia*. Ithaca, NY: Cornell University Southeast Asian Publication Series.

Latus, Janine. 2007. *If I Am Missing or Dead*. New York: Simon & Schuster.

Leach, Edmund. 1954. *Political Systems of Highland Burma*. Boston: Beacon.

Nash, June. 2007. *Practicing Ethnography in a Globalizing World*. Boulder, CO: AltaMira.

Newman, Katherine. 1988. *Falling from Grace: The Experience of Downward Mobility in the American Middle Class*. New York: Vintage.

———. 2000. *No Shame in My Game: The Working Poor in the Inner City*. New York: Vintage.

———. 2008. *Laid off, Laid Low: Political and Economic Consequences of Employment Insecurity*. New York: Columbia University Press.

Newman, Katherine, and Victor Tan Chen. 2007. *The Missing Class: Portraits of the Near Poor in America*. Boston: Beacon.

Newman, Katherine, Cybelle Fox, David J. Harding, Jal Metha, and Wendy Roth. 2004. *Rampage: The Social Roots of School Shootings*. New York: Basic.

Ortner, Sherry. 1998. "Identities: The Hidden Life of Class." *Journal of Anthropological Research* 54(1): 1–17.

———. 2005. *New Jersey Dreaming: Capital, Culture, and the Class of 58*. Durham, NC: Duke University Press.

Rubin, Lillian B. 1994. *Families on the Fault Line: America's Working Class Speaks about the Family, the Economy, Race, and Ethnicity*. New York: Harper.

Zweig, Michael. 2000. *The Working Class Majority: America's Best Kept Secret*. Ithaca, NY: Cornell University Press.

Contributors

Douglas Bolender teaches, does research about, and publishes on the topics of property and social inequality, households and agricultural production, Scandinavian and North Atlantic archaeology and history, geochemistry, landscape archaeology, and geographic information systems. He is currently a postdoctoral fellow at the Field Museum in Chicago. His latest book is *Eventful Archaeologies: New Approaches to Social Transformation in The Archaeological Record* from the SUNY press at Albany, 2010.

Barbara J. Dilly teaches cultural anthropology at Creighton University. Her research focuses primarily on rural issues. She is currently writing a book on the social and cultural transformation of the farmer's daughter iconic image in American agriculture.

Dimitra Doukas is a semiretired anthropologist who continues to study and write about class cultures, politics, local economies, and the impact of corporate capitalism in the United States. She has taught at New York University, Cornell University, Dalhousie University, and the University of

Denver. Her latest book is *Worked Over: The Corporate Sabotage of an American Community* from Cornell University Press at Ithaca, NY, 2003

Paul Durrenberger is a professor of anthropology at Penn State University. He has been working with his wife, Suzan Erem, on various ethnographic projects with the labor movement in the United States. Together they have published several books and numerous papers. Their latest book is the second edition of their introductory anthropology textbook aimed at working-class students that sells for about a fourth of the price of most, *Anthropology Unbound: A Field Guide to the 21st Century*, and an accompanying reader, *Paradigms in Anthropology*, both from Paradigm Publishers, 2010.

Kate Goltermann is an instructor in the anthropology department at Seattle Central Community College. She earned her BA from New College in Sarasota, Florida, and her MA from the University of Florida in Gainesville, Florida.

David Griffith is a senior scientist and professor of anthropology at East Carolina University. He combines work on local knowledge and local history with work on international labor migration in Veracruz, Mexico, and Olancho, Honduras; research on Latino settlement and entrepreneurship in North Carolina; the study of Iñupiaq seal hunters of Kotzebue Sound, Alaska; and ethnographic profiles of South Atlantic fishing communities. His most recent book is *American Guestworkers: Jamaicans and Mexicans in the United States* from Penn State University Press, 2006.

Josiah Heyman is a professor of anthropology and chair of sociology and anthropology at the University of Texas at El Paso. He has written many scholarly articles, book chapters, and books on engaged anthropology, class, power, migration, and border society.

Ann Maxwell Hill teaches anthropology at Dickinson College and does ethnohistorical fieldwork in southwestern China. She recently coedited a book on China's affirmative action policies in minority education.

William Honeychurch is an assistant professor at Yale University and specializes in the archaeology of Inner Asia, complex societies, and inter-regional interaction. He has worked in Mongolia since 1991 and focuses on nomadic states and empires. His projects in northern Mongolia and most recently in the Gobi Desert have emphasized regional survey, seasonal campsite excavation, and mortuary archaeology to better understand the local foundations of steppe politics.

Sharryn Kasmir is a professor of anthropology at Hofstra University. She has carried out research on issues of work, class, and politics in the Basque region of Spain and in the southern United States.

Paul Trawick is a senior lecturer in environmental anthropology at Cranfield University in England. Most of his research to date has focused on the comparative study of farmer-managed irrigation systems in different parts of the world (the Andes, Spain) and, more generally, the study of successful forms of collective action at the community level. He has a strong interest in exploring the role that worldview can play in making people willing to exercise self-restraint in their consumption of goods and services and to move toward more sustainable lifestyles.

Index